Chinese Consumers

Ashok Sethi

Chinese Consumers

Exploring the World's Largest Demographic

palgrave
macmillan

Ashok Sethi
Illuminera Institute
Shanghai, China

ISBN 978-981-10-8991-6 ISBN 978-981-10-8992-3 (eBook)
https://doi.org/10.1007/978-981-10-8992-3

Library of Congress Control Number: 2018943397

Cover illustration: © TECHDESIGNWORK / Getty Images
Cover Design by Tom Howey

This Palgrave Macmillan imprint is published by the registered company Springer Nature Singapore Pte Ltd.
The registered company address is: 152 Beach Road, #21-01/04 Gateway East, Singapore 189721, Singapore

Acknowledgments

It has been a privilege to be able to observe the changes in the consumer and market landscape in China for the past 15 years. I would like to thank two of my senior ex-colleagues, John Smurthwaite and Wander Meijer, who were responsible for my relocation to China, motivated by their significant trust in my abilities to grow the business, as well as a strong desire to avoid having to move to the country themselves.

I have had the pleasure of working with some of the best Chinese and global marketing professionals in this period, who have generously shared their astute insights and observations which I have liberally and unashamedly used in this book. While the mention of all their names will add significant bulk to the book, I would specifically like to express my gratitude to Paul Zhou, Sandy Chen, Morris Mo, Shawn Wang, Simon Wang, Cindy Liu, Lisa Li, Lynn Zhu, Michael Muller, and Klaus Paur who enriched my journey of trying to fathom the Chinese consumers through their observations, inputs, and sheer companionship and friendship.

My friends and classmates from my alma mater, IIM Ahmedabad, who have been loyal readers of some of my writing, always encouraged me to write more, and I am indebted to them for their support.

I would like to thank my wife, Renu, and my daughter, Shreya, who are as fascinated by China as I am, though often see it differently, providing me with an alternative perspective.

Last but not the least, my gratitude goes to the Chinese consumers, who generously welcomed me and my colleagues to their homes, agreed to let us accompany them on their shopping and consumption missions, and answered the barrage of our questions, to enable us to have a peek at their habits, motivations, and preferences, which are summarized in this book.

Contents

About the Author

Ashok Sethi leads the Illuminera Institute in Shanghai, an organization dedicated to skill-building, consultancy, and thought leadership in the area of consumer insights and marketing. Ashok has over 30 years of experience in providing consumer insights and marketing advice to a wide range of multinational and local companies. He has been studying Chinese consumers for the last 15 years and hence had the privilege of observing firsthand the vast change in the consumer and marketing landscape. Ashok has held a number of senior-level positions including Managing Director of TNS China, Regional Director of Methodology and Consumer Insights at TNS Asia-Pacific, and Managing Director of GfK China—Consumer Experience.

List of Figures

List of Tables

CHAPTER 1

Introduction: The Yin and the Yang of the Chinese Consumers

I could have called this a foreword, a preface or even a prologue, as most erudite books choose to. However, an introduction is what it really is, and that is what I would call it. It is an introduction to 1.4 billion consumers—the products that they like to consume, the forces and urges that drive their behavior, and the opportunities it creates for the marketers, from both within China and elsewhere in the world, who have so far not succumbed to the attraction of the land.

Economists, particularly those in the West, may find the book a bit strange as one of their key laments is that the Chinese consumers do not consume enough and the country's prosperity is entirely based on exporting cheap merchandise to the West and wasteful infrastructure spending, including building bridges to nowhere. However, the fact that in the past decade China has become the most important market, or at least among the top three markets for many of the global manufacturers, has probably wrested the argument away from these economists and paved the way for the relevance of this book.

The Yin and Yang of Chinese Consumers

China is a large and heterogeneous market, which makes talking about Chinese consumers a task which is fraught with dangers and risk of overgeneralizations. Given the size and complexity of China, Newton's law of Consumer trends applies to China. For every consumer trend that you see,

A. Sethi, *Chinese Consumers*,
https://doi.org/10.1007/978-981-10-8992-3_1

there is an opposite, though not necessarily an equal, trend. Hence, if we notice that Chinese consumers are becoming more health-conscious—and that is absolutely a valid trend—we also need to acknowledge that Western junk food restaurants have been growing in the country at a phenomenal rate. The apparently opposing trends may apply to two different segments of the market—both of which are growing swiftly. In fact, they could even apply to the same consumers, who display different behaviors at different occasions and may explain the apparent contradiction by saying that they are often forced to eat junk food as normally they are too busy to cook, but as a rebound also try to engage in compensatory healthy habits by practicing yoga or go for jogging.

Similarly, we may say that the Chinese consumer is getting Westernized—which is evident, at least in terms of adoption of Western food (not just junk food) or customs (all Chinese brides don the Western style, white wedding gown for the ceremony). Even religious festivals are embraced whole-heartedly—the largely atheists Chinese celebrate Christmas with great gusto and festivity. Valentine's day elicits significant enthusiasm, in spite of the fact that the Chinese also have their own Valentine's day (七夕节or qixijie). The Chinese believe having two Valentine's days allows you to celebrate the joy of romance twice in a year—possibly with two different partners. But we also need to point out that there is a resurgence of interest in traditional Chinese culture—including studying Confucian philosophy and Chinese art and design.

Nation on the Move

The reason for the apparent contradiction is that apart from being large and heterogeneous, China is also a nation on the move and is hence perpetually changing. The fact that different parts of it are changing at a different pace presents a collage of contrasting and captivating pictures. One part of it has progressed far ahead of the rest and it has given China much to be proud of. It has achieved an economic miracle by clocking an average annual growth rate of 9% every year for more than two decades. It has lifted 350 million people out of poverty and achieved almost all millennium development goals set by the United Nations Development Program (UNDP). But another part of the country is still languishing and has formidable challenges that it needs to address. The most significant aspect of China's development perhaps is that while it has achieved growth, the effect of this growth is not uniform. The growth is much more visible in large cities and in the coastal areas—the large rural populace and the Western provinces are relatively untouched by this bountiful progress. Within the cities itself, there are yawning gaps between the haves and the have-nots causing tension and social strife. This dual picture presents opportunities for both luxury and premium products, as well as the low-priced basic necessities.

Numerator or Denominator

So while we all look at China with awe, celebrating its status as the second-largest economy in the world, we cannot but acknowledge that it is a long way from being a developed economy. If we temper its economy with the size of its population, we see that as it still ranks around 90th in the world, in terms of per capita gross domestic product (GDP). As an economist remarked some time ago, China looks great when its bulk (such as its population) is in the numerator but looks miserable if the same heft shifts to the denominator.

In the media, we often see pictures of young, attractive, modern urban Chinese consumers gleefully carrying a basket full of goods in their hands. This is the picture that the Western companies like to see—they dream and hope that such consumers will lap up their products, possibly compensating for the Western consumers' thriftiness after the financial crisis. But are these typical Chinese consumers? Or the typical consumers are the 600 million rural residents, with an average annual disposable income of US$1000?

And then we realize that both pictures are true. China is now the largest luxury goods market in the world (if you add what the affluent Chinese buy outside of China in their frequent jaunts abroad). It is estimated that there are more than a million Chinese with a million dollars in their pockets. But when you look at 45% of the Chinese population which lives in rural areas, we see that even their entire annual income will not be adequate to buy them a Louis Vuitton bag.

In This Book

This book is a result of being a witness to the evolution of Chinese consumers from thrifty survivalists to global luxury powerhouses. The book looks at the trends which have been shaping the Chinese consumers and attempts to look ahead and imagine the shape of things to emerge.

It starts by looking at the megatrends. Megatrends are broad economic, demographic and environmental changes which are normally beyond the control of the consumers and the marketers. In Chap. 1 I start by looking at a mega-shift, which is at the top of everyone's mind—the slowing Chinese economy and whether it spells doom. I examine the big facts and figures from the point of view of marketing companies, which really hope for the continuation of the dream run, and do not want the party to end. While everyone acknowledges the slowdown, its implications on the consumer market are not clear. Will it mean an end to the era of growth in consumer goods or even a decline, or merely a slowdown or in fact a transition to a new set of consumer goods, as the profiles and priorities of the Chinese consumers shift?

As incomes and urbanizations are intrinsically linked mega forces, the same chapter analyzes the trends in urbanizations and the effect it is likely to have on China's consumer market. While all developing nations have succumbed to the forces of urbanization, it is the scale and pace of the phenomenon in China, which amazes as well as poses unique challenges to its government and interesting opportunities to the marketers. Every year, for the past 20 years or so, as many as ten million additional Chinese have become a part of urban communities and at the same time a part of the consuming class. However, what is relevant from a marketing point of view is what it does to the minds of these newly urbanized consumers, who often display behavior and preferences which neither resemble the urban consumers, not the rural brethren that they have left behind.

A unique aspect of the Chinese development is the rapid change in the demographics. Economists often like to say that China is one of the few countries in the world which has become old before it became rich. The contrasting reference is to the Western economies and also Japan, which also show some of the same demographic shifts as China (particularly aging) but are already upper-income countries, and hence in a much better position to cope with the demographic shift and look after the elderly. The economists also worry about the loss of demographic dividend (a favorably high ratio of economically active, working population as a proportion of the total population) as a result of low birth rate and increasing longevity. The Chinese working population actually declined for the first time in 2013 and is expected to continue to decline in the coming years. What implications will it have on the consumer incomes and spending? Of course, the biggest policy change of allowing all Chinese to have two children instead of one is expected to alter this course to some extent, and I examine the expectations that this and further loosening of state's grip on the public reproduction habits is likely to result in. As a part of the analysis of the megatrends, I examine the story of the Chinese demographics and its implication on the shape of Chinese consumer market to come (will more chocolate be consumed by the elderly than children in China?).

The one-child policy coupled with traditional Chinese preference for the male child has created a gender imbalance in China that is not seen in many other parts of the world. It is estimated that because of China's gender imbalance, 30 million men will fail to secure a bride in the coming 20 years or so. At the same time increasing education levels among the Chinese women (52% of undergraduate and graduate students in China are female) along with growing career ambition, leads to late marriages and often no marriage at all, leading to a group of women disparagingly referred to as leftover women or shengnv剩女. Add to this the trend of late marriages and rising divorce rates, and you see that China is becoming a nation of singles. I examine the implications of these changes in the family structure on companies who want to market to them.

China has seen several different revolutions, the most hallowed of them being the People's Revolution of 1949 which liberated the country from years of subjugation and misery and gave birth to the modern Chinese nation. It then witnessed a less hallowed and more hellish cultural revolution which brought misery and mayhem of an unprecedented nature to millions of Chinese and put the country back by several decades. In Chap. 2 I talk about the latest revolution in China—the digital and mobile revolution and the way it has transformed the country, not just economically but also socially, given its citizens a voice (albeit a trifle muffled one) and unleashed the excitement and rapturous delights of shopping anywhere and anytime. Digital has ceased to be an additional or peripheral aspect of the Chinese consumers, and just another "channel" that the marketers need to use to reach the Chinese consumers. Digital is now an all-pervasive environment, and all traditional channels of communication are converging into digital (as more and more Chinese watch popular television dramas on their computers or mobile phones) just as traditional channels of distribution are trying to transform themselves into seamless omnichannel offerings.

China has 1.4 billion consumers. It will be naïve to paint all of them with the same brush. Segmentation, a commonly used but often misunderstood marketing technique, offers a useful way of looking at a large consumer mass in smaller more manageable parts. Most usefully segmentation needs to be applied for a specific product category and in fact even more specifically from the point of view of examining and evaluating opportunities for a particular company or brand, in relation to its strengths and weaknesses. However, applying segmentation in this manner will lead to China being divided into hundreds of segments, which will make the task of studying them an arduous undertaking. Hence I choose the middle path (the right path to take in a book about the Middle Country or 中国Zhongguo, as the Chinese call their country in their own language). With this perspective, in Chap. 3 I look at a few broad, specific segments of Chinese consumers and attempt a general, and not a product-specific classification of the Chinese consumers, with an objective to look at certain specific groups which may offer a certain degree of homogeneity of needs and warrant a commonality of approach for developing the marketing strategy directed at them. Specifically, this book examines the following consumer groups, and tries to explain their importance and their peculiar characteristics which could be relevant for marketing to them:

- Chinese women consumers, who because of their own means of income (China has one of the largest proportion of women working outside the home) have created an enormous market
- Chinese millennials and centennials, who may have very little in common with their Western counterparts, as they grew up and came of age in an entirely different environment
- Gray consumers, who through sheer numbers offer a huge and untapped market, which most marketers are slow to exploit
- Young couples, who are one of the largest consumer groups
- China's singles—who are getting more numerous and hence more important as a consumer group

(I do not look at the popular group of "middle class"—as firstly, I do not think that China has a middle class the way it is commonly understood. When marketers and economists talk about China's middle class, they are really referring to its "consuming class" which is highly skewed to the higher end of the population spectrum, as I will explain later. And secondly this "consuming class" is not one homogeneous block, but a highly heterogeneous group which is spread over all the other specific consumer groups that I do talk about).

Apart from looking at specific target groups, it also makes sense to look at some specific industries which are benefitting from the trends and changes in China. As the Chinese market is maturing, some product categories are facing stagnation, or even decline, but some other categories are booming (to take an example, beer and instant noodles are declining in urban China, but yogurt and makeup are growing healthily). Many of these new industries are services and have grown from practically nothing in the last 10 or 15 years. These include travel (particularly international travel), financial investments, education and learning (apart from the basic school education, which has been compulsory in China since 1986), premium beauty care (including cosmetic surgery), and entertainment. In Chap. 4 I examine some of these industries, the factors which are driving their growth, and their future prospects.

One of the most interesting and intriguing marketing phenomena in China has been the ballistic rise of the luxury goods market. The global luxury goods market has been sustained on the basis of unfettered enthusiasm and passion from the Chinese consumers. Are there any specific attitudes and socio-cultural factors that have led to the Chinese embrace of high priced gloss and luxury? However, the latest figures have jolted the industry leaders as Chinese consumers are exhibiting a more restrained behavior perhaps driven by the anti-corruption stipulations on the Chinese officials or a softening of the incomes. The factors responsible for the growth, as well as for the slowdown, are important to analyze to understand how long will the sheen last, how will its character change in the coming years, and what opportunities will the Chinese consumers offer for luxury and premium goods in the future. This subject, I felt, deserved a chapter by itself and I devote Chap. 5 to the luxury consumers of China.

In the second part of the book, I look a bit more deeply into the consumer mind, and specifically their changing values and preferences with implications on the shape of things to come in China. It is a common refrain among marketers and China experts that China is different and Chinese consumers are different. You cannot, therefore, assume that the Chinese consumers will be guided by the same functional and emotional needs that make the consumers in the developed markets reach for their wallets. As we will see through various pointers and insights, that while there is some truth in this assertion, there is also a whole lot of commonality which binds the Chinese consumers to their brethren in the rest of the world. And that is because the Chinese human beings espouse to, more or less, the same values that people in the rest of the world claim as their own. Even though the Communist Party may urge them to adopt and give more priority to socialistic values than anything else, the Chinese consumers are guided by universal values.

The Chinese consumers share the same conscience and scruples whether determined by a goodness of heart, or selfishness about ensuring a healthy, safe, and pollution-free environment for their children. In Chap. 6 we look at certain strong consumer trends and values which need to guide all marketing and branding in China. This chapter collates data from various surveys and research studies done by numerous research organizations, who have all been trying to fathom the Chinese mind and understand what makes the Chinese consumers tick.

The Chinese consumers are often seen as fickle, promiscuous bargain hunters and marketers often spend more on short-term tactical promotions than long-term brand building in China. In Chap. 7 I look at the task of branding in China. The key fact that we need to acknowledge about marketing in China is that the history of marketing in China is very short. When Mao Zedong's red guards acted on his call to destroy the "four olds" (old customs, old culture, old habits, old ideas) they inadvertently destroyed the "four P's of marketing" too—in fact, the whole discipline of marketing. In the chaos that ensued and the era of scarcity and rationing, there was little to buy and little to market. It was only after Deng Xiaoping gave out his permission that, "let some people get rich first", and started enacting the "four modernizations" (in the areas of agriculture, industry, national defense, and science and technology) that the four P's resurfaced and the story of marketing was reborn in the 1980s. In the 30 years that followed, China has been transformed from a land of acute scarcity to a place of overwhelming abundance. People born in the 1960s and 1970s have been catapulted from not seeing any brand to being exposed to a bewildering array of products from every part of the world.

As a result, the consumers are often confounded by the choices that confront them and sometimes follow decision rules which are not found in any marketing textbook. Marketers, therefore, often find the task of brand building and winning the Chinese consumers' loyalty a daunting proposition. Chinese consumers are known to be notoriously promiscuous, abandoning their favored brand for another which woos them with even trifling price-offs. The question hence is—is it really worthwhile to build a brand in China, and if yes, how to address this challenging task in one of the most crowded and competitive markets in the world.

One key characteristic of the Chinese market has been technological leapfrogging that one has been witnessing in the country. China bypassed the era of home phones and went straight to mobile phones. Film cameras never had an opportunity to photograph the Chinese, as, by the time the Chinese managed to acquire the money to buy cameras, digital cameras were already mainstream. And of course, most recently, the Chinese bypassed the personal computer and started surfing the net directly with their smartphones. The smartphone-based internet has had an impact on the consumer lives, the like of which has perhaps not been seen in several decades. In essence, it has totally transformed the manner in which the Chinese consume entertainment and information, and also changed their shopping and social lives. This has two major areas of implications. One of which is marketing—several of the traditional marketing concepts and ideas do not appear as relevant as they did in the pre-digital era. Does the consumer really have the time for a 30-second commercial in the fragmented way in which she consumes entertainment and information? Do traditional approaches to segmentation still make sense when the digital approach allows us to treat each consumer in his or her own segment? In Chap. 8, I examine the implications of the digital leapfrog on the practice of marketing in China, deriving implications on how it needs to change in the digital era.

This leapfrogging also has implications on the shape of things to come and the kind of products and services the Chinese consumers are likely to veer toward in the future. Now we see that China is no longer trailing the developed markets in technology which is relevant to the consumers. The largest number of industrial robots are in China as are the largest number of users of sharing economy.

In Chap. 9 I try to look ahead in some specific areas where China and the Chinese consumers seem to be leading the world—the embrace of artificial intelligence (AI), connected and self-driving cars, and growth of the sharing economy. These trends are important not just for technology products, but for all products and services, as keeping pace with technological changes and trends becomes a necessary condition for keeping pace with the Chinese consumers.

I conclude, in Chap. 10, by drawing a few portraits representing some key segments of Chinese consumers. I hope this will add body to and complete the picture that I have painted in the previous chapters, and leave the reader with an enriched and more intimate understanding of the consumer, provide a better empathetic feel, and lead to the development of more effective marketing strategies.

A Note of Caution

Research studies and surveys often compare China and the rest of the world in terms of attitudes, preferences, and behavior. I have used these liberally in trying to analyze the Chinese consumer mind. However, when most of the studies compare the Chinese and the German or the American consumers, they omit to mention that while in the developed markets the views are representative of the entire population (as the surveys are mostly done with a nationally representative sample), in China they more often than not, just represent the urban Chinese—and in fact sometimes just those who live in large cities like Shanghai and Beijing. However, this is a reality not just of the surveys but of the general discussion about the Chinese consumers. When most people talk about Chinese consumers, they are really talking about the urban Chinese consumers. Despite furious urbanization, 42% of the 1.39 billion Chinese still live in rural areas. Most marketers are essentially concerned about the urban consumers. This book is also about the 810 million urban Chinese consumers—and does not include the, still substantial, 580 million rural consumers.

CHAPTER 2

The Mega Forces

The Chinese consumer behavior is shaped by many diverse forces. Some of them are cultural and stem from the quintessence of being Chinese. Some of them pertain to the unique history of China—both its political history and the very short marketing history. However, some of these are even more powerful and all-encompassing than these and stem from the broader environment in which China and the Chinese consumers exist today. While there may be several such mega forces with a relevance for shaping the Chinese consumer, this book discusses the nature and the impact of four such mega forces:

- The economy and especially the consumer economy
- Urbanization
- Changing demographics
- Digital environment

The first three of these are analyzed in this chapter and the digital environment is discussed in the following chapter.

Chinese Consumer Economy: Still Striding Ahead

The Largest Economy in the World

In 2010, China's economy grew 10.6%—to reach $5.88 trillion (nominal gross domestic product [GDP]). Japan in comparison grew 3.9% to reach

A. Sethi, *Chinese Consumers*,
https://doi.org/10.1007/978-981-10-8992-3_2

$5.47 trillion, which led the economists to declare that China has overtaken Japan to become the second-largest economy in the world (China overtakes Japan as world's second-largest economy 2011). The media touted it as another feather in China's cap and reported it with a mix of grudging admiration and trepidation. Just a few years later, in 2014, came an even more awe-inspiring news about the strides being made by the Chinese economy. After 140 years of American dominance, International Monetary Fund (IMF) declared China to be the largest economy in the world (Bird 2014). IMF figures put China's economy at that time at $17.6 trillion in 2013, slightly higher than the $17.4 trillion estimate for the USA. Of course, this favorable comparison for China only holds if these figures are calculated using the purchasing power parity (PPP) (Callen 2017) method, which adjusts for the different purchasing power of money in different countries. Without the adjustment, China's economy still stood a distant second at $10.4 trillion as compared to $17.4 trillion for the USA (statisticstimes.com 2015).

However, the overall size of the economy does not portray an accurate picture of the living standard or purchasing power of the Chinese. When the same GDP is put along with a denominator of the Chinese population, it is clear that while China may be the largest economy in the world, its per capita GDP is only around 20% of America's (Nye 2014) and only around 90th in the world in terms of per capita GDP (worldbank.org n.d.). While sheer population and a modest income and spending have already made China the largest economy in the world, and one of the largest consumer markets in the world, its continued growth and attractiveness critically hinge on its ability to sustain its growth of the economy as a whole, and consumer incomes and spending specifically.

What Do the Economists Worry About

The recent global and domestic winds have been less than favorable. The Chinese economy is slowing down distinctly, its currency has depreciated, and its stock market behaving like a temperamental widow. In 2015 the Chinese GDP grew by 6.9% and further slowed down to 6.7% in 2016 (worldbank.org n.d.) though it rebounded to 6.9% in 2017.

However, the reassuring news for the students of consumer markets in China was that the consumer per capita disposable income grew significantly faster than the GDP, by 7.3% from 23,821 renminbi in 2016 to 25,974 renminbi in 2017 (stats.gov.cn 2018). Similarly, the retail sales in

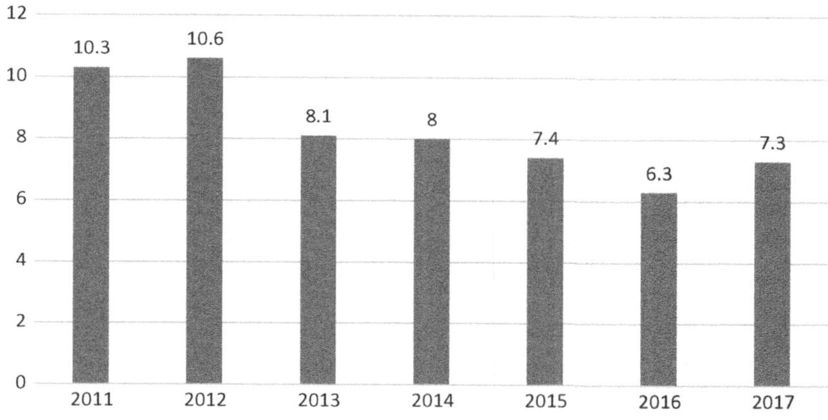

Fig. 2.1 Real growth rate of per capita disposable income (%)

2017 grew by 10.2%—up 10.0% in urban areas and 11.8% in rural areas (stats.gov.cn 2018). Hence while the overall economy may be stuttering, the consumer engine at its core is still firing admirably (Fig. 2.1).

China's per capita GDP has already reached $8000 per annum, and economists worry that it will be a struggle to take it further to a level of around $12,000, a standard which the World Bank uses to classify a country as upper-income. Economists worry that China will fall into what is called as the "middle-income trap". The origin of the thinking is based on the fact that of the 101 economies that the World Bank defined as middle-income in 1960, only 13 managed to wriggle their way into high-income countries by 2008, and the others continued to languish in middle-income mediocrity (The middle-income trap 2012). When the countries were starting at a low starting point, it was easy to shoot ahead, with many easy wins and low hanging fruits. However, now China has perhaps fully exploited the growth potential of the easy wins, such as low-cost production on the strength of impoverished villagers, happy to work on abysmal wages to escape the rural poverty, and exports to a hungry global middle class, looking to enjoy more products and more comforts but at a cheap price. Further substantial areas of growth from this level are going to be harder to find. Many experts are forecasting doom and disaster at worst, or at least stagnation for years to come and posit several apprehensions about the future of China's economy.

Why Do Not the Chinese Buy Like the Americans?

Even when the growth in China was at its best, the Western economists always worried that China's growth was riding on an export and investment boom and the domestic consumption's contribution to the GDP was disproportionately low. On the face of it the contribution of consumption to the GDP (only 39% in 2016, which in fact declined from 46% in 2000) (Household final consumption expenditure, etc. (% of GDP): World Bank n.d.) looks frighteningly low, and fuels the idea that the Chinese owe their economic growth only to the furious investment spree including building ghost cities, erecting bridges to nowhere, and launching high-speed trains to locations where no one wants to go. A number of hypotheses attempt to explain the relatively low share of consumption in GDP—including cultural proclivity of the Chinese to save rather than to splurge, or that the Chinese are forced to tuck away a large proportion of their income as they lack the social security net, and want to safeguard against the possibility of being hit by a large expense because of major illness or any other unforeseen eventuality. While surely there is some truth in these hypotheses, the fact is that the Chinese consumer spending has been increasing with the economy and in the later years, when the GDP growth has been sluggish, has been growing a few points higher than the economy.

The problem is that Chinese consumers look a bit feeble in comparison with the American consumers, who served the world well over the past few decades. They bought in large quantities, extravagantly and indiscriminately. They bought regardless of where the product came from (and a large proportion came from China), what it did for them, and whether they had a place in the house to keep it—which led to their having to buy larger and larger houses to keep the things that they bought.

The workers in China and other developing countries toiled away in Dickensian conditions to satiate the American consumer demand. They worked 12 hours a day in sweltering workshops, with no overtime or social security, to provide affordable goods to American consumers, who in turn obliged by consuming in prodigious quantities. When will the Chinese consumer spin the same magic as the American consumer and save the world? The advocates for designating the Chinese consumer as the replacement of the American sustainers of world economy argued that the fact that there are four times as many Chinese as Americans is a good starting point. And it was any way partly the Chinese money that the

Americans were spending. Hence it was not really the American consumer but actually the Chinese consumer who was providing the growth to the world economy! The Chinese consumers toiled in sweatshops and gave a part of their hard-earned money to the Americans who used it to buy the goods that the Chinese workers sweated to produce. So it all worked out quite well—the Americans did what they did best and are known for, and the Chinese did what their culture and tradition guided, giving them the satisfaction of following their values of hard work and moderation.

However clearly the fact that for most consumer goods, China is already the largest market in the world, or at least among the top five markets, it is time that we put a stop to this lament that the Chinese consumers are not spending enough. When focusing on the relatively low share of consumption as a proportion of the economy, what is often overlooked is that the low share is not so much because of the abstemious nature of the Chinese consumers (as we will see later in the book, contrary to popular perception, "thrift" as a value is not any more cherished in China than the rest of the world), but the overwhelmingly large contribution of investment into the economy, which pushes the consumption share to look relatively tiny, though in absolute terms it is significant. In fact, as Arthur R Kroeber (Kroeber) argues in his book—China's Economy: What Everyone Needs to Know—other Asian economies such as South Korea and Japan, which also went through a model of investment-led growth, including the development of a huge manufacturing sector, went through a similar phase, when domestic consumption as a proportion of the total GDP was rather small.

So while it is true that the Chinese consumers are not as profligate as the Americans, overdrawing on one credit card to pay the installment on another one is not the norm of financing one's lifestyle, actually the Chinese do want to consume, but they also want to eschew the Western style, debt-fueled over-consumption preceding the global financial crisis of 2008 (though there are some segments among the Chinese youth, which are playing as recklessly with debt as the American consumers).

China's Debt Problem

The Western economists have furrowed brows because of China's high debt—which increased from 150% of the GDP in 2008 to over 300% at the beginning of 2017 (Amaro 2017). In May 2016, the official People's Daily (China cannot accelerate economic growth by increasing leverage, says 'authoritative insider' 2016) also acknowledged the problem by publishing an article from an official from the Central Leading Group for Financial and Economic Affairs (of the National Development and Reforms Commission) worrying about China's dependence on high leverage and expressed an urgency to swerve away from credit-driven growth. The problem, it said, is particularly pronounced in industries like housing and emerging industries revolving around the use of the internet. Also of concern is the growth of some financing platforms which have been feeding real estate, some of which have ambivalent legal status. Apart from corporate debt, also of concern is the very high leverage of the local governments, which, the economists feel, may lead to an "L-shaped" growth for China in the future, rather than "U-shaped" or "V-shaped" leading to a plateauing or even a decline of the consumer economy.

However, what is important from the point of view of the health of the consumption is that the consumer debt is relatively modest. While Chinese attitude to debt is changing (almost all houses are bought with over 70% of the price as mortgage and new mortgages worth 2.2 trillion yuan accounted for 45% of the increase in total loans at 14 of the largest Chinese banks in 2015, because of easing of home purchase restrictions and easier access to mortgages), the use of credit card debt is relatively limited, and most Chinese pay the entire credit card bill on a regular basis. A large number of them also need to worry about the absence of adequate social security, the fearsome cost of housing, and the specter of major illness bankrupting them and ruining their lives.

Many economists worry that China is not mustering up enough courage to undertake real fiscal and structural reforms and continues to rely on the easier but superficial administrations of monetary policy tinkering and investments. On the other hand, there is a feeling that the government is showing increasing concern for supply-side reforms and reducing overcapacity and willing to make the required changes to address the problem which will protect the consumer economy.

The Way Ahead

The further pace of growth of China's consumer market is intrinsically linked to the consumer confidence and optimism about the future. According to the Boston Consulting Group (BCG) Consumer Sentiments Surveys, while the consumers are feeling the effect of the slowing economy in terms of reduced growth in their incomes, three-quarters of consumers had plans to maintain or increase their spending in 2016. In a similar survey in 2015, this figure was 81% (Walters and Kuo 2016). Hence, while there is a softening of the consumer sentiment, there is no meltdown. If the economy continues to restrain the growth of the consumer incomes, they are likely to tighten their purse-strings, though the trend of growth is likely to continue as the mindset will encourage consumption.

The Chinese government has set itself a target of doubling the 2010 per capita income by 2020, that is at the end of the 13th five-year plan. Even if it is not able to meet this target and the economy merely chugs along at a more modest pace of 5–6% a year, the overall growth and hence the opportunity for marketers is substantial. Economists such as Justin Yifu (former World Bank Chief Economist) (Yifu Lin & Triechel) are rosy about the future and see many engines of growth for incomes, which will propel China from a middle-income to a high-income country. These engines of growth include:

- Urbanization
- Continued infrastructure development
- Economic reforms
- Social reforms such as the hukou or the household registration system
- Expanding coverage of social services

BCG, a consultancy, in their New China Playbook (Kuo et al. 2015), a report on the Chinese consumers, estimate that China's consumer economy is expected to expand by about half, to \$6.5 trillion by 2020—even if the GDP growth slackens to 5.5% a year. This will lead to an incremental consumer market of \$2.3 trillion which is equivalent to adding a consumer market 1.3 times the size of today's Germany or the UK.

What Factors Are Likely to Continue to Drive the Chinese Consumer Markets

Chinese Consumers Are Still Optimistic

The Chinese consumers remain some of the most optimistic in the world. According to the McKinsey 2016 China consumer report (Zipser et al. 2016), 55% of the Chinese consumers were confident that their income will increase over the next five years—just 2% lower than 2012, when the economy was still growing at nearly 10%. The level of positive attitude still stands at an extraordinarily healthy level, and is indicative of an optimistic consumer mindset. In another research from zhaopin.com (a leading job-hunting website) which tracks the white-collar workers' confidence in job opportunities, it emerged that the confidence index was the highest in early 2017, in comparison to the previous three years (Zhaopin: Nearly 80% of China White Collars Trying to Switch Jobs 2017).

Infrastructure Spending Will Continue to Fuel the Consumer Market

While excessive infrastructure spending is often bemoaned by the economists, a fair amount of this investment creates the foundation of consumer spending. For instance, utilizing the high-speed rail network, Chinese made 5 billion trips on China's bullet trains in the eight years since high-speed rail services began in China in 2008. China Railway Corporation plans to double its length of high-speed railway by 2025. Forty-five percent of all rail trips in China in 2015 were by high-speed trains. Four thousand two hundred bullet trains operate every day, with 4 million passenger trips. China has 19,000 km of high-speed rail tracks (out of the total track of 120,000 km) accounting for 60% of the global high-speed rails (China's bullet trains make five billion trips 2016). It plans to increase it to 38,000 km by 2025, accounting for one-fifth of its 150,000 km network. This spending will continue to provide fuel for the growth of the Chinese consumer market.

The $1.4 trillion investment in the "one belt, one road" or the OBOR program, which aims at creating an economic belt, encompassing the countries on the historical silk route through East Asia, Central Asia and onto Middle East and Europe, as also a maritime route, that links China to India, Africa, and the Mediterranean, will give a boost to exports and help in regaining some of the export-oriented jobs which China has been losing in the recent years (China's US$1.4 trillion 'One Belt, One Road' set to make bigger impact than US' Marshall Plan to rebuild post-war Europe 2016).

Continued March of Urbanization

In 1978, just before the country started veering away from economic and political insanity toward a more sensible direction, only 18% of China's population lived in cities. In 2013 China's urban population exceeded the number of people living in its cities and by the end of 2017, 58.5% of China's population was classified as urban (stats.gov.cn 2018). Another 240 million consumers are likely to be added to urban China over the next 15 years, elevating the urbanization rate to around 70% by 2030 (Sun et al. 2017). This continued march of urbanization, while creating many challenges, is likely to provide continuous fodder for the consumer market.

Growth in the Premium Categories

In its high growth honeymoon period, China's consumer market had been driven by certain very basic factors—such as increasing number of urban households and increasing penetration of basic products of everyday use, particularly as the lower tier cities caught up with the more developed cities in terms of adoption of a range of products. However, many of these basic factors are now playing a much lower role in driving growth, as urban markets approach saturation. Particularly for non-discretionary fast-moving consumer goods (FMCG), there is a level beyond which penetration and usage frequency and volume will not grow any further. It is also expected that the proportion of the income which is spent on basic FMCG products will plateau and not continue to increase with incomes. However, certain drivers of growth are still strong and are likely to continue to drive the market.

According to the fifth China shopper report from Kantar Worldpanel and Bain & Company, the value growth of FMCG in 2016 was a five-year low at 3.0% in terms of value (further decrease from the 3.6% growth in 2015), in urban China. In comparison, the growth in 2014 was 5.4% and in 2012 as high as 11.8% (Lannes et al. 2017).

Looking further, the report reveals that almost all of this growth came because the consumers were buying more premium products—the volume growth was actually only 0.6%—volume growth was flat in 2015 and 2014 too, though before that the FMCG market was growing at around 4–5% a year. As the category largely consists of basic essentials, the plateauing of its growth is expected. Some categories which are typically consumed by the lower end of the consuming class are actually declining—according to the China Shopper report, the volume of instant noodles actually declined in 2015 by 12.5%. Similarly, beer, the lower middle-class tipple, also lost volume to the extent of 3.6%.

On the other hand, the pet food category saw an 11.7% increase in value and yogurt by 20.6%. The makeup category grew by 15.5% and skin care by 13.3%. Even the more routine personal care category is benefitting from a trend of premiumization—showing a 9.5% value growth in spite of a 1.5% drop in volume.

Urbanization: A Mega Force Driving Consumption

Urbanizing with Haste

China has been urbanizing at a furious pace. The figures indicate that in the last two decades or so, around 10 million people were added to the urban population every year. Not all of this is contributed by an actual migration of rural folks into cities; a significant proportion is also accounted for by administrative reclassifications of erstwhile rural areas into urban ones. However, on the whole, it is well established that urbanization has taken place at an unprecedented pace.

It is also well recognized that it has contributed immensely to economic growth, particularly in a country like China, where most rural residents have rights to very small parcels of land, tilling which can only provide a survival-level existence. This migration of rural Chinese to China's cities, to work as cheap labor in its export-oriented factories, has been a key contributor to China's growth and will continue, as still, 600 million Chinese live in rural areas with a per capita disposable income of less than US$150 a month.

Historians and sociologists have always said that man prefers the modern conveniences of the city than the harsh rural existence. What is surprising is the scale and speed with which urbanization has happened in China—with over 10 million consumers added to urban China every year. China's migrant workforce was estimated at 286.5 million in 2017. The growth was rapid after economic liberalization, though in recent years the pace of growth has slackened (1.7% in 2017) (stats.gov.cn 2018). This definition includes everyone whose hukou or household registration is in a rural area but who works in a non-rural area for more than six months in a year.

Driven by the export boom, millions of rural Chinese have been leaving their farms to toil in urban workshops and construction sites, sending money home to supplement the meager agricultural income. The workers left home as their income from tilling their small farms was woefully inadequate to provide them with a comfortable existence and even a modicum of savings and security. The median per capita rural income in 2017 was a little more than a third of what the urban Chinese enjoyed (stats.gov.cn 2018). Despite the harsh conditions of work and stay in the cities and the emotional pain of living away from their loved ones, they willingly accepted this existence to be able to provide their families with a better quality of life.

Will the Economic Slowdown Also Decelerate Urbanization

The growth was interrupted by the 2008 crisis in which Wall Street brought down the Main Street, which in turn resulted in the closure of factories in China which churned out products enjoyed by American consumers with borrowed money and 20 million of these workers lost their jobs and faced the unwelcome prospect to return to their rural homes. The languishing countryside and the widening urban-rural income gap was always an area of anxiety for the Chinese government. Guided by this concern, the party leadership raised slogans like "the new socialistic countryside" accompanied by supportive actions such as abolishing the tax on agricultural income. The government also helped out by infrastructure spending in the 4 trillion Yuan stimulus package—including expansion of railways, building roads, and housing—compensating for some of the jobs lost in the export industry. It also invested in trying to boost domestic consumption and cheer the rural masses by offering a 13% subsidy on a range of home appliances ranging from washing machines to mobile phones. On the whole, the significant brakes in the economic vehicle did not restrain urbanization.

The export growth in China has been faltering again and domestic consumption, though increasing significantly, has not been able to compensate for the decline in exports. At the same time the cry of "supply-side reforms" means that workers will face an axe as obese steel mills slim down in response to excess capacity and faltering demand. The workers need an alternative to a miserable though lucrative toil in the cities and leisurely but penurious existence at home. Much is being done to equip the laid-off workers with new skills which make them eligible for other employment opportunities in and around their homes. Hence even if some of the laid-off workers return to the countryside, it will not stem the tide of urbanization.

Home But Not Really: The Rurban Chinese

While it has attracted 287 million workers to cities and towns, China has so far discouraged its rural population to totally abandon their rustic homes and move to the cities—possibly out of a fear that if not restrained, it will lead to a deluge, converting cities into shanty towns as seen in much of the developing world. The movement is controlled by a draconian system of household registration known as the hukou, which ties you to your place of birth for all essential benefits and services (Special Topic Paper: China's Household Registration System: Sustained Reform Needed to Protect China's Rural Migrants 2005). The system is a continuation of the Maoist era when impoverished villagers were prevented from flooding the cities to maintain order and also the privileges of the ruling urban elite. The system is highly discriminatory against the migrants, as a result of which rural Chinese living in urban areas cannot send their children to the same schools as the city folks do, nor can they go to the same hospitals and enjoy the same subsidized health care that the city folks benefit from. If the family needs a passport or loses their identity card, they again need to trudge back to their home village to sort this out. These rural-urban residents (or rurbans) have one foot in the city and the other back home, creating a unique target group with interesting marketing possibilities.

Education and care of children is perhaps the biggest of the problems that the rurban Chinese face. If their child needs to sit for the gaokao (高考 the frightening college entrance examination, that is seen by almost all as a ticket to prosperity) he or she must go back to their home province and take the test in a location near their home. As a result, the parents who migrate to the cities, often leave their children behind in the care of the grandparents. The concern in the media has been rising for these "left-behind" children (referred to as 留守儿童 or liushouertong).

In fact, the fear of the authorities of a horde of rural Chinese flooding the cities is misplaced. Most rural families are tied to the villages by a piece of land which they do not own but have a right to till and hold on to forever. The land cannot be sold by them to get some cash to make an investment in a house in the cities. As soon as they relinquish their rural hukou and take a transfer to the city, they lose the right over that piece of land and also the choice to come back to their rural home if things do not work out in the city or if they wish to retire back to a slower pace life back home. According to a research done by the Chinese Academy of Social Sciences in April 2016, more than half of the rural hukou holders interviewed were reluctant to part with their land binding certificates and move to a life of modern city revelry. The chief reason for this reluctance was the land in their villages. The land though not really owned by them, allows them to till it, or even rent it to obtain an income. Once they embrace the generally highly coveted urban hukou, they lose this source of income (economist.com 2016).

In spite of the hukou obstacle, 260 million rural migrants live in the cities—as is evident from the fact that though 55% of China's population is urban, only 36% have an urban hukou. Further urbanization is not only likely but planned. By 2050, 75% of China's population is expected to be urban. In fact, hukou reforms are one of the key changes that the government is under pressure to implement, which will further accelerate urbanization, contributing further to the growth.

In 2016, China's State Council said that it plans to ease the restrictions on permanent residency in cities for university graduates, skilled technicians and those returning after receiving an education overseas, as well as restriction on rural workers. The new residency permit became operational in 2016, which entitles holders to free education, health care, employment, and legal services in the city in which they live.

The March of Urbanization and the Opportunities for Brands in the Smaller Cities

The continuation of urbanization will naturally offer myriad opportunities to brands. According to a report by Ogilvy, an advertising agency, half of world's GDP growth, and consumer power over the next decade will come from smaller cities in the emerging world—nearly all this growth happening in fast-growing economies in Asia, with China and India leading the way.

The initial wave of migration from rural to urban areas normally hits the larger cities as that is where the largest and the most visible economic opportunities lie. The Chinese government, while recognizing the inevitability and economic benefits of urbanization, is also keen to prevent their showcase cities from degenerating into soulless sprawls and shanty towns. As a result, the official policies encourage enticing the rural migrants into smaller cities surrounding the first-tier cities like Shanghai and Beijing. The development of the smaller cities has been providing much fodder for economic growth and will continue to do so in the coming years, as official policies encourage their development and lower prices (particularly for housing) and better living conditions attract the migrants.

In the past several years, while top-tier cities like Shanghai, Beijing, and Guangzhou have been exhibiting signs of saturation for many product categories, the smaller cities have been providing the growth. While the China Institute for Employment Research (CIER) Index decreased in Q4 of 2017, compared to a year ago, in tier-1 cities, it increased in tier-2 and tier-3 cities. In fact the highest increase was registered in tier-3 cities (Source: Zhaopin and CIER at Renmin University of China) (morningstar.com 2018).

Envisioning Shanghai's Future

Shanghai is the largest city in China with a population of 24.3 million in 2014. The population has grown by more than 8 million since 2000. However, the Shanghai government has set a target to keep the population under 25 million—a figure it expects to achieve by 2020. Instead, it has decided to contribute and help grow the surrounding cities in the Yangtze River Delta, a cluster which comprises 26 cities, including parts of Jiangsu, Zhejiang and Anhui provinces. According to the 2016 Shanghai Blue Book, The Yangtze River Delta City Cluster houses 16.7% of China's population, has only 3.7% of the country's area, but contributes 21.2% of China's GDP, with a per capita GDP of over $10,000 in 2014. Shanghai plans to channel some of the investment it attracts to other cities in the Delta. Beijing also looks at its future development in the form of a broader area, which encompasses the city of Tianjin as well as parts of the adjoining Hebei province (the combined area referred to as JingJinJi government also plans to cap the population of the city and is actively investing in neighboring areas to take the pressure off the capital city). In 2017 it announced a plan to develop Xiongan New Area in Hebei province, and move some key functions from Beijing to this new development.

Changing Demographics

Dwindling Demographic Dividend

China's population increased by 2.52% by the end of 2015 since the census in 2010 to 1.37 billion. The figure has been forecast to peak at about 1.45 billion by 2030, while India is expected to take the dubious crown of being the most populous country in the world from China around 2028. Many economic analyses postulate that population growth was a major driver of consumer markets in the last millennium. However, population growth is something that has slowed down to such an extent that the fertility rate in China today is below the required replacement rate—the rate at which the population can be maintained at the current level (fertility rate of 1.2 according to Census 2010, as compared to the required replacement rate of 2.1 to prevent the population from shrinking). While China continues to be the manufacturing center of the world, the one thing that the Chinese are producing a lot less of than before, is more Chinese citizens.

While the so-called one-child policy comes readily as an explanation, some people will argue that there never really was a one-child policy as many people were exempt from it or were able to dodge it. This is true as those belonging to a minority group or living in rural areas and with the first child a girl are allowed to have another go at producing a male heir. Secondly, neither the million millionaires nor the 700 million who only earn less than $2000 a year have one child—as usually, it is the middle class which succumbs to the strictures. However, the policy is rather strictly applied in cities and it is rare to see an under 30 city dweller today who has a sibling. This has resulted in two specific demographic peculiarities in China—one of which is a disproportionately large proportion of the elderly and the other is an awfully skewed gender ratio in favor of males, because of the traditional preference of the male child.

The demographic dividend is a term coined by demographers to describe to what extent a country's economic growth is fueled by the fact that it has a large number of people in the working age (normally considered 15–59 or 15–64 years) and not many in the non-contributing age of less than 15 years or the aged. Due to various factors including historical and policy-related, particularly China's policy to discourage its citizens to have more than one child, it has peculiar demographics. In China, the onset of demographic dividend started in the 1970s when China took

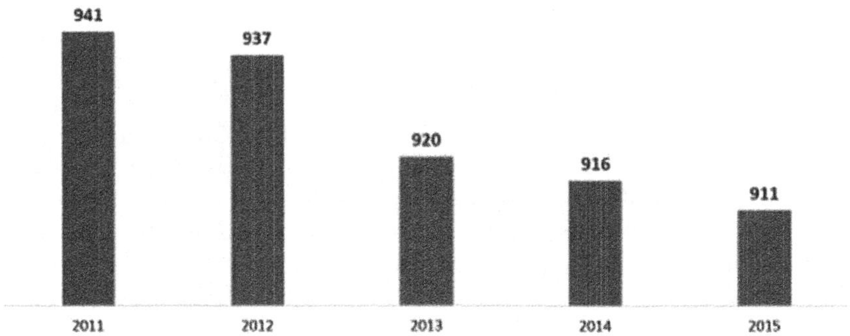

Fig. 2.2 Workforce population of China. Source: Green book of population. 2011–2012, 15–59 years; 2013–2015, 16–60 years

strong measures to control the birth rate and fewer children were being born, but the previous generation had many children, who were members of the working age group. According to a World Bank report, China's demographic dividend has been estimated to have contributed one-quarter to the country's per capita GDP growth during 1982–2000 (Wang 2010).

However, the demographic dividend is diminishing because of two reasons—fewer people are entering the working age population and secondly as the health standards and health care improves, people are living longer and the numbers of the non-productive aged is increasing. In 2012 the number of people in the age group of 15–59 years actually declined to 922 million from 925 million in 2011. This figure continues to diminish and stands at 911 million in 2015, and is expected to sink to 830 million in 2030 (Myers 2016) (Fig. 2.2).

Graying Population

China has the largest gray population in the world. The share of population 60 years or above increased by 3% between the sixth population census of 2010 and the 2015 survey-based assessment. China is graying—in fact, it is one of the few countries which is graying before it can get rich. This is important as with aging comes the responsibility of looking after the senior citizens who are not able to contribute to the economy but need to be taken care of. But one-child policy is not the only reason for China's graying. China has achieved amazing improvement in health standards and a resultant increase in life expectancy. Today the average life expectancy of a woman in Beijing or Shanghai is over 80 years—something that any man is well advised to keep in mind if tempted to propose to one of the attractive residents of the city (Dehua 2018).

The graying population has enormous implications on the economy and is of immense importance for policymakers. But from a marketing point of view, graying consumers offer unique opportunities as they have unique needs—both physically and emotionally (the marketing opportunities for gray consumers is further discussed in Chap. 3 of this book). These needs need to be recognized while designing products and services for them.

> In fact, the need for the children to visit their elderly parents became a law in China in 2013. In 2016, Shanghai Municipal government introduced an amendment to the regulation on the Protection of the Rights and Interests of the Elderly in Shanghai, making it compulsory for children to regularly visit or at least be in contact with their parents, Shanghai alone has a 4.36 million people aged 60 or above. The unfortunate unvisited parents can take their children to court, which has the ability to impose fines or even reduce their credit rating, making it difficult for them to secure mortgages and personal loans. This enforcement of Confucian values elicited a mixed reaction from the Chinese citizens, with some feeling that "filial piety needs to be felt from the heart, not enforced by the stick of the law". A 77 years old woman from Wuxi (a city in Jiangsu province in Eastern China) became the first senior citizen to assert this right by taking her son to court for neglecting to show his face to her periodically. The court promptly issued an order asking the son as well as his wife to make bi-monthly visits to her.

The Two-Child Policy

China's top legislature approved a draft amendment to the country's family planning law on December 27, 2015, which will allow all couples to have a second child from the start of 2016, ending the three decades of "one couple, one child" policy. According to the data from the National Health and Family Planning Commission (NHFPC), 90 million women will become eligible to have a second child as a result of this relaxation.

However, 54 million of these women will be at least 35 years old or older. Seventy-two million of them have an intrauterine device (IUD) or ligation and would be unable to have a second child without undergoing a surgical procedure (though the State has offered to provide free surgery for fertility recovery [Xiaodong 2016]).

However, the issue goes beyond physical ability and fertility—the key question is whether the newly eligible women want to give birth to a second child? In 2016, Zhaopin.com, China's leading recruitment website conducted a survey among 14,290 working women to inquire about their plans to raise a family. Sixty percent of the working women said that they do not want to have a second child. In fact, 20% said that they do not want to have a child at all. The biggest reason for desisting to have a second child was stated to be the cost of raising a child. Other stated reasons included the demand on time and energy to raise a child, concern about the career, and fear of childbirth. According to forecasts by the standing council of the China Population Association, under the NHFPC, even after the change of policy, the workforce (those aged between 15 and 59 years) will drop to 700 million by 2050 from the current 911 million.

Despite the deterrents that many parents feel for producing the second child, clearly, the change in regulation will create additional consumption for products and services targeted at children. While the authorities and demographers are still studying the response from prospective couples and crunching the numbers, it is estimated that around 2 million additional kids will be borne every year in the coming years.

While this is good news for companies which target children, such as the infant milk formula manufacturers (already a huge and booming market) and companies offering child-care and educational services, on the whole, the two-child policy is not expected to have any significant impact on the demographic profile and the problem of dwindling workforce population.

Gender Imbalance

While the communist revolution and Mao Zedong may be blamed for much suffering in China, even his sternest detractors acknowledge the dramatic changes in women's rights seen after the liberation of the country in 1949. Mao Zedong famously said that "women hold half the sky" in 1950, and took some concrete action to maintain this celestial order. However, all the proclamations and exhortations of the Chairman were

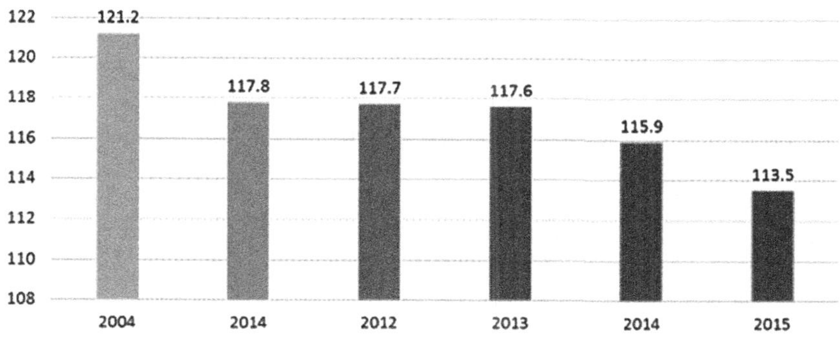

Fig. 2.3 Gender ratio at birth. Source: National Health and Family Planning Commission

not able to wipe the strong preference for the male child in China. This preference has been further exacerbated by the one-child policy which has resulted in a huge gender imbalance. While in the population as a whole, there are only 105 males to 100 females in China, the gender ratio at birth tells a different story—according to figures from the National Bureau of Statistics, China's gender ratio at birth remained one of the worst in the world and in 2014, with 115.9 boys born for every 100 girls (a normal ratio is 103–107 boys for every 100 girls) (Fig. 2.3).

Gender imbalance is particularly serious among those of a marriageable age (legal age of marriage is 22 years for males and 20 years for females). The sixth nationwide population census conducted in 2010 showed that the ratio between unmarried men and women born in the 1980s was 136 to 100. According to various estimates, there will be 30 million more single men than women by 2020 across China. Sociologists feel that this can become an incendiary factor for threatening the social stability. It is also common now for men from China, particular the southern provinces such as Guangxi, to go across the border to Vietnam in search of brides (not a part of the official OBOR initiative!).

However, marketers see the gender imbalance as an opportunity to sell products and services to the single men, who are in a fiercely competitive market to woo the much fewer women in the marriage market. The women in cities like Shanghai have raised the stakes and demands of an apartment and a car is the basic eligibility requirements for them to consider the case of a potential suitor. Some economists feel that the enormous price surge in the real estate market in Shanghai and Beijing is at least partly caused by the demand created among young men of marriageable age, who are desperate to acquire an apartment to further their prospects for marriage. In rural areas, the problem is particularly acute, as the preference of the male child is even stronger in the villages and the one-child policy was not enforced as rigorously. Though the price of housing in rural China may not be as daunting as in the large cities, the prospective grooms are required to put up a substantial "bride price" to win the hand of a local maiden.

Changing Family Structure

As many young women fail to find suitable young men who meet their exacting standards, they choose a life of singlehood. The fact that young women are often better educated than men (52% of undergraduate and graduate students in China are female) along with growing career ambition and the fact that women mostly want to "marry up", that is, seek a partner who is better educated and earns more than them, lead to late marriages and often no marriage at all. This is leading to a group of women disparagingly referred to as leftover women or shengnv 剩女. Add to this the trend of late marriages and rising divorce rates (Kai 2016), and you see that China is becoming a nation of singles. This change has a huge implication on the way marketers design and promote their products in China.

Not only has this created a huge market to appeal to the aspirants, who need to compete for a partner, it has also created a market to win favor of those who have willingly or unwillingly reconciled to a life of remaining single rather than succumbing to the parental and societal pressure and enter into a marriage of convenience. SKII, a brand of skin care and cosmetics, created a series of online videos on the Chinese video sharing websites, which portrayed marriage as a choice, not an obligation. The videos, which touched a chord with the audience and soon went viral, attempted to remove the stigma attached to singlehood, while at the same time paved the way for enhancing their brand appeal to this target group, which is increasing in terms of size and importance. IKEA, the Swedish furniture store, on the other hand, was berated by the Chinese netizens for airing a television commercial in which a mother reprimands her daughter by saying, "Don't call me your mom if you cannot bring a boyfriend".

The Tyranny of Demographics

The unique history of China, the strong controls that the government has exercised on the citizens' reproductive practices, as well as the rapid advancements in economy and health care, have left China with a rather peculiar set of demographics. Understanding of these demographics is essential for any marketer to identify the most lucrative opportunities and design effective marketing strategies to exploit them. China presents a unique demographic profile which needs to be reflected in the marketing plans.

References

(n.d.). Retrieved from worldbank.org: https://data.worldbank.org/indicator/NY.GDP.PCAP.CD?name_desc=false&view=chart

(2015, January 10). Retrieved from statisticstimes.com: http://statisticstimes.com/economy/united-states-vs-china-gdp.php

(2016, March 26). Retrieved from economist.com: https://www.economist.com/news/china/21695556-ambitious-plan-social-change-has-run-trouble-reformu2019s-big-taboo

(2018, February 28). Retrieved from stats.gov.cn: http://www.stats.gov.cn/english/PressRelease/201802/t20180228_1585666.html

(2018, January 18). Retrieved from morningstar.com: https://www.morningstar.com/news/pr-news-wire/PRNews_20180118CN91509/china-labor-market-index-hits-record-high-in-the-fourth-quarter-of-2017.print.html

Amaro, S. (2017, June 28). *China's debt surpasses 300 percent of GDP, IIF says, raising doubts over Yellen's crisis remarks*. Retrieved from cnbc.com: https://www.cnbc.com/2017/06/28/chinas-debt-surpasses-300-percent-of-gdp-iif-says-raising-doubts-over-yellens-crisis-remarks.html

Bird, M. (2014, October 8). Retrieved from businessinsider.com: http://www.businessinsider.com/china-overtakes-us-as-worlds-largest-economy-2014-10

Callen, T. (2017, July 29). *Purchasing Power Parity: Weights Matter*. Retrieved from imf.org: http://www.imf.org/external/pubs/ft/fandd/basics/ppp.htm

China cannot accelerate economic growth by increasing leverage, says 'authoritative insider'. (2016, May 10). Retrieved from en.people.cn: http://en.people.cn/n3/2016/0510/c90780-9055625.html

China overtakes Japan as world's second-largest economy. (2011, February 14). Retrieved from www.theguardian.com: https://www.theguardian.com/business/2011/feb/14/china-second-largest-economy

China's US$1.4 trillion 'One Belt, One Road' set to make bigger impact than US' Marshall Plan to rebuild post-war Europe. (2016, August 6). Retrieved from scmp.com: http://www.scmp.com/news/china/policies-politics/article/2000835/chinas-us14-trillion-one-belt-one-road-extends-beijings

China's bullet trains make five billion trips. (2016, August 1). Retrieved from chinadaily.com.cn: http://www.chinadaily.com.cn/business/2016-08/01/content_26292785.htm

Dehua, C. (2018, January 24). Retrieved from gbtimes.com: https://gbtimes.com/shanghais-average-life-expectancy-reaches-record-high

Household final consumption expenditure, etc. (% of GDP): World Bank. (n.d.). Retrieved from worldbank.org: https://data.worldbank.org/indicator/NE.CON.PETC.ZS?locations=CN

Kai, G. (2016, July 12). Retrieved from chinadaily.com.cn: http://www.chinadaily.com.cn/china/2016-07/12/content_26055052.htm

Kuo, Y., Walters, J., Gao, H., Wang, A., Yang, V., Yang, J., …Wan, H. (2015). *The New China Playbook.* Boston Consulting Group; AliResearch.

Lannes, B., Ding, J., Kou, M., & Yu, J. (2017). *China Shopper Report 2017.* Bain & Company & Kantar Worldpanel.

Myers, J. (2016, July 25). Retrieved from weforum.com: https://www.weforum.org/agenda/2016/07/china-working-ageing-population/

Nye, J. S. (2014, November 6). *When will China overtake the US?* Retrieved from weforum.org: https://www.weforum.org/agenda/2014/11/will-china-overtake-us/

Special Topic Paper: China's Household Registration System: Sustained Reform Needed to Protect China's Rural Migrants. (2005, October 7). Retrieved from cecc.gov: https://www.cecc.gov/publications/issue-papers/cecc-special-topic-paper-chinas-household-registration-system-sustained

Sun, D., Zhou, L., Li, Y., Liu, H., Shen, X., Wang, Z., & Wang, X. (2017). New-type urbanization in China: Predicted trends and investment demand for 2015–2030. *Journal of Geographical Science.*

The middle-income trap. (2012, March 27). Retrieved from economist.com: https://www.economist.com/blogs/graphicdetail/2012/03/focus-3

Walters, J., & Kuo, Y. (2016, June 20). *China's Consumers Stay the (slightly slower) Course.* Retrieved from bcg.com: https://www.bcg.com/publications/2016/globalization-center-customer-insight-china-consumers-stay-slightly-slower-course.aspx

Wang, F. (2010, September 30). *https://www.brookings.edu/articles/chinas-population-destiny-the-looming-crisis/.* Retrieved from brookings.edu: https://www.brookings.edu/articles/chinas-population-destiny-the-looming-crisis/

Xiaodong, W. (2016, January 25). Retrieved from en.nhfpc.gov.cn: http://en.nhfpc.gov.cn/2016-01/25/c_69360.htm

Zhaopin: Nearly 80% of China White Collars Trying to Switch Jobs. (2017, February 27). Retrieved from prnewswire.com: https://www.prnewswire.com/news-releases/zhaopin-nearly-80-of-china-white-collars-trying-to-switch-jobs-300413855.html

Zipser, D., Chen, Y., & Gong, F. (2016). *2016 China Consumer Report.* McKinsey&Company.

CHAPTER 3

Digital China

The Teeming Netizens

In 2008 the China Internet Network Information Center (CNNIC) gleefully reported that the number of internet users in China, estimated by them at 253 million, has surpassed the number in the USA (Barboza 2008). At that time, the news was greeted with a fair amount of exclamation and wonder. Just the next year the same organization reported that the number of internet users in China now was greater than the entire population of USA. The feeling of awe, almost disbelief, grew further. In 2016 CNNIC reported that now the number of Chinese internet users, counted as 710 million, was twice the number of the entire population of USA (CNNIC—China Internet Network Information Center 2016). Clearly, the pace of adoption of the internet by the Chinese has been astonishing and now more than half the population of the country has access to the internet, though the penetration in large cities such as Shanghai and Beijing, as well as prosperous provinces such as Zhejiang and Guangdong, is over 60%.

However, it is not just the pace of adoption which causes amazement—it is the strength of the embrace and the whole-hearted enthusiasm and pervasiveness of the different ways in which the Chinese have taken to the internet, which inspires awe.

A. Sethi, *Chinese Consumers*,
https://doi.org/10.1007/978-981-10-8992-3_3

Leapfrogging China

The term "leapfrog" refers to advancement or progress, which does not follow the usual, sequential steps, which had been observed in previous similar developments and hence one would normally expect to see. In the Western world, the consumers had their first taste of the internet through a dial-up modem connected to their phone line, which they then upgraded to a broadband connection, and finally started tentatively accessing the internet on their mobile phones after Steve Jobs showed them that it was not only possible but also pleasurable. In China, the consumers leapfrogged from no internet (no phone, no broadband connection at home) straight to the mobile internet. Technological access shot ahead of the traditional path of progress and increase of incomes which would have led to consumers installing a landline at home and then buying a modem to connect to the internet. Today, more Chinese access the internet on their mobile phones as compared to a PC, with 90% of the 710 million internet consumers using their phones to get online (Fig. 3.1).

There have been a number of factors responsible for the leapfrogging (which incidentally is also observed in several other areas in China, including, for instance, a nearly total by-pass of film cameras, to move to digital cameras and of course, from no phone directly to mobile phone). These factors include:

- The landline and broadband infrastructure development lagged behind the development of mobile internet infrastructure

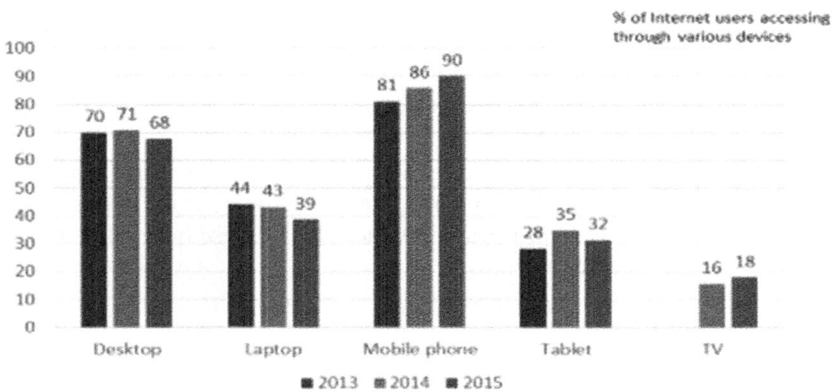

Fig. 3.1 Access of internet through various devices. Source: CNNIC

- Low penetration of computers meant that even those with a telephone landline were not in a position to access the internet
- With over 200 million migrant workers, living in dormitories and temporary accommodation, computer access of the internet was impractical, but mobile access was handy
- China innovated to produce smartphones at a fraction of a price of an iPhone or an Android phone from a global brand, which made it affordable for nearly all
- The main draw of the internet, which was and remains social networking, transitioned very easily and well to the mobile due to strong efforts made by the application providers such as Tencent (provider of QQ and WeChat) and Sina (provider of SinaWeibo, a Twitter-like service).
- The state-owned mobile service providers offered mobile internet at an affordable price, and in fact enabled the users to even save money, as they moved mobile messaging and even calls to the internet

As a confluence of these factors, China has become essentially a mobile internet nation (a path that another giant market, India, is also embracing, with the help of Chinese smartphones!). Data suggests that among the internet users, two-third of the time spent on the internet is on the mobile phone. While it was mostly the social networking which happened on the mobile, clever innovations from the Chinese internet companies, including clever mobile-based payment options, have also resulted in e-commerce morphing into mobile-based e-commerce (mCommerce).

Reaching the Consumer on the Internet

With the increasing reach of the internet, the amount of time that the consumers are spending on the digital media has overtaken the amount of time that the consumers spend on traditional media in urban China. There are several reasons for this and one of the more important reasons is that the television content is now all available on the internet (in a paid and unpaid, legitimate or pirated manner).

A few years ago, when the internet audience numbers became interesting, most companies were hurriedly trying to put together a digital strategy to connect online with the consumers. Most of these companies were acting too slowly and their strategies were short-lived in their effectiveness.

With 710 million internet users, the need of the hour is not to develop a digital strategy, but to comprehensively overhaul the strategy with digital at the core of it. According to a research conducted by eMarketer, a research firm, in 2015 for the first time, the amount of time a Chinese consumer spent on digital channels outstripped the time that was spent glued to the television. The average Chinese, according to their data, spends six hours and six minutes consuming media in various forms, and out of this three hours and five minutes is devoted to the partaking of social media and digital content (eMarketer 2016).

GroupM, a part of the WPP group, estimates that online advertising expenditure was 277 billion yuan in 2016, an increase of 30% over the previous year. In 2007 digital media spend was expected to account for 57.2% of the media spend—a significant increase from the 38% share of the pie that digital secured in 2015 and almost the same as the proportion of time that consumers spend on digital (GroupM 2017). Correspondingly the share of television was forecasted to decline from 41% in 2015 to 31.4% in 2017. This growth trajectory is likely to be maintained in the coming years and the online ad spend is expected to nearly double in 2019 to 543 million yuan from the 2016 figure. This comes at the cost of traditional media advertising, which declined by 2% in 2016 (after seeing a growth of 1% in each of the preceding years).

Rural Internet

According to the latest CNNIC report, over 200 million of the 710 million Chinese Internet users lived in rural areas (28.4% of the internet users as against 45% of the total population). However, while the urban growth in the number of Internet users is now sluggish, the rural netizens are growing at an impressive 9.5% in 2015—twice as fast as the urban growth (CNNIC—China Internet Network Information Center 2016).

However reports shows that China ranks relatively low in terms of average internet speed and peak connection speed. This is particularly so in the rural areas. In fact, the goal of inclusion of the rural population into the group of fast internet access through better broadband and mobile access is one of the stated objectives of the Chinese government and an avenue of further growth in China.

With the exception of email, which never took off as a significant personal application in China, the range of activities the Chinese consumers engage in on the internet is quite diverse. Instant messaging (mostly through WeChat) and search (where local search engine Baidu dominates) are the most common applications (Fig. 3.2). Apart from these, news (a lot of which is shared on WeChat and Weibo), video, and music engage the consumers. The extent to which internet consumption has become video consumption is amazing—and a surprisingly large proportion of this is legitimate paid and unpaid content (still mostly unpaid but with a steadily increasing paid portion). Low data costs on mobile, ability to download, and significant financial investments from the well-endowed video websites (owned or funded by the largest Chinese internet companies) are some of the key factors responsible for this video bonanza. Also awe-inspiring is the fact that nearly two-third of the internet users do online shopping on their mobile—one of the highest incidence in the world.

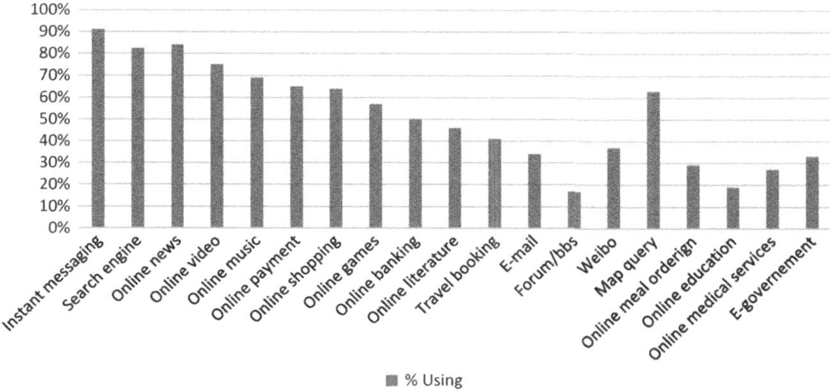

Fig. 3.2 Key online activities of the Chinese internet users

Live Streaming

The pace at which the online media scene continues to change in China is really amazing. 2016 seemed to have been the year of live streaming. According to a report from the CNNIC released in August 2016, 325 million Chinese (46% of the 710 million internet users) watch live streaming (CNNIC—China Internet Network Information Center 2016). The report mentioned that a total of 106 live streaming apps secured a funding of 2.37 billion yuan ($350 million) in 2015. A new live streaming platform was established every three days in 2016. According to some experts, this represents a trend toward "fragmented entertainment" where the audience can choose a streaming star or content which matches their individual preferences much better than any of the mass broadcasts. In addition, it allows you to socially engage with the performer, send her rewards and pay her and feel a degree of social interaction, which is ruled out in a mass television broadcast.

Fragmented Life: Unified Experiences

What is peculiar in China is not just the content that the consumers are partaking, but the whole manner in which this consumption takes place. This has significant implications on the way marketers can reach their messages to the digital consumers.

The internet and especially the mobile internet has entirely transformed all key aspects of the consumers' lives. We briefly examine the impact in four key areas of life—entertainment, information, shopping, and social interaction.

Essentially the power of the mobile phone makes it possible to do whatever the consumer wants, whenever she wants it and wherever she wants it. This has removed the boundaries of time and place and consumers seamlessly flit from one activity to another at their whim.

Entertainment

Right Through the Day. Emergence of Micro-content

The Chinese consumers' homes are likely to be adorned with a large LCD display (often more than one) but the consumption of the television content is more on the tiny screen of their mobile phone or a tablet. While the majority of the consumers partake the free content, China had 81 million paid online video service users in 2017 subscribing to online platforms such as iQiyi, Tencent video, and Youku. The largest of these, iQiyi itself has a monthly reach of nearly 250 million. The growth of 4G, low mobile data costs and the facility to download the content on phone and watch later have all contributed to this shift. The Metro lifestyle of long commutes also encourages mobile video watching during the journey.

Of course, the availability of content is a key contributor—not only the online platforms host all the major film and television programs, they also have their own content, which is competing with the traditional television fare. The video websites produced 112 drama series in 2016, and 22 of them could find a place in the top 120 dramas of the year (GroupM 2017).

Most importantly, the distinction between play time (entertainment) and work time has been blurred, as entertainment is always at hand. Play and work are often intermixed, with entertainment consumed in small bites squeezed in between work (or sometimes equally small bites of work). Entertainment has been transformed from a discrete activity done in focused leisure to a near-continuous indulgence stolen in small pieces throughout the day.

Naturally, the entertainment content has also transformed itself to suit the changing consumer habit. It is hardly possible to watch an entire film or even an entire episode of your favorite television drama, during a quick break, but it is definitely possible to partake the copious amount of micro-content which has penetrated the internet now.

Information

Personalized News in Bite-Sized Chunks

The conversion from the discrete to the continuous is true for other activities also. The digitally connected do not wait for the newspaper to arrive every morning. Information continuously trickles to them through myriads of forums, websites, emails, newsletters, and sharing and updates from their friends and even strangers. As in many other parts of the world, the young Chinese often imbibe more news from social networking websites than the news channels themselves.

Here again, the shape of the content has been transformed to accommodate the changing habits of the consumers. One of the fastest growing news apps is JnriToutiao (今日头条), which serves algorithmically selected, personalized, bite-sized content to suit the individual preferences of the readers (Feng 2017).

Shopping on the Net

Grabbing Every Opportunity for a Deal

The Chinese never really adopted the Western consumers' shopping habits and weekend trips to the hypermarkets and buying a carload of groceries. However, hypermarkets (including Walmart and Carrefour) established a significant presence in China and the Chinese—though for Chinese consumers basket sizes remained small and shopping trips were more frequent. E-commerce fitted the Chinese shopping habits to the tee. It is not surprising that the Chinese have become the most enthusiastic embracers of online shopping.

Additionally they can now buy as often as they want, and the basket size can be even one item.

Like entertainment and seeking information, shopping too now is a near-continuous activity and the consumers can enjoy the experience whenever and wherever they are online and with their mobile. In fact, shopping anywhere, anytime is becoming the norm, as technology places the world's supermarkets in the hand of the Chinese consumers, with ordering and payment through the mobile phone. Though China is a distant second to the USA in terms of the size of its total consumer market, it is already the world's largest e-commerce market. The value of online sales of physical goods increased by 28% to 5.481 trillion yuan, accounting for 15% of the total retail sales in China (Source: National Bureau of Statistics. Statistical Communique of the People's Republic of China on the 2017 National Economic and Social Development 2018).

Along with shopping, a near revolution has taken place in the way the consumers pay for their purchases. Online payment tools like Alipay have proven to be so successful that they have practically taken over not just the online payments but also a huge share of offline payments. As behavioral economics tells us, payment by methods other than cash reduces the pain associated with parting with money and leads to more liberal spending (Ariely and Kriesler 2017). This phenomenon is clearly on display in China.

Social Interaction

The young Chinese (particularly the post 1990s) grew up digital and display a closeness to the internet like no other generation. The absence of siblings, aunts, and uncles is all compensated by continuous interaction with a large number of friends and acquaintances on the internet. In fact, a common sight is a young couple having a meal together in a restaurant, each one absorbed in his or her own mobile phone, neglecting physical interaction for the sake of the virtual companionship.

As for the other activities, mobile internet has converted this discrete activity to a continuous interaction with friends, relatives, and even strangers. The phenomenal growth of the main tool for facilitating social interaction, WeChat, and the time consumers spend on it (about half the WeChat users spend more than two hours on it every day), bears clear testimony to it (emarketer.com 2017).

Unified Experiences: It Is All Social

It is well established that one of the key drivers of the growth of internet and mobile internet in China has been social media. Data suggests that instant messaging, search, news, social networking, and online video are the most popular uses of the internet in China (CNNIC—China Internet Network Information Center 2016). News and online video are also often channeled through social media, as sharing of news and video is one of the most common activities on social media. This will suggest that in fact nearly all internet use in China is social—and in fact internet and social media in China are nearly synonymous. One can surmise and perhaps explain the "social" nature of the Chinese internet by the fact that most Chinese under the age of 35 years are a single child, and absence of a sibling to socialize at home, inevitably drives them to the internet in search of companionship. Whatever may be the reasons, the net result is a 700 million large social internet-based community, which is sharing news, watching online videos, and commenting on it (referred to as danmu 弹幕—or bulleted comments which fly past on the screens when the viewer is watching the video) giving each other suggestions and recommendations on what to watch, what to buy and what is in vogue. It is as if a traditional, tightly knit social community has transformed itself into a mobile internet-based community where all the traditional dynamics of sharing and social interaction are having a play with the help of technology.

Hence while consumer life has been fragmented and the consumer flits from one activity to another, the experiences are getting more unified—under the umbrella of social, and actively and astutely led by WeChat. In fact, apps like WeChat have made sharing so easy, that all activities on the internet now have a social flavor. Shopping merges into social, as consumers click on the links shared by their friends, work merges into pleasure as colleagues connect on WeChat, and content which is shared straddles personal as well as pleasure.

The reason is that social media is highly addictive. Once the consumers experience the joys of "likes" and social connections, they find it difficult to switch off. Research indicates that social media activity, such as likes, tweets, and comments, activates the brains' reward center in the same way as a hug, smile, or compliment. A study published in Psychological Science reports that people had a higher "self-control failure rate" with social media as compared to sports, spending, and even sex! Another study indicates that social media addiction shares features with substance and gambling addictions, and both activate the amygdala-striatal brain system which the drive for impulsive behavior.

In fact the addictive features of social media are so strong that consumers look for social media features in other digital (and even non-digital) media. Video watching now comes with screen bullets "danmu" 弹幕 (user comments which flash on the screen); even offline TV viewing of popular programs is accompanied by simultaneous comments and bantering on WeChat among friends. Shopping has become a social activity as consumers seek out friends and acquaintances for usage experience, recommendations, and sharing. In fact, the survival of the non-social digital (and non-digital) media critically hinges on them being able to tackle the challenge of successfully inducing social elements in their domain, so that they are not rejected by the consumers when they find that they cannot get that gratification of social interaction, to which they are hopelessly addicted. Marketers used to debate how they should allocate their resources to social media and other parts of digital media. But the Chinese digital world has been overrun by social media and it is difficult to draw a line between social and non-social. Chinese consumers have developed a strong bond with social media—basically WeChat on their phone. Social media almost acts like a drug—shooting up the oxytocin and endorphins levels and putting the consumers on a permanent hold.

This social character of the web along with the fragmentation creates a unique environment, as well as unique consumer state of mind. For brands to get their messages across in this environment is a challenging task and definitely, a very different task than what they have faced so far—and definitely showing TV advertising on the digital platforms is not a good way to do it.

E-Commerce

In 2017, Forbes released its annual list of the 100 richest tech billionaires in the world. Nineteen of these 100 global tech wizards are from China, which proves that not only is tech thriving in China, it is also making money for the entrepreneurs who are leading the tech businesses. Of course, e-commerce is one of the main ingredients of this tech revolution and Jack Ma is ranked seventh in this pack of 100 (Vinton 2018).

The USA is witnessing a huge tussle between the might and reach of the traditional brick and mortar retailer Walmart and the muscle and aggressiveness of Amazon. While Walmart's might is still able to withstand the onslaught of e-commerce, the less powerful traditional US retailers like Macy's and Gap are suffering. Walmart itself is able to resist the onslaught by actually converting itself into an online retailer—with an added advantage of 5000 physical stores to enhance the customer experience. On the whole, e-commerce seems to be winning, whose share in the US market increased from 9.3% in 2014 to 10.4% in 2015 (Source: Economist, June 2016).

While the Chinese GDP grew by only 6.9% in 2017 (one of the slowest pace of growth in 25 years), the value of online sales of goods and services in this period reached 5.481 trillion yuan, up by 28% year-on-year (Statistical Communique of the People's Republic of China on the 2017 National Economic and Social Development 2018). The Chinese market will become the world's first $1 trillion online retail market by 2020, according to a forecast by Forrester Research, a market research firm (Meena 2017).

According to China's National Bureau of Statistics, online retail transactions in the country are larger than the combined online sales of USA and Europe.

In 2015, four of the world's top ten internet companies ranked by market capitalization were Chinese (Seth 2018). China is now the world leader in e-commerce, with ordinary Chinese using their phones to invest, buy groceries or pay for street food.

Alibaba, which dominates the e-commerce scene in China, raised $21.8 billion in its initial public offering, which valued the company at $231.4 billion, larger than Amazon and eBay combined. Its initial public offering (IPO) stands as the world's largest at $25 billion, beating the record set in 2010 by the Agricultural Bank of China (Mac 2014). This made the brand a household name outside of China and the fourth most valuable tech company by market cap, ahead of Facebook, IBM, and Oracle. Alibaba-owned websites now hold an estimated 80% of the total online shopping market share in mainland China. Its 2017 Singles Day promotion alone generated more than US$25 billion in sales—a 39% increase on the previous year and more than double of the combined Black Friday and Cyber Monday sales in the USA.

It Is Not Just Books and Apparel

Certain categories enjoyed a natural advantage in selling their products online—particularly those like books and apparel, where the internet offers you endless shelf space to accommodate every taste and preference. Similarly, transparent and attractive pricing, and poor service from brick and mortar intermediaries, propelled the consumers to the online world in the areas of airlines and hotels.

Some categories such as FMCG did not have a natural advantage for migration to online. As a result, the share of online channels for FMCG sales is relatively modest and the Kantar World panel e-commerce report indicates that global online FMCG sales only account for 4.6% of the total FMCG sales, with a value of $48 billion (The Future of eCommerce in FMCG 2017). It is forecasted that this share will reach 9% of all FMCG sales even by 2025 (double of what it is today) with a value of around $150 billion. Unlike in many other things digital, China does not lead the way in FMCG online sales—the share of online FMCG is comparable to other developed markets such as France and UK but lags behind Asian developed markets (Korea—19.7%; Japan—7.5%). However it showed a very strong growth in 2016, and if this growth continues, it will resemble more like the Asian developed markets than Europe or America, and will shift more heavily to online for FMCG too. Another interesting aspect of the Chinese online grocery sales is that 50% of the value is from the sale of beauty products. The relatively low purchase of food and daily household necessities online is linked to the Chinese habit of small and very frequent purchase of daily necessities, which is itself greatly influenced by the high importance accorded to freshness, especially for food products. There is a developed infrastructure of stores and markets selling grocery products, including wet markets, mom and pop stores, as well as modern trade. Increasing share in the FMCG and fresh foods hinges on faster deliveries—so that the consumer does not have to compromise on the primary need of freshness.

Hairy Crabs Online

Hairy crab, as the name suggests have bristles on their legs, but their scrawny bodies are infused with an extraordinary taste and flavor, which makes them hugely popular among the Chinese when they are in season around Autumn. Consumers mostly buy them from the supermarkets, hypermarkets or wet markets, where they are invariably sold alive, as no Chinese consumer will accept the creature when already dead. Given this one would think that it will be a difficult category to shift online. However, JD.com and Alibaba are doing precisely that and developed the ability to deliver live hairy crabs from Yangcheng Lake in Jiangsu province, which is known to produce the best quality of the crustaceans. In the beginning of the season in 2017, Tmall sold 140,000 hairy crabs within a minute of making them available online. JD.com sold gift cards for two million hairy crabs in the first 24 hours. With innovative marketing and huge consumer appetite, there are no limits on what can be sold online in China.

Haitao, Daigou, and Tourism

It has been mistakenly reported that 122 million Chinese tourists went overseas in 2016 (Chinese Outbound Tourism Statistics in 2016: 122 Million Chinese Tourists Make Outbound Trips, Spend $109.8 Billion 2017). Actually, only around 20 million real tourists who went abroad, and the remaining 100 million were shoppers in the guise of tourists. The most popular way of buying imported goods remains personal overseas trips, ostensibly for tourism but firmly revolving around the task of securing coveted products that the Chinese are not able to find on the domestic shelves. It is estimated that Chinese cross-border sales reached $100 billion in 2017 and are expected to increase by 15% in 2018 (Cross-Border Retail Ecommerce Sales in China, 2016–2021 2017)

Plastic bags with distinctive patterns and logos (commonly referred to as luxury products in the industry because of their excessive price) have been a perennial favorite. Louis Vuitton stores in Paris, Bloomingdales in New York, Selfridges in London, and now also the Japanese departmental stores all hire Chinese speaking shop assistants to welcome and service the droves of Chinese shoppers.

However what the Chinese consumers buy overseas is becoming curiouser and curiouser. The latest item on the popularity charts among the tourists to Japan was toilet seats. The Chinese want to experience everything—including the pleasure of sitting on a warm toilet seat which performs the required hygiene tasks through water jets, as the consumers play Angry Birds on their iPads. Japanese rice cookers also figured high on the list. And so did Japanese rice, in spite of being 10 to even 100 times more expensive than the domestically grown variety. It is difficult to say whether the popularity of Japanese rice was driven by a belief that Japanese toilets work best in expelling the digestive residue of Japanese rice, preferably cooked in Japanese rice cookers.

When the Chinese are not traveling overseas, they quench their thirst for imported goods through haitao 海淘. Haitao refers to the phenomenon of scouring the global websites to buy the products that the consumers want. International e-commerce websites like Amazon now allow the Chinese to directly purchase from their international site and have the products shipped to China. Other websites require a local address and do not ship directly to China. Logistic companies have cropped up which provide a local address where the website can ship to, and the company then transfers the product to China.

More and more Chinese are also purchasing imported goods through overseas contacts and agents—a phenomenon referred to as daigou 代购. Daigou is preferred to buying goods which are already imported by dealers who hawk their wares on Taobao or import them as per the request and demand of the buyers. Daigou and haitao offer consumers a sense of assurance of quality and authenticity. Daigou agents can also be contacted on Taobao but are now being increasingly reached through WeChat.

The most popular ingredient of the daigou and haitao baskets is baby milk formula (Xia, Cross-border e-commerce is luring Chinese shoppers 2016). In fact, according to a recent survey conducted by PayPal Inc, the US-based payment service provider, Chinese parents, especially those with children under the age of six, have become the largest spenders on overseas online stores. Chinese parents want to buy only foreign goods for their babies, as the domestic producers have lost their trust. Not just the melamine scandal from a few years ago, but intermittent and frequent news for various types of contaminations and adulteration has put parents on the edge and they want to do everything to protect their children.

The Chinese behavior of buying foreign goods is driven by certain basic needs. Foremost of them is a desire to buy the safest possible products for themselves and their families. It is also driven by a curiosity and a desire to experience new delights and a quest for a better life. Domestic manufacturers need to up their game if they also want a good share of the new Chinese consumers.

Social Buying

Leveraging social media for e-commerce has been a challenge in the developed markets. Social media is the personal space of consumers, where they go to enjoy emotional warmth and interaction with their friends and loved ones. How do they react to messages from brands in such an environment? What can brands do so that they are not seen as intrusive and blend well with the natural social interaction?

In sharp contrast to the developed markets, most consumers in China have already embraced commerce in social media. One of the key reasons is that in China word of mouth is the most important influences on consumer choices. Recommendations and endorsements coming from your friends and acquaintances on social networks are trusted—which is important particularly at a time when brands and companies are facing a crisis of trust. Repeatedly quality scandals ranging from the melamine milk to swill oil or 地沟油 digouyou put the consumer in a dread (Chinese restaurant staff jailed for cooking with 'gutter oil' 2017). In fact, it is not just a Chinese or Asian crisis, the developed world has been treated to horses eaten under the label of beef.

In this context consumers are looking for assurance; they are looking for familiar voices that they can trust. They want to know from their friends what they are using which is not going to poison them or make them sick. And that is the reason why social commerce is growing and is likely to grow further.

To a great extent, the credit also goes to the online platforms, which have been trying hard to create a social character within their ecosystem. Taobao, for instance, has added a feature called wendajia or "ask others" within their shopping platform ('Social Commerce' Blossoms On Mobile Taobao 2016).

Brick and Mortar Retailers Shift Online

While Alibaba seems to have cornered a large proportion of the online market, the traditional brick and mortar stores, including global players such as Metro are upping their ante in China. In 2015, Metro China launched a flagship online store on Alibaba's Tmall Global platform. Walmart acquired full ownership of Yihaodian (yhd.com), a Shanghai-based online supermarket, in 2015 and has entered into a strategic partnership with JD.com, one of the largest shopping platforms in China. The French supermarket Carrefour launched its own e-commerce website and also a mobile app.

Bridging the Gap

While online shopping does have lures, the joy of actually browsing through stores, picking up and examining products as you wish, trying them out to assess what they will do to your sex appeal and interacting with charming sales staff remain strong factors in favor on the traditional modes of shopping. Online stores are trying their best to try to bridge this gap through technology. Several online stores already offer the ability to see yourself virtually wear the clothes that you are considering to buy, if you upload your pictures and dimensions for the website to create your avatar.

In July 2016, Alibaba revealed a planned offering of "Buy+" virtual store which leverages virtual reality (VR) technology to enhance the customer experience. Buy+ users need to don a VR headset to enter a virtual shopping environment, a 360 degrees view and almost all the attractions that the shopper may miss from the traditional store. This includes a pretty shopping assistant called Xiaoyu, who will guide you through your experience and help you try out the products which catch your fancy. In fact, it goes beyond what the brick and mortar stores can offer—and includes a virtual catwalk, where models are strutting wearing the apparel on sale (Store 2016).

Rural E-Commerce

While urban e-commerce is booming, the rural activity is also significant. The CNNIC report indicates that there are over 200 million internet users in rural areas and 22.4% of the online shoppers live in townships (zhen 镇) and villages (cun 村) (CNNIC—China Internet Network Information Center 2016). However it is not just as consumers, the rural Chinese are also becoming active suppliers of goods on the internet. Qingyanliu village (a part of Yiwu city, which is well-known around the world for being a center of trade in small commodities), in Zhejiang province, has been proclaimed as China's number one online village. Most of the villagers are Taobao store owners. Lei Jin, the founder of Xiaomi feels that the internet businesses run from rural areas will be the next big thing after the mobile internet. Xiaomi has been actively investing in rural internet startups in rural China.

In April 2016, the State Council issued a statement saying that the government will accelerate its spending in establishing rural broadband networks. This is seen as a part of the program that aims to integrate the internet with the logistics sector, with an eventual aim of reducing costs, increasing income of the rural producers, and stimulating consumption through providing low priced products. As bridging the urban-rural income gap is one of the key challenges for the government, ensuring better market access and prices to rural producers is seen as a route to addressing the challenge.

Chinese e-commerce giants such as Alibaba, JD, and Suning are increasingly investing in rural areas, both to buy from and sell to. Similarly, logistic companies are salivating at the prospect of catering to the gigantic rural population, which was so far at the mercy of China Post as the only delivery mechanism.

Double Eleven Festival

No discussion on China's e-commerce can be complete without the mention of the Double Eleven festival. How is the date (November 11 or 11.11.), which appeared like a natural symbol of singlehood, got transformed into a shopping bonanza is a miracle—but a man-made miracle, and a great testimony to the marketing prowess of the Alibaba group, which tentatively tried to cook up a festival in 2009, trying to boost their sales in the relatively quiet period after the National day and before the new year. The consumer enthusiasm for the stimulus was incredible, and they started lapping up the goods as if there was no tomorrow. The bells and whistles that Alibaba kept on adding, and the range of brands which kept on enrolling in the orgy, further stoked the consumer appetite and frenzy. The year 2017 was marked by a focus on cross-border e-commerce, allowing the Chinese consumers from buying from all over the world. On the single's day of 2017, Alibaba sold goods worth 168.2 billion yuan—a 39% increase over the previous year. The phenomenon is not restricted to Alibaba, every e-commerce platform has joined the fray, and JD.com, China's second largest online retailer, also managed to offload 127 billion yuan of merchandise to the consumers.

Mobile Commerce

It is well established that mobile has a disproportionately high importance in this part of the world. Often because of low incomes and lack of availability of broadband, mobile is not a supplemental but often the sole mode of connecting to the internet. It is not surprising, therefore, that the biggest change that China has seen in e-commerce is the growth of shopping with the smartphone, rather than on the computer. There are several factors responsible for this, foremost of which is that the Chinese internet market is now heavily a smartphone access market. Ninety percent of the 710 million internet users in China access the net through their smartphones. And over 80% of online shoppers shop with their mobile phones. The fact that a large number of Chinese consumers in large cities have long commuting, most of which is spent glued to the phone, also definitely contributes both to phone internet access and phone shopping. Three-fourths of the Chinese online shoppers now say that the mobile phone is their most important shopping tool.

At the same time, the online retailers have improved their mobile stores, which are no longer the squeezed (Virtual red packets are most popular way to gift money in China as digital disruption hits tradition 2018) versions of their full-screen websites, designed for display on large computer screens. Every retailer now has a specific Android and OS app, which makes smartphone shopping much more interesting and comfortable than before—sometimes even more so than shopping on the computer.

The intrinsic portability and versatility of the mobile device makes it a much more powerful shopping aid than a PC could ever hope to be. Its unique characteristics boldly take e-commerce where it has never been before—right into the heart of a traditional store. The fact is that consumers are bent on using their mobile device as a tool for e-commerce. The traditional stores can fret about it, try to block the usage of internet in their stores, or they can take a more positive attitude and actually encourage internet use in the store by providing free wi-fi connectivity and ensure that the consumers use the internet to the best advantage of the store. A mobile phone in the store can become as much a useful tool for the consumers as it can for the retailers. With large screen smartphones, retailers can display their catalogs on the shoppers' mobile phones, send them discount coupons and special offers, and use it as a payment device. By leveraging the shoppers' mobile the retailers can actually reduce their investment in expensive and short-lived equipment and devices.

Mobile becomes more powerful when combined with locational services and social media—SoLoMo which utilizes mobile but then supercharges it by recognition of the specific location and opportunity to interact with your friends at that location makes a potent mix. Retail stores such as Starbucks are already utilizing the power of SoLoMo to lure the shoppers to their stores.

The growth on online payment methods, which do not require the consumer to enter their credit card details on the smartphone, has given a phenomenal fillip to mCommerce. Most websites allow you to shop using online payments such as Alipay (or Zhifubao) with merely imputing a pin or with just your thumbprint. In fact, one of the most significant and dramatic changes in the buying habits of the Chinese consumers in the past few years has been the mode of payment. While Apple Pay was introduced in China in early 2016, Alipay (or Zhifubao) is already a nearly universally accepted method of payment for both online and offline shopping. WeChat money (also called Tenpay) is also catching up after heavy promotion and usage for exchanging hongbaos or red envelopes, a common practice during the Chinese new year (Virtual red packets are most popular way to gift money in China as digital disruption hits tradition 2018). Among urban online shoppers, the usage of Alipay and WeChat is higher than the use of credit card. Alipay enjoys a market share of 63%, and WeChat Money has cornered around 23% of the market. WeChat as the challenger has been trying to catch up with attractive promotions—most of which involve winning sums with a number of 8s in them (8 being considered the luckiest number by the Chinese). Eighty-six percent of online shoppers in China claim to use online payment methods. According to the research firm, Analysys, China's third-party mobile payment market reached 23 trillion yuan in the second quarter of 2017, up 22.5% from the previous quarter (China's third-party mobile payment market continues rapid expansion 2017).

The key attraction of these online payment methods is that they are considered easier and faster. There is no need to input credit card details. Payment with a mobile phone is particularly easy and can be made merely by a finger print touch or by scanning a QR code. The two payment methods have had a tremendous effect on the cash management practices of the young Chinese, with many of them directly transferring their monthly salary to their Alipay account, then transferring a part to eBao, the savings product linked to Alipay, which offers a much better interest than the banks, and using the remaining for all payments—from McDonald's, convenience stores, taxis to online shopping. Expectedly the millennials have embraced these payment systems most enthusiastically and often go about without any cash or just a few kuais in their pocket. According to research findings released in August 2016, by IPSOS, a research firm, and Ogilvy, an advertising firm, 12% of college students go around with absolutely no cash in their pockets. Among the older consumers, aged 23–29 years, 30% normally have only 100 yuan or less in their wallets. Another research done by Tencent shows that 84% of the Chinese netizens have no qualms or fears about leaving home without any cash at all (IPSOS 2017).

The implication of the embrace of cash-less payments is not just on the mode of payment. Behavioral economists tell us that consumers tend to spend more liberally when it is not by cash. The American problem of credit card debt is a clear proof of this phenomenon. When the consumers are confronted with an attractive target of purchase, two parts of the brain get engaged in a frantic activity. One of these is the nucleus accumbens, which is a part of the dopamine-reward system of the brain. The extent of the activation of this part of the brain is an indication of how strong is the consumer desire to acquire the object on sales. However, at the same time, another part of the brain called insula, which is associated with negative thoughts is activated at the thought of paying the price for the product (Lehrer 2009). The activation, it seems, only takes place when paying with cash, and scanning a barcode or paying with a mobile app, which puts distance between the product acquisition and actual payment, prevents the insula from exercising the restraining effect. The growth of mobile payments hence is not only making shopping more convenient, it is possibly also boosting the economy, by insulating the consumers from the pain of payment and thereby encouraging consumption and boosting the economy.

References

(2017, April 16). Retrieved from emarketer.com: http://www.emarketer.com/Chart/Average-Daily-Time-Spent-on-WeChat-According-WeChat-Users-China-2015-2016-of-respondents/207293

Ariely, D., & Kriesler, J. (2017). *Dollars and Sense: Money Mishaps and How to Avoid Them*. Pan Macmillan.

Barboza, D. (2008, July 16). *China Surpasses U.S. in Number of Internet Users*. Retrieved from nytimes.com: http://www.nytimes.com/2008/07/26/business/worldbusiness/26internet.html

China's third-party mobile payment market continues rapid expansion. (2017, October 4). Retrieved from xinhuanet.com: http://www.xinhuanet.com/english/2017-10/04/c_136658500.htm

Chinese Outbound Tourism Statistics in 2016: 122 Million Chinese Tourists Make Outbound Trips, Spend $109.8 Billion. (2017, February 3). Retrieved from travel168.net: http://news.travel168.net/20170203/43145.html

Chinese restaurant staff jailed for cooking with 'gutter oil'. (2017, June 12). Retrieved from scmp.com: http://www.scmp.com/news/china/society/article/2091125/chinese-restaurant-staff-jailed-cooking-gutter-oil

CNNIC—China Internet Network Information Center. (2016). CNNIC.

Cross-Border Retail Ecommerce Sales in China, 2016–2021. (2017, October 25). Retrieved from emarketer.com: http://www.emarketer.com/Chart/Cross-Border-Retail-Ecommerce-Sales-China-2016-2021-billions-change/212844

eMarketer. (2016, April 27). *Digital Overtakes Traditional Media in China, but TV Consumption Holds Strong*. Retrieved from emarketer.com: https://www.emarketer.com/Article/Digital-Overtakes-Traditional-Media-China-TV-Consumption-Holds-Strong/1013881

Feng, E. (2017, May 10). Retrieved from ft.com: https://www.ft.com/content/04b55fdc-28b7-11e7-9ec8-168383da43b7

GroupM. (2017). *China Media Market Summary*. GroupM.

IPSOS. (2017). *2017 MOBILE PAYMENT USAGE IN CHINA REPORT*.

Lehrer, J. (2009). *How we Decide?* HOUGHTON MIFFLIN HARCOURT.

Mac, R. (2014, September 12). *Alibaba Claims Title for Largest Global IPO Ever With Extra Share Sales*. Retrieved from forbes.com: https://www.forbes.com/sites/ryanmac/2014/09/22/alibaba-claims-title-for-largest-global-ipo-ever-with-extra-share-sales/#1f33fb438dcc

Meena, S. (2017, February 8). *Forrester Data: Online Retail Forecast, 2016 to 2021 (Asia Pacific)*. Retrieved from forrester.com: https://www.forrester.com/report/Forrester+Data+Online+Retail+Forecast+2016+To+2021+Asia+Pacific/-/E-RES137063#

Seth, S. (2018, February 16). Retrieved from investopedia.com: https://www.investopedia.com/articles/personal-finance/030415/worlds-top-10-internet-companies.asp

'Social Commerce' Blossoms on Mobile Taobao. (2016, July 16). Retrieved from alibabagroup.com: http://www.alibabagroup.com/en/ir/article?news=p160726

(2018). *Statistical Communique of the People's Republic of China on the 2017 National Economic and Social Development.* National Bureau of Statistics of China.

Store, C. G. (2016, July 22). Retrieved from alizila.com: http://www.alizila.com/consumers-get-first-peek-alibabas-buy-vr-store/

(2017). *The Future of eCommerce in FMCG.* KantarWorldpanel.

Vinton, K. (2018). Retrieved from forbes.com: https://www.forbes.com/pictures/5997308731358e60d7766b1c/2017-richest-in-tech-top-/#7551c0f63f85

Virtual red packets are most popular way to gift money in China as digital disruption hits tradition. (2018, February 13). Retrieved from scmp.com: http://www.scmp.com/business/banking-finance/article/2133219/virtual-red-packets-are-most-popular-way-gift-money-china

Xia, C. (2016). Cross-border e-commerce is luring Chinese shoppers. *McKinsey Quarterly.* Retrieved from mckinsey.com: https://www.mckinsey.com/industries/high-tech/our-insights/crossborder-ecommerce-is-luring-chinese-shoppers

CHAPTER 4

Key Segments of Chinese Consumers

In this chapter, I look at a few broad specific segments of Chinese consumers and attempt a general classification of the Chinese consumers, with an objective to look at a few groups which may offer a certain degree of homogeneity of needs and warrant a certain degree of uniformity of approach for developing marketing strategies and tactics. These segments described here are not mutually exclusive and collectively exhaustive. For instance, millennials is a large group, which straddles young couples as well as singles, and is a critical target group for marketing for most brands. Similarly, women consumers are a part of all the other groups. However, women and millennials have been described separately as they have some special characteristics which deserve separate examination. Specifically, this book examines the following consumer groups, and tries to explain their importance and their peculiar characteristics which could be relevant for marketing to them:

- Gray consumers, who through sheer numbers in China offer a huge and a largely untapped market, which most marketers are slow to exploit
- Young couples, who are not only large in number but also at or approaching the peak of consumption, as they buy to get the best out of life as well as nurture the family
- China's singles, which is a growing population as more and more people lead their life by themselves, voluntarily or by force of circumstance as they are unable to find a mate

A. Sethi, *Chinese Consumers*,
https://doi.org/10.1007/978-981-10-8992-3_4

- Chinese centennials, who are the youngest and the most distinctive of the consumer groups

  (These four groups mentioned above are mutually exclusive and collectively form the large part of the consumers in China)
- Chinese millennials, who may have very little in common with their Western counterparts, as they grew up and came of age in an entirely different environment
- Chinese women consumers, who because of their own means of income (China has one of the largest proportion of women working outside the home) have created an enormous market
- Lower tier city consumers and migrant workers, who offer unique characteristics because of their background and where they come from

While these segments may not represent the whole of China, as they do not strictly meet the criteria of being non-overlapping and collectively exhaustive, they are the key target groups that most brands are trying to woo. Additionally, by virtue of belonging to a particular group, they all display a degree of uniqueness in behavior and attitudes, which is relevant from the point of view of marketing to them, and hence merits a discussion.

All these segments, of course, are a part of the Chinese consuming class, often labeled as the Chinese middle class. Hence it is worthwhile to first briefly look at this broad group, before profiling the specific segments.

Consuming Class or Middle Class

A lot has been said about China's middle class and surely the importance of middle class in the Middle Kingdom cannot be overestimated. Of course, the key question that a lot of analysts have given some thought to is—how one should define the middle class—beyond the obvious criteria that it is in the middle (presumably of the income spectrum). But I can think of an even more important question that we must address—why should we bother to define the middle class? Why is the middle class important? The term middle class is normally used in two different contexts—economic and socio-political. In the socio-political context, the term middle class is applied to the relatively educated, white-collared workers, with little or no inherited wealth, who lie somewhere between the working class and the landed nobility or "old world" wealthy. Higher levels of education and ambition normally make this group of people politically active and vociferous about their rights. The middle class has also been facetiously referred to as "meddle-class", in reference to their prudish morals, and tendency to meddle with others' affairs if they are not seen to hold up to their strict moral standards.

This book is about China's consumers not about its politics, and hence I will confine myself to the economic context only. Even in the economic context, the terms basically originated in the class-based societies of Europe and the UK, and were synonymous with the emergence of a group of people, who through their education and professional skills were able to elevate themselves from working class misery and begin to enjoy the same goods and services, and lead a similar lifestyle as the nobility, or the class with inherited wealth and privilege because of its birth.

If you see this in the context of China's recent, post-liberation history, there has been no such emergence of middle class—basically because there was no upper class to start with and everyone was equally penniless at the end of the Cultural Revolution. Only in 1979 when Deng Xiaoping started the process of reform and opening (Reform and Opening Up 2014) (改革开放 gaigekaifang) and raised the idea of "let some people get rich first", shoots of prosperity started to manifest themselves. Subsequent to that China has witnessed the emergence of ***not a middle class***, but of a ***consuming class***, that is a group of people who were able to leave behind their penurious existence as peasants or low-paid factory jobs or even white-collared low-paid government jobs, and have now the wherewithal of leading a comfortable lifestyle resembling the relatively well-off in the Western economies. Clearly, some of these new consumers made more money and made it more swiftly (under Deng's blessing of "let some people get rich first") than others and have reached the status of the affluent. However—this affluent class differs from the global affluent class in several important aspects—that they had no inherited wealth, are entirely self-made, and they moved from penury to affluence in a relatively short time span of time within the last 30 years. Secondly, even though this nascent affluent population has amassed vast wealth and even catapulted China to be the largest luxury market in the world, in relation to China's total population, this group is insignificant in size—it is estimated that there are around 1.6 million Chinese with a net worth of $1 million—a mere fraction of the 1.4 billion population (Bain & Company; China Merchants Bank 2017).

Hence, China's consuming class is not in the middle at all—but it is lumped at the upper end of the spectrum. Essentially if you leave out the bottom x% of the population or so (mostly rural) which is only able to consume the basic products essential for survival and live under a shelter, the remaining Chinese can all be classified as the consuming class. I would hence argue that it is wrong and misleading to talk about China's middle class—it is a term devoid of its traditional meaning and significance in the Chinese context—and much more useful and practical to talk in terms of China's consuming class.

The key question is what should be the value of this bottom x%, which should not be included in the consuming class. The Chinese government counts around 70.17 million, most of them in rural China as living below the poverty line as at the end of 2014, based on the criteria of 2800 yuan in annual income. If you exclude these households, it makes a 1.3 billion out of 1.37 billion as the consuming class. And surely for some basic product categories, this entire mass of 1.3 billion is indeed the consuming class, as for some products every Chinese consumer or household is relevant—as is evident from the universal penetration of products like color televisions and mobile phones. At the next level, products like washing machines and refrigerators have an 80% penetration among Chinese households (National Bureau of Statistics of China 2016). Whereas at the other end of the spectrum, 49% of the households own a computer (710 million Chinese or 52% are internet users) and only 17% of the households have an automobile. Hence it is futile to define one middle class or even one consuming class in China—the basic fact is that there are a large number of consumers whether you want to sell washing machines or luxury automobiles and the definition of the consuming class really depends upon what product or service is being sold.

Definitions Galore

However, several different definitions of the middle class or consuming class exist to guide (or to confuse) the marketer. The World Bank defines the middle class most interestingly but almost completely uselessly for any practical market purpose as between the poor in Portugal/Italy and the rich in Luxembourg: with an income of $10 to $100 a day, 2005 PPP$ (purchasing power parity) (Kharas 2017). According to this definition and the World Bank forecasts, by 2020 54% of the global middle class will be in Asia and by 2030 66% of the global middle class will be in Asia. Further based on this criterion, only 12% of the Chinese could be classified as middle class in 2009, a figure which the Bank forecasts to increase to 70% by 2020.

Credit Suisse Research Institute, in their Global Wealth Report estimate the Chinese middle class to be around 109 million individuals (around 8% of the Chinese population) as compared to 92 million in the USA (around 30% of the population) (Credit Suisse 2015). Credit Suisse, however, defines the middle class in terms of investable assets of $50,000 to $500,000. BCG, on the other hand, defines the middle class in China as those who have a household income between $16,000 and $46,000 a year which will put the number of middle-class individuals at five times the number estimated by Credit Suisse (BCG 2016).

McKinsey, a consultancy, uses a practical definition based on the annual household income of 60,000 yuan to 106,000 yuan (at 2012 prices) to define "mass middle class" and 106,000 yuan to 229,000 yuan to define "upper middle class". According to this definition, 68% of all urban households could be classified as middle class (54% in the mass middle class and 14% in the upper middle class). This would put the number of urban middle-class households at around 175 million in 2012. McKinsey have since then updated their figures and now use an income band of 75,000–280,000 yuan ($11,500–43,000) and estimate that as many as 225 million households can be defined as middle class in 2016, compared to just 5 million in 2000. This is an astoundingly large number and clearly ties up with the market size and penetration of most product categories than one sees in China. It also implies that over three-fourths of the urban households are middle class. However, it also underestimates the total number of consuming class households in China as surely a significant proportion of the more than 200 million rural households are also in the consuming class (Barton et al. 2013).

As urban disposable incomes continue to increase at a rate higher than the GDP growth, it is expected that the mix between "mass consuming class" and "upper consuming class" will change significantly. Hence while only 20% of the consuming class could be classified as "upper consuming class" in 2012, it will constitute as high as 70% of the total "consuming class" in 2022. Urban China hence is already a largely consuming class society and is gradually transforming itself from mass consuming class to upper consuming class, which will increase the consumption of higher value products and services, as well as give a fillip to premium brands as compared to the low priced mass brands.

Not only is the upper consuming class endowed with higher affordability, they are also different in terms of their attitudes. They are more open to spending on discretionary products, spending on services such as travel and entertainment—markets which are currently booming in China and are likely to continue to do so in the coming years. A report from McKinsey (McKinsey Annual Consumer Survey 2012) also suggests that these consumers also have a different mindset and criteria of choice while selecting brands and services. While the mass consuming class relies heavily on the functional attributes such as durability in making their choices, the upper consuming class goes beyond functionality and is driven by emotional benefits.

Blue Book 2016 from the Chinese Academy of Social Sciences, has its own way of defining Middle Class and concluded from a recent study that, the earning of an average middle-class citizen is 200,000 yuan (Beijing earns 256,016 yuan (US$39,600) a year, in Shanghai 219,770 yuan a year, and in Guangzhou 170,037 yuan). According to the report, 55% of people Beijing are middle class, in Shanghai it is 51% and Guangzhou 42.5%.

The report indicated that more than 60% of middle-class are home-owners and more than half own cars, while 14% from groups below the medium strata have cars. The majority of middle-class citizens work in the private sector which is different in its makeup to that in Europe or the United States.

The Gray Market

The Demographics and Segment Size

A graying population is an important demographic trend in China, which on one hand poses extraordinary challenges for the government and the policymakers, but on the other hand, presents major implications for marketers, offering them both unprecedented challenges and unique opportunities. Normally countries age as they grow richer—the proportions of consumers who are less than 15 years old are more than twice as many in the Philippines as compared to Japan. Other developed economies such as

Korea, Hong Kong, and Taiwan also have significant graying populations. However, as a result of the one-child policy, China is in a unique position of aging before it becomes well-off and the society is able to bear the cost of the elders. Even more important is the fact that China is committed to a continuation of population control policy (now modified to a two-child policy) with an objective to control the total population to under 1.4 billion which will further skew the population to the elderly.

The current senior population (aged 60 or above) in China is estimated to be at 241 million—17.3% of the total (Statistical Communique of the People's Republic of China on the 2017 National Economic and Social Develoment 2018). The situation is more extreme in certain cities—in Shanghai 30% of the population is over 59, and this group is the fastest-growing segment of the population, augmented by over 100,000 every year. By 2020, about a third of Shanghai's residents will be over 59. On the whole, even though it is only 17% of the total population, it is a staggeringly large consumer base. Possibly they are a set of consumers with limited purchasing power today, but still an enormous market if appropriately targeted and addressed.

According to a report from McKinsey, as reported in the Harvard Business Review, consumers aged 60+ are one of the key demographic groups, which will account for growth for consumer products in the coming 15 years. And this is as true in China, as it is in the USA and Western Europe. In developed countries their number is expected to increase to 222 million by 2030, accounting for 51% of the total urban consumption growth, equivalent to more than $4 trillion (Dobbs et al. 2016), whereas in China, it is already a 241 million strong consumer base.

Distinctive Lifestyle, Physical, and Emotive Needs

Interestingly, the group corresponds to the "baby boomer" cohort in the USA, many of whom are now coming into retirement with a fair amount of wealth and resources. However, the over 60s are often referred to as the "lost generation" in China. The roughly 150 million Chinese born in the ten-year period after the 1949 Communist Revolution were dubbed the Lost Generation (Roland and Yang 2017). They did not have much of a childhood, a family, or an education, and the experience had left them without the skills needed to succeed in this new China. After having struggled to eke out a living and raise a family, many of these consumers, possibly for the first time in their life, will have resources and ability to spend on themselves. Most of these will be living alone or with their spouse.

These consumers have special needs and marketers who succeed in winning their franchise will be those who are able to accurately read and understand them. Marketing is founded on the principle of satisfying consumer needs. Consumer needs exist at several levels or layers. The most obvious layer is, of course, the functional needs, which the products and brands meet through their features and product attributes. Clearly, with biological changes, the functional needs of the elderly consumers acquire some unique characteristics. This alone has significant implications—special foods and supplements are required, product labels and instructions need to be legible to fading eye-sights, buttons on phones large and easy to press, and packaging should not pose the same challenges which the younger consumers are able to tackle in their stride.

However, apart from functional needs, consumer behavior is also governed by social and emotional needs which assume a high level of uniqueness and complexity for the older consumers. The psychological changes create a set of unique needs which few marketers are exploiting today. These consumers have throughout their lives bought products for their children—their emotive needs have centered around protecting and nurturing their families. They chose brands which offered emotive benefits of helping to be a good mother, a responsible father or a conscientious home-maker. But with the children now leading their separate lives, the elders need to look elsewhere for emotional sustenance. Relatively affluent older consumers' state of mind often broadens to include ideas of social responsibility and philanthropy, broadening their caring gaze to beyond their own children. At the same time, they are learning to pamper themselves, without the gnawing feeling of guilt. Marketers need to understand these emotive needs with sensitivity and tap them through thoughtfully designed brand propositions and communication.

The "Gray" Market Opportunities in China

This "gray market" generates special opportunities for products and services which are specially designed for the elders in several areas and sectors.

Health-care services. With the changing social dynamics in China, more and more elders live on their own. They cannot rely on their children for physical care, but need to fend for themselves and will be forced to buy elder "care" services. The traditional stigma and reluctance to live in old age homes are rapidly disappearing. This will create a huge market for elder care homes and clinics.

Health supplements. This is already a huge market—with not only the elderly buying for themselves but the children splurging on huge, extravagantly packaged health products to gift to their parents in an attempt to assuage their guilt of abandoning them.

Targeted services. An opportunity exists for many services where the elders are likely to have special needs—that is, travel and tourism. In the absence of children and grandchildren, a huge market exists for leisure activities and entertainment for elders. This could be in the form of TV programs, shows, and even gaming.

Special product design. Product design, especially for products the older consumers did not grow up with, needs to be guided by special considerations for the need of the elders. Mobile phones and computers—important tools for the elders to keep in touch with their children, living away from them—need to have large buttons and be easy to use and products without getting lost in the labyrinth of complex interfaces would have a promising future.

FMCG. Opportunities also exist for consumer products like chocolates, snacks, and drinks—in fact, the marketers of these products, whose traditional market is the young, may be compelled to look at elders as a consequence of shrinking youth population. According to medical research reports, the number of active taste buds declines with age. The use of more exotic spices or the addition of herbs may be required to enhance the flavor, without increasing fat or sodium levels.

Retail. Implications also exist for design of retail aisles, and physical positioning of products. The product labels need to be large and easy to read and the store shelves designed to provide easy access without challenging contortions of the body.

Financial services. Financial needs of this group are obviously unique as the group needs to carefully weigh the possibility of running out of resources in case of long life and leaving a large sum behind without an opportunity to enjoy it. Carefully designed financial and insurance products could address these concerns and tap the market.

A Portrait of Health

Health is the most important concern for Zhang Yan, a 60-year-old retired middle school teacher, who lives with her husband in Shanghai. Food and exercise, she feels, are the two most important determinants of health, and she goes to great length to shop every day for the freshest vegetables and live fish to prepare a healthy meal for herself and her husband. She draws a pension of RMB 2000 (US$285) per month and lives with her husband. Their only child is married and lives in the neighborhood with his wife and a daughter. Zhang Yan leads a gregarious life with a sizeable set of similarly retired friends, many of whom are her ex-colleagues or classmates. They meet regularly, exercise and sing together, shop together, and often holiday together. She is a voracious user of the mobile phone, mostly uses text to keep the monthly bill in check but has now shifted to Weixin. She loves to travel and especially likes to visit the farms around Shanghai where she and her friends can enjoy a peaceful time in the lap of nature and away from the noise and pollution of Shanghai. When she grows older she wishes to live in an old people's home and not be a burden on her son.

Zhang Yan is healthy, has reasonable, though modest amount of money, and if we go by the average longevity of females in Shanghai, still has at least 20 more years of consumption ahead of her. While India celebrates its 500 million strong youth, China is grappling with an aging population. However, this large group of healthy individuals with modest but collectively enormous means also represents a growing market segment for marketers if they could read their special functional and psychological needs and address them with intelligently designed products and services.

The "Gray" Market Comes of Age

One important factor likely to fuel the gray market is the changing attitudes of consumers. According to a research done by Hurun, a research firm, and Taiping, an insurance provider, only 15% of high net-worth individuals (those with ten million yuan in net worth) in 2105 said that they will consider elder care homes as an alternative for retirement. Within a year in 2016, this figure increased to 28% (Hurun Report; Taikang 2016).

This indicates an increasing desire to continue living well in one's advanced years and also an openness to stay independently, rather than rely on the children (or in most cases the child). This change of attitude will definitely give a boost to the gray market.

Traditionally marketers in China have tended to ignore the older consumers and focused their energies on trying to woo the young. However, with the changing demographics, marketers have no choice but to find the market for their products among the elderly. Many companies have already taken notice and are changing gear. The marketers are not going to endear themselves to this segment by decrying age and glorifying youth. They need to embrace age and cater to the needs of this segment with sensitivity and care.

Interestingly, the two brands clearly positioned for the elderly in China are notorious for their dubious benefits and extremely repetitive and irritating advertising. Both Huangjin Dadang 黄金搭档 and Naobaijin 脑白金, target the elderly, but through their children by encouraging them to gift these to their parents, especially around the Chinese new year, when going home laden with gifts is de'riguer for the Chinese. Apart from atrocious advertising, the products are also known for their excessive packaging—to make them look large and impressive as gifts to win parental approval and appreciation.

The Young Chinese Couples

The Demographics

For the purpose of this book, we define young couples as individuals born in the 1980s and 1990s (balinghou 八零后 and jiulinghou 九零后, respectively, as they are referred to in China) who are married or are living together. Most of those born in the 1980s would already be in a permanent relationship, whereas most of the post1990s may not have yet tied the knot, but many may already be in a relationship and may be living together. The average age of marriage in large cities like Shanghai is climbing and is as high as 30 years for women (nearly 33 years for men) though it would be significantly lower in the smaller cities. In fact, most Chinese feel that a woman should be married by the age of 27, and unmarried women more than 27 years of age are often disparagingly labeled as "left-over women".

The average age of marriage has been rising because of many reasons. Firstly, because of strong parental preference for boys, there are around 20–30 million fewer women under 30, than men, which prolongs the search for a mate. Secondly, women are often better educated (52% of the undergraduates and master's degree students in Chinese universities are women) and more successful than men and mostly want to "marry up", which narrows the choice. Another factor resulting in a delayed marriage is the increasing acceptance of pre-marital cohabitation—nearly 40% of married couples lived together before marriage (Wang 2015) (Source: Zhenai.com—a marriage website). However unlike in some developed countries, cohabitation is in no way a substitute of marriage, but only a delay of marriage. Unless unable to find a mate, most Chinese still prefer to tie the knot and face an enormous social pressure to do so. This results in a number of desperate marriages, where the couple does not really enjoy compatibility, leading to rising divorce rates.

There are several factors which will have a role in determining the size of this group of young urban couples in the coming years. Firstly, the tide of migration from the countryside to cities, which has already resulted in over 250 million migrant workers, is likely to continue, albeit in a slightly subdued manner. The World Bank estimated that increased productivity in agriculture will drive another 100 million rural residents to the cities in search of employment till 2030.

The organic size of this segment in the cities may decrease over time and the population of singles may increase because of the paucity of women as well as overambitious demands and requirements from a spouse. In a survey by the matchmaking site, Zhenai.com 34% of singles felt that they hold too high an expectation for a spouse, and nearly a quarter are willing to prod through life in a state of singlehood rather than compromise on their ideals. Lastly, the size of this segment will also be constrained by an increasing divorce rate, which increased by 63% in the past decade.

The most peculiar demographic characteristic of the young couples in China, of course, is that at least in urban areas, both the partners come from single-child families. As the one-child policy was less rigorously enforced in rural areas, migrant couples in the cities will often have siblings. However, the majority of children born to young couples will never know an uncle or an aunt.

Economically, it creates a relatively beneficial situation for them as they have few financial obligations with no siblings to look after and parents normally at least being able to look after themselves with their modest earnings or pension. The parents of the young couples come from an era where the housing was granted by the state, and hence they have no rent to pay, and if they were lucky and wise in trading and upgrading of property, could well be sitting on a pretty piece of real estate. In addition, the couples are the sole inheritors of their parents' wealth. The parents were not only able to afford to provide them a good education, they are also able to give them a good start to their married life, including helping with the down payment for the apartment.

Not Just One Target Group

Young urban couples in China are definitely not a single target group with uniform behavior and preferences but come in several colors and shades. Some variables on which they can be segmented are obvious—the city tier they come from and whether they are local to the city (have the hukou) or have migrated from another place. Similarly having or not having a child makes a big difference. And of course, education and profession make huge differences to the kind of consumers they make.

While the internet has brought everyone closer together and put everyone on an equal footing in terms of access to information and products, in has also tribalized the youth by allowing them to pursue their own very individual interests in smaller connected groups, which was not possible before. Brands would do well to recognize the key tribes on the internet and attempt to develop a relationship with those with which they can interact meaningfully.

The City Tier Divide

China has around 650 cities (apart from over 2000 smaller towns), whose urban population ranges from over 20 million in Shanghai to less than a hundred thousand in a small county-level city. Like the rest of the Chinese population, only a small minority of these couples live in the tier-1 cities, with the largest proportion spread across over 250 prefecture-level cities of the country. While increasing transportation links (including the network of high-speed rail) and the reach of the internet has substantially reduced the differences between consumers living in large cities in relation to the smaller cities, the distinctions in some areas of the lifestyle and the mindset can be significant.

One key difference is the difference in employment opportunities and the resulting incomes. Multinational companies and large well-paying private Chinese companies tend to be concentrated in the larger cities. The opportunity for livelihood in smaller cities is, therefore, mostly with the government or small private enterprises, which pay much lower. The money in lower tier cities is mainly from entrepreneurship, including moonlighting by the underemployed employees of the government and the public sector.

Despite these differences, the young couples in smaller cities have caught up with the larger city residents in terms of consumption of basic products and services. According to data from Kantar Worldpanel, which measures household purchases of consumer goods, the lower tier cities which were playing the catch-up game, have now reached a similar level of saturation as the larger cities and are no longer able to provide the volume growth to the commonly used product categories.

Young Couples and the Internet

The fact is that there are no young couples in China—there are only threesomes—the couple and the mobile internet. The post-1990s have never seen a world without the internet and the post-1980s have also embraced the net at an early age and with unbridled enthusiasm. The young consumers (20–39 years old) constitute 54% of all internet users in China and are early adopters of the innovations and businesses developing around the internet. The internet and especially the mobile internet has entirely transformed four key aspects of the consumer's lives—entertainment, information, shopping, and social interaction.

The distinction between playtime (entertainment) and work time has been blurred, as the two are often intermixed, and entertainment and information is consumed in small bites in between bouts of work. Shopping and social interaction have also been transformed from discrete activities done in focused leisure to a near continuous indulgence grabbed in small doses right through the day.

Lifestyle, Aspirations, and Values

The turning point of the lifestyle of young couples is the arrival of the child—before which the house is merely a place to come and sleep, and the focus of life, including nearly all meals, is outside the house rather than inside the house. Interestingly while the desire to own a house is very strong (in fact almost a pre-condition for getting married) the amount of time a typical couple without a child spends in the house is rather limited, and the location for social interaction and entertainment is outside of the home.

A big differentiator of the lifestyle as well as aspirations is the type of city the couple resides in. The absence of long hours frittered away on commuting provides much more time to lower-tier city consumers. As a result, traditional offline shopping and entertainment are more popular in smaller cities. Similarly working for the government and smaller private companies, does not put the same competitive pressure that is faced by those working for large companies in cities like Shanghai and Beijing. However, most young couples living in lower tier cities look up to the big cities and long for the money and lifestyle that these cities provide, but compromise to stay in their home cities for various reasons. A micro-trend now is some couples from tier-1 cities, moving to lower tier cities for a more relaxed lifestyle.

Marketers often debate whether the Chinese consumers in general and particularly the relatively unique set of young consumers have the same fundamental needs as consumers in the rest of the world. Needs are determined by a number of factors, and one of the important determinants of needs are the basic values that we subscribe to. Values are all-encompassing beliefs which determine the consumer lifestyle, the consumer behavior and preferences.

Numerous surveys have been conducted which measure the Chinese consumers' values in comparison to the rest of the world (including the World Values Survey as well as periodic surveys by research organizations such as GfK and Illuminera). The most interesting aspect of the findings from these studies is that unlike the common perception, the Chinese are not wired entirely differently from those in the rest of the world. Just as people all over the world, the Chinese value the family, honesty, friendship, self-reliance, and open-mindedness. There are some differences and in general, the findings do support the popular beliefs that the Chinese consumers place more in store on values such as duty, hard work, and respecting elders. The values remain surprisingly consistent across different age groups. The key change is that duty and filial piety, though remain important among the young too, lose somewhat at the cost of learning and fulfilling work, which gains salience in this group.

The importance of fulfilling work gets further magnified among the younger couples—particularly those born after 1985. A zhaopin.com (a job-seeking website) shows that while remuneration and growth prospects are important choice considerations for all working people, interesting and fulfilling nature of the work is much more important to the younger office workers.

Young Couples and Consumption

The All-Consuming House

A peculiar phenomenon in China is the obsession with purchasing a house—in particular, the implicit association of a house with marriage. Psychologically, ownership of a house is considered almost a pre-condition to getting married. Hence among the Chinese couples, house purchase tends to occur much earlier than the lives of couples in other countries, where they only start contemplating a house purchase after several years of working and saving. While this has been a boon for the real estate industry in China and has led to house pricing in Beijing and Shanghai to rival those in London and New York, it has also placed a huge financial burden on the couples, and with a significant proportion of their salary going toward mortgage payment, many refer to themselves as fang nu 房奴 (house slaves).

On this aspect usually, there is a huge difference in the financial situation of local residents of large cities like Beijing, Shanghai, and Guangzhou, where their parents already own a house and are often able to help their children acquire one. The couples coming to these cities from smaller towns and villages do not have this advantage as their parents themselves only have small and low-value dwellings.

House But No Housewife

As most married women work in urban China, there is no concept of a housewife as known in other countries. In fact, while the desire to acquire a home is very high, as is the eagerness to decorate it, the inclination to look after it (and even live in it) is muted. Many young couples have all their meals outside the home, and their idea of a good time is outside the home rather than in the home. Most Chinese couples, therefore, tend to save on the purchase of common home care products. But as mentioned earlier, the whole perspective changes with the arrival of the child, when the key concern and focus change into the protection of the child.

Payment Revolution

The embrace of online payments has led to the wider opening of the wallets of this generation and it likes to spend much more than the previous generations (behavioral economists tell us payment with cash hurts, but when you put a distance between purchase and actual payment, the consumer is much more liberal in his purchases). According to data from iResearch, an online research organization, it is not just the online purchases which are paid through online payments, 42% of in-store purchases are non-cash. Additionally, mobile payments have sprinted ahead of non-mobile payments methods and account for three-fourths of the online payments.

Premiumization

The young couples in urban China can swing from extreme price sensitivity to almost complete disregard of the price. A vivid example of the latter is the way the category of infant milk formula moved from low priced local brands to very premium imported ones. The trigger for this premiumization was the unfortunate case of contamination of the product with melamine in 2008, which lead to the death of six children and caused illness among many others. Since the incident, parents have been going to great lengths to avoid domestically produced products, often trying to source directly from retailers outside of China. It is evident that the Chinese consumers will readily pay an enormous premium for some products and will scrounge for others. Premiumization is key to the growth of many companies, as the market is getting saturated in terms of penetration as well as geography. Data from Kantar Worldpanel shows that the categories benefitting most from premiumization in the recent years have been foods such as yogurt and biscuits, skin-care and makeup products, and certain personal care products. On the other hand, the consumers are not spending more on products used in the confines of home such as fabric care, toilet tissue, and kitchen cleansers.

Consumption of Services

One key aspect in which the young couples differ from the previous generations is the higher consumption of services—which includes travel, hospitality, health care, entertainment, and personal care.

The number of international tourists from China increased ten-fold from 2001 to 2015, with 122 million Chinese visiting an international destination in 2016. Some reports indicate that the Chinese account for nearly one-fourth of the global outbound consumption. It is not surprising, therefore, that hotels and tourist attractions all across the world are going an extra step to cater to the Chinese tourists' tastes, including the provision of an electric kettle in the room (so that instant noodles can be cooked) and bedroom slippers.

Cross-Border Purchases

A major development in the recent years has been the enormous increase in the Chinese consumers buying from outside China. Of course one of the most important ways to acquire goods from outside China is to buy them on trips abroad. The Chinese tourists are one of the most profligate shoppers in the world, and stores from Tiffany to Bloomingdale to Galeries Lafayette are hiring Chinese speaking sales assistants to woo the Chinese consumers. While luxury goods remain the perennial favorites for overseas shopping, the consumer choice varies from time to time—recent favorites for purchase in Japan included rice cookers, toilet seats, and Japanese rice.

The direct online cross-border purchase has also gained momentum. Haitao 海淘 refers to the phenomenon of browsing the global websites to buy the products that the consumers want. International e-commerce websites like Amazon now allow the Chinese to directly purchase from their international site and have the products shipped to China. Another popular channel for purchase is daigou 代购—where other consumers buy and bring the desired goods from other countries. These "daigou", who promote themselves on Taobao and WeChat, make frequent shopping trips abroad and some of them may even live abroad (e.g. as a student) and are trying to make an extra buck by offering this service.

Cross-border sales were forecast to hit 432 billion yuan in 2016, up from 259 billion yuan in 2015, according to McKinsey & Co (Xia, Cross-border e-commerce is luring Chinese shoppers 2016). The most popular ingredient of the daigou and haitao baskets is baby milk formula. In fact, according to a recent survey conducted by PayPal Inc., the US-based payment service provider, Chinese parents, especially those with children under the age of six, have become the largest spenders on overseas online stores. Chinese parents want to only buy foreign goods for their babies, as the domestic producers have lost their trust. Not just the melamine scandal from a few years ago, but intermittent and frequent news of various types of contaminations and adulteration has put the parents on the edge and they want to do everything to protect their children. Marketers in China, particularly for premium products, need to take a global perspective of the marketplace and their competition.

The Changing Face of the Young Couples

The "young couples" is possibly the most dynamic of the various segments of Chinese consumers, and their global exposure, internet, and social media make sure that they are always in tune with the rest of the world. At the same time, their relatively high levels of education, and absence of traditional prejudices makes them extremely open to change and embracing new ideas and services with eagerness and promptitude.

Sharing Not Owning

The previous generations of Chinese consumers were exposed for the first time to an array of goods which they never had an opportunity to possess, and hence single-mindedly went after acquiring without any qualms or concerns with a motto of "if you can afford it, buy it". However, the post-1980s couples place less in store on acquisition and more on experiences. This has resulted in a booming sharing economy, particularly in transportation—firstly with cars and now with bicycles.

Participants, Not Just Recipients of Marketing Messages

The older generations were content to sit in front of the TV and patiently absorb the messages thrown at them from brands. The digital world has changed this by transferring the control to the consumers from the marketers. Consumers today choose what content they consume and what ads they see, and most importantly what messages they share with others. Consumers hence have a say in what messages are worth talking about and transmitting about a brand. In fact, the internet is a boon for the real product enthusiasts who have access to all the information about a category or a brand, and may decide themselves what is worth saying about a brand—and hence becoming creators not just recipients of messages. This has resulted in experienced and expert users turning into key opinion leaders (KOLs) who not only transmit brand messages but often also distribute the product. Marketers need to recruit the help from these KOLs to leverage their marketing efforts (Escabado 2017).

Shortening Consumer Journey

Urban Chinese couples, particularly in the larger cities are time poor. Long commuting, demanding work and overtime, exhausting entertainment, parental care, and, most demandingly, "tiger-mom" child care leave little time to pause and think about anything—leave alone brands. Marketers need to rethink their traditional strategies to reach the consumers in sequential, linear steps, and give up trying to slowly push the consumers along traditional marketing models such as awareness, interest, desire, and action (AIDA). Today's young consumers have a mind of their own, and confidence and impetuousness to try the brand even when they may see it for the first time. On the other hand, the stubbornness to ignore its repeated messages and refusing to be lured by its overtures, if the brands fail to resonate with them.

Increasing Environmental Consciousness
At a country level, China seems to be keen to take up the global leadership position on environmental concern, which has been vacated by Donald Trump. However, in China, the country's stance is based on solid support and even demand of the middle class. In most global surveys, the Chinese consumers espouse strong environmental concern and also demand responsible behavior from companies and their government. The rare protests that are seen in China mostly pertain to government projects which the consumers see as harming their environment. The key question really is whether this conscience can translate into revenue and profits for marketers. In many areas, it is already doing so. Couples with a small child have an extremely high degree of concern about pollution and the safety of the environment. The roaring sale of air purifiers bears a strong testimony to this. The sale of alternate energy vehicles is also increasing steadily. The key to selling green products to the Chinese consumers is to link them to a core benefit which is of high value to them—protecting the health of their family. With this at the core, the future is bright for green energy vehicles, grass-fed beef, low energy lamps and a greener lifestyle.

The Lonely Hearts: China's Singles

The Demographics and Size

China today has over 200 million single adults. Many of them are only temporarily single and sooner or later will settle to a life of domesticity and start raising a family. However, many will choose to remain single, often because of the inability to find a suitable partner, but sometimes also because of a choice. Even those who will eventually marry will not be in a hurry to do so, often choosing to live with their partner for a couple of years, before formally tying the knot. On the whole, this is one demographic, one can bet will continue to increase in size because of several reasons:

- With the embrace of Western values and sexual mores, pre-marital cohabitation is now widely practiced and accepted. While many of these cohabitations eventually lead to matrimony, many do not as couples lose the passion and break up.
- The gender imbalance (discussed in Chap. 1) will anyway rule out millions of men out of the pleasures of marriage. Additionally, the higher education levels and well-paying white-collared jobs among women make them more demanding in qualities of the desired mate, plunging them into the status of what the society calls as "sheng nv" or leftover women (Fischer 2014).
- The standards of marriage in terms of material possessions are high in China and a major hurdle is the ownership of an apartment. According to a well-publicized survey of mothers of marriageable girls in Shanghai, over 70% of mothers will not accept a son-in-law who cannot produce the keys of an apartment for the wedded couple to live in. The price of housing in large cities is already beyond the reach of most young men, and the trend suggests that it will continue to be more and more so, making the task of persuading a prospective mother-in-law even more daunting.
- The divorce rates are rising, putting the couples back into singlehood.

Lifestyle, Aspirations, and Values

The young singles often have many concerns and worries—which vary by the kind of city they live in. For those dwelling in big cities, other than those who belong to the fuerdai 富二代 (second generation rich) group, embracing a lucrative and fulfilling career and achieving economic prosperity to be able to settle down in the big cities is the strongest area of concern. The concern is much higher among those who do not belong to the city, as their parents are less likely to be in a position to help them with buying a house. In fact, this is prompting many of the young singles to look for opportunities back in their hometown or lower tier cities and many of these cities are actively wooing the young talent (Ganand Hu 2017).

The turning point of the lifestyle of young singles is the start of cohabitation and preparing to settle down in marriage (a desire and intention which may or may not materialize). Before this, the focus of the consumption for men is mostly to woo and court a girl, and the focus for women is to look as attractive as possible. Products which serve an obvious role in these tasks are of major interest.

Apart from finding a partner, career is the other area of focus and the young single workers often spend on products and services which may be seen as a help in advancing their careers—including education. This is a major industry in China as a large number of youth invest in skill-enhancement courses to further their career prospects. Like the young couples discussed earlier, the young singles also aspire to fulfilling work, and they feel that enriching their skill-sets will help them in achieving their goal.

The young singles are also big consumers of restaurants and food delivery services, as they seldom have a functional kitchen at home and dining is a natural activity in courtship. Additionally bonding with friends mostly takes place at restaurants.

The importance of fulfilling work gets further magnified among the younger singles—particularly those born after 1985. A zhaopin.com (a job seeking website) shows that while remuneration and growth prospects are important choice considerations for all working people, interesting and fulfilling nature of the work is much more important to the younger office workers.

Chinese Centennials

The Demographics

Centennials are the under 20s, the cohort after millennials—born from 1997 (Hong Kong's handover to China) to now. This population has been declining due to the lowering birth rate. The centennials are normally in education, though there are a large number of them, especially from rural China and smaller cities, who have abandoned education and are working as migrant workers in the factories and service industry in larger cities.

The Mindset

"I still can't understand," said Mr. Six to his son, in a 2016 film called Mr. Six. "Tell me what do you kids think about the whole day, besides chasing money, chasing girls, what else do you chase?" "We just chase a good time, whatever makes us happy," answered Bobby, his son. "What if your chasing of happiness, causes pain to someone else?" "Then it has nothing to do with me," answers Bobby.

Bobby is a Chinese centennial—sometimes also called as Generation Z'er. Globally this cohort came to age around the time of the great recession of 2008, the collapse of Lehman Brothers and global terrorism. But in China, this cohort came to age at the time of the glory of Beijing Olympics, and as China was relatively unsinged by the fires of the global slowdown, this generation in China has not really seen any real hardship or unemployed parents fretting about trying to make the ends meet.

In fact, the paradox of this generation comes from the fact that while they are truly born in an era of plenty and opportunity, to really exploit those opportunities is becoming harder and harder. Unless they belong to the second generation rich (富二代 or fuerdai) the competition for them has never been as intense. The quick get rich opportunities are gone, and now the only way to get ahead is through real toil to get into the best universities and then compete with the 8 million graduating every year to get a decent job. Additionally, this is a generation which does not necessarily see the need to compete and is happy to look for alternatives ways of leading their lives.

Globally this cohort is seen as more considered and less compulsive spenders as compared to the millennials. They have been witnesses to the hardship caused by the financial crisis and show more resilience and realism. However, in China, the cohort is more pampered and easygoing. They do not always want to take the beaten path, which they feel is tough and competitive. Many of their parents also have the wherewithal to send them to universities abroad rather than the grind of the Chinese college entrance exam (高考 or gaokao).

Global in Values and Desires

Despite these differences, this is the first Chinese generation which is truly global in their basic values and desires. The most striking difference the centennials have from the Chinese millennials is their quest and respect for freedom. The millennials' sensitivity to freedom was numbed by economic progress and the absorbing opportunities they saw for themselves to create a better life than their parents. However, centennials take economic well-being, as well as the conventional routes to this well-being (as also the usual accouterments of learning and fulfilling work) for granted and aspire for higher level needs such as freedom, open-mindedness and social tolerance on one end and creativity on the other. Centennials truly want to lead a different life from the millennials—guided not by material security and wealth, but by freedom, creativity, and open-mindedness. This generation is also likely to be more concerned and respectful of the environment, and expect companies to do the same.

True Digital Natives

Like their counterparts in the developed world, this cohort was born with a mobile phone in their hand. Their lives revolve around their mobile phones and its usage for social media, e-commerce, and entertainment comes naturally to them.

Like the global cohort, the Chinese centennials are spoiled by personalization, through the internet. They do not have the patience to wade through the myriad of options, an elaborate evaluation process and choose what fits them the best. They are used to brands offering them targeted products and services and take that for granted. They are willing to offer feedback to make the experience even more personalized. For marketers, it is critical that they treat the centennials as a diverse set of individuals, and work on targeted offerings rather than a mass positioning.

Chinese Millennials

The Demographics

The millennials cohort refers to those born between 1981 to the late 1990s, who are in the age group of 18–35 years in 2016. In China, this cohort is often divided into the post-1980s (八零后 or baling hou) and the post-1990s (九零后 or jiulinghou). In the USA, this group follows the Baby Boomers and Generation X, and is followed by Generation Z (also called centennials) and is the largest generational cohort (92 million, compared to 61 million Generation X'ers and 70 million Baby Boomers). This a very large and diverse segment in China too and the young couples, as well as the singles, described earlier largely belong to this cohort. The cohort spans a large age range and both in China and globally it is recognized that it is not really a homogeneous group, and there are distinct differences between the different age groups in this cohort.

Chinese Millennials' Mindset

"I haven't removed my makeup in 18 days, my monthly contact lenses have been in for two and a half years, my biological clock is in total disorder, yet I'm getting fatter than ever," croons a Chinese chorus song called "My body is hollowed out" with the English title "So far, the sofa is so far." The popular online video describes the exhaustion of young Chinese office workers, a common theme, and lament among this cohort (Xingjian 2016).

The importance of this group in China is even greater than their global significance. This is the first generation of educated, modern Chinese, most of whom come from one-child families. Almost all the workforce in private companies in China, particularly the multinationals, belongs to the millennials cohort. Another large part of this cohort is the rural migrant workers—this is the first generation which left their agricultural land in droves and populated export-oriented factories of companies like Foxconn (largest contract manufacturer for Apple and other electronic brands) which gave China the consistent export earning economic growth in the 1990s and early 2000s.

There are a number of distinct features which define this generational cohort in China, and many of which are very different from the unique aspects of the millennials in the developed markets. In the USA and the Western markets, millennials faced lower rates of employment and in fact lower disposable incomes as compared to their parents. However, in China, this is the first generation which was able to afford a living standard which was distinctly economically better than their parents. They grew with China's economy and were right there in the lap of increasing opportunities.

Most millennials in China do not have a brother or a sister, and are under exclusive attention from their parents, and benefitted from all the family resources going toward their education. As a result, a very large proportion of millennials are university graduates and populate the white-collar jobs in urban China. In general, millennials are appreciative and thankful for the opportunity that they had to be economically better off than their parents. Millennials, therefore, feel a rather heightened sense of filial piety, but which is largely reflected economically, by ensuring that their parents also live well, and not so often by actually spending a lot of time with them. Most of them live separately from their parents and try to make up for the lack of adequate time spent with parents, by helping them financially and ensuring that they lead a better lifestyle.

However, in this aspect, there are distinct differences between the two sub-segments of millennials—the post-1980s and the post-1990s. The post-1990s are entering employment and trying to make their fortune in a time when China's economy is slowing down and competition becoming intense. When someone born in the early 1980s graduated from university in 2001, there were only about a million university graduates looking for a job. But a person born in the early 1990s who graduated ten years later had to compete with nearly 7 million university graduates. Clearly, the opportunities had also multiplied but so had the competition and the cost of living. The post-1990s are therefore less thankful and in fact sometimes resentful of the competition and high cost—particularly the cost of buying an apartment in large cities like Shanghai and Beijing.

Women Consumers

Traditional Role

An old Chinese saying goes 重男轻女 or zhong nan qing nu, implying the importance of men. This preference translates into a preference for the male child and has been further exacerbated by the one-child policy which has resulted in a huge gender imbalance created in China. If you look at the population as a whole, there are 105 males to 100 females in China (Statistical Communique of the People's Republic of China on the 2017 National Economic and Social Develoment 2018). But the gender ratio at birth tells a different story—according to figures from the National Bureau of Statistics, China's gender ratio at birth remained one of the worst in the world in 2015, with 113.5 boys born to every 100 girls (a normal ratio is 103 to 107 boys for every 100 girls) (Shumei 2017).

Much chaos and bedlam is attributed to Mao Zedong but historians agree that he deserves praise for the dramatic changes in women's rights seen after the liberation in 1949. Mao Zedong famously said that "women hold half the sky" in 1950 (azquotes.com n.d.), and women did follow his advice and plunged themselves into mainstream economic activity. The

New Marriage Law enacted by the People's Republic of China guaranteed women equal rights in marriage, divorce, and property. A clear result of this was an external unleashing of women's potential or power, and a clear escape from a tradition of polygamy and concubines. Two specific factors were key contributors to the improvement of the status of women—equal opportunity for education and equal opportunity for employment (which though is still to translate to equal rights and benefits once in employment). Most women of working age became a near equal participant in economic activity in China. School enrolment for girls and boys is identical, in fact, there are more women pursuing a university degree than men (52.1% of undergraduate students and 51.6% of postgraduate students are women) (The State Council Information Office of the People's Republic of China 2015). The government continues to provide support through legislation, as seen in a 2016 act, which provides ten days' child-care leave to new fathers, with an intention to reduce the burden on women.

That attitudes have changed is evident from the fact that among the modern couples of urban China, boys are referred to as 建设银行 Jianshe Yinhang (the Chinese name of China Construction Bank, implying that the boys need money to construct a house) and girls as 招商银行 Zhaoshang Yinhang (the Chinese name of China Merchants Bank, implying that the girls will invite money). A 2012 Boston Consulting Group report estimated that female earnings in China grew from $350 billion in 2000 to $1.3 trillion in 2010 (Silverstein 2012). The earnings are further projected to reach $4 trillion in 2020. However, while the external signs and indicators point positively to the status of women in China, the traditional attitudes are hard to obliterate.

Looking For Love

Signs of gender imbalance are serious among those of a marriageable age (legal age of 22 for males and 20 for females). The sixth nationwide population census conducted in 2010 showed that the ratio between unmarried men and women born in the 1980s was 136 to 100. According to various estimates, there are more than 30 million single men across China (Shumei 2017) and this huge group is believed to become a dangerous factor for authorities and even threaten social stability. It is also common now for men from China, particularly the southern provinces of Guanxi are crossing the border to Vietnam in search of brides.

In spite of the sex ratio in favor of men, it is the "leftover women" (剩女 Shengnu) rather than the leftover men (光棍 guanggun) that the Chinese are concerned about. The term "leftover women" (剩女 Shengnu), which is often seen in media, became a derogatory term for women in their late 20s or 30s, who have failed to secure a groom for themselves. Leta Hong Fincher, author of the book "Leftover Women: The Resurgence of Gender Inequality in China" (Fischer 2014), condemns the label as pejorative and fears that it is indicative of a retrograde tendency in China and inimical for women's rights and equality. The derogatory reference is a suggestion that these women are too proud and too choosy to deign to accept any of the men around them, or are so busy with their jobs and careers that they do not even have time to look around them to see if any eligible males could make a decent husband for them. The term, in fact, was first used by the All-China Women's Federation, which first employed the term in this disparaging manner, implying that these women exhibit misplaced priorities by neglecting to get hitched in favor of career and education advancement and in fact are to blame for the millions of poor "bare branches" (guang gun 光棍—referring to unmarried men), who are not able to find a bride.

However, the Chinese young women are increasingly individualistic and hate to define themselves in terms of their relationships with men. Many young women, despite enormous social pressure, are happy to lead a life as a single, rather than succumb to social pressure and accept the hand of any convenient male who crosses their path. Brands are increasingly echoing the changing attitude and in 2016 SKII ran a series of videos depicting women who would normally be considered of a marriageable age, but who are happy to find satisfaction and meaning in life outside marriage.

SKII

In 2016, SKII, the global luxury cosmetics and skin-care brand, ran an online campaign in China called "Marriage market take-over". The videos, which are a part of the global #ChangeDestiny campaign, portrays a number of unmarried women, who are under pressure from parents and society to tie the knot. The key message conveyed is that marriage is a choice for women and it is perfectly possible to lead a life of dignity and responsibility without getting hitched. The film ends with the women attending the Shanghai Marriage Market, a weekly fair held in the premises of city's People Park. But the women go there not to search for partners, but to proclaim and celebrate their single status and ask for the parents to accept it with understanding.

Women Spenders

From a marketing point of view, the importance of women as a segment also emanates from the fact that most women in urban China are in employment or business and have their own independent source of funds. Women constitute 45% of the workforce in China. In fact, a quarter of all entrepreneurs in China are women, and more than half of online entrepreneurs are women (Source: All-China Women's Federation). Female entrepreneurs from China accounted for 60% of businesswomen worldwide who have more than $1 billion in wealth, (Source: Hurun Research Institute). This coupled with the fact, that in most cases women also control the husband's purse-strings, imparts them with an enormous spending power in China.

This has prompted some companies to initiate gender-differentiated strategies in the Chinese market as illustrated by a smattering of appliances and computers in feminine colors and designs. However, appealing to female consumers is not just a question of adding a brush of pink color to the brand, or streamlining the shape to more closely resemble the female body. There are several factors that marketers need to consider in China while marketing to the female consumers:

- Female consumers in China are not less but more educated than male consumers, and hence do not need a simplification or feminization of the products. In fact, in many cases, such tactics will work contrary to the interest of the brand, and women may consider these touches as indications that the product is over-simplified and less sophisticated than what it should be. What they do need is a clearer explanation of the benefits and operating instructions, particularly for categories in which they have traditionally been less involved, such as automobiles.
- The hard-selling strategies often employed by manufacturers and dealers do not cut much ice with female consumers, as these raise suspicion and make it difficult to win their trust. On the other hand softer, non-aggressive sales tactics, which are rich in information, work much better in China. One of the reasons for women's preference of the online channels is lack of aggressive sales assault.
- The assurance and the quality of after-sales service carry even a higher appeal among female consumers, as they want to ensure that they are not blamed by the husband or other family members for buying a product which is lying unused because of a break-down.

- While women may not be any more price sensitive than men, their need for having got a deal (what the behavioral economists refer to as transactional utility as against the pure acquisition utility for acquiring the product) is higher than that of men. It is necessary, therefore, to design careful sales promotions and offers, which lets the consumer go home with a sense of self-congratulation and satisfaction for having made a deal.
- The priority and concerns of the women consumers shift dramatically as they go through different life stages, and a specific moment of change is the birth of a child. However, unlike in some of the other markets, the childbirth only brings about a transient shift in focus as the consumers learn to cope with motherhood. Most women in urban China return to work four to six months after the birth of the child, and regain focus on self (of course now in addition to the child) as a consumer.

References

(n.d.). Retrieved from azquotes.com: http://www.azquotes.com/quote/324531

Bain & Company; China Merchants Bank. (2017). *China Private Wealth Report.*

Barton, D., Chen, Y., & Jin, A. (2013). Mapping China's Middle Class. *McKinsey Quarterly.*

BCG. (2016, November 2). *Capitalizing on Asia's Booming Upper Middle Class.* Retrieved from bcg.com: https://www.bcg.com/publications/2016/globalization-growth-capitalizing-asias-booming-upper-middle-class.aspx

Credit Suisse. (2015). *Global Wealth Report 2105.*

Dobbs, R., Remes, J., & Woetzel, J. (2016). Emerging Demographics are the New Emerging Markets. *Harvard Business Review.*

Escabado, J. (2017, May 22). *Nearly $150K Per Post? What You Need to Know About China's Key Opinion Leaders.* Retrieved from forbes.com: https://www.forbes.com/sites/joeescobedo/2017/05/22/key-opinion-leaders-in-china/#388a8e9272ee

Fischer, L. H. (2014). *Leftover Women: The Resurgence of Gender Inequality in China (Asian Arguments).* Zed Books.

Gan, N., & Hu, T. (2017, July 4). *How China's smaller cities are going all out in the race to win young talent.* Retrieved from scmp.com: http://www.scmp.com/news/china/policies-politics/article/2101208/chinas-smaller-cities-offer-cash-incentives-race

Hurun Report; Taikang. (2016). *The Healthcare pension Combo Trend.*

Kharas, H. (2017). *The Unprecedented Expansion of the World Class an Update*. Brookings Institution.

National Bureau of Statistics of China. (2016). *China Statistical Yearbook 2016*.

Reform and Opening Up. (2014, November 18). Retrieved from china.org.cn: http://www.china.org.cn/english/china_key_words/2014-11/18/content_34158784.htm

Roland, G., & Yang, D. Y. (2017, May). *nber.org*. Retrieved from CHINA'S LOST GENERATION: http://www.nber.org/papers/w23441.pdf

Shumei, L. (2017, February 13). *Single men to number over 30m by 2030*. Retrieved from globaltimes.cn: http://www.globaltimes.cn/content/1032677.shtml

Silverstein, M. J. (2012). *Driving Growth – the Female Economy in China and India*. The Boston Consulting Group.

(2018). *Statistical Communique of the People's Republic of China on the 2017 National Economic and Social Development*. National Bureau of Statistics of China.

The State Council Information Office of the People's Republic of China. (2015). *PRC State Council, WhitePaper – Gender Equality and Development in China*.

Wang, L. (2015, November 19). *More Chinese couples cohabit before marrying: survey*. Retrieved from chinadaily.com.cn: http://www.chinadaily.com.cn/china/2015-11/19/content_22485696.htm

Xia, C. (2016). Cross-border e-commerce is luring Chinese shoppers. *McKinsey Quarterly*. Retrieved from mckinsey.com: https://www.mckinsey.com/industries/high-tech/our-insights/crossborder-ecommerce-is-luring-chinese-shoppers

Xingjian, Z. (2016, July 28). *'So far, the sofa is so far' strikes a chord with overworked professionals*. Retrieved from chinadaily.com.cn: http://www.chinadaily.com.cn/culture/2016-07/28/content_26256174.htm

CHAPTER 5

Key Industries for Future Growth

In this chapter, I look at certain specific industries which have already reached an exceptional stature in China, and are likely to continue to grow further and offer significant opportunities to companies. The number of such industries is large and it is overambitious to try a comprehensive listing of such industries. The choice is definitely biased by my own perspective, though I have attempted to be as objective as possible. Additionally, I have tried to focus on those industries, for which important factors fueling the growth include some specific features of the Chinese economy or distinctive consumer characteristics.

Beauty

While the overall urban FMCG market in 2015 only grew by 3.5% in value, the skin-care and the makeup product categories grew by 13.2% and 15.5%, respectively (Bain & Company; Kantar Worldpanel 2016). In fact, the Chinese consumers were not content with the marginal polish or uplift that these products provided for their looks. HSBC expects China's cosmetic surgery industry to double in market size by 2019, reaching 800 billion yuan (US$116.3 billion), making it the third largest in the world behind the USA and Japan (He 2017).

It is commonly believed that the Chinese have a very high concern about beauty and place a lot of importance on appearance. The industry data does support this hypothesis with China having the second largest

A. Sethi, *Chinese Consumers*,
https://doi.org/10.1007/978-981-10-8992-3_5

beauty industry in the world. According to a research done by research firm Mintel two-thirds (65%) of Chinese consumers spent more on facial skin care in 2015 than they did in 2014, and driven by this growing consumption, China's beauty retail market is expected to be worth 338 billion yuan (US$50 billion) by 2020.

To what extent is this size and growth driven by the importance of beauty in China? The data from the GfK Consumer Life study, with 27,000 consumers over 22 markets, suggests that the overall perceived value of beauty in China is not very different from elsewhere in the world (beauty ranks 34 out of 50 values in China and 35 globally). Nevertheless, it still has a huge industry in skin care, cosmetics, and now also plastic surgery. Hence unlike the common perception, the Chinese do not spend more on beauty and grooming because they care more about their beauty—beauty is equally desired and sought everywhere in the world. There are several other factors which propel this market in China.

Eight Reasons Fueling the Growth of the Beauty Products Market in China

The Chinese and North East Asians, in general, have higher standards of beauty. Hence what may be considered perfectly charming in other parts of the world may come under critical scrutiny and disapproval in China. According to research, while 22% of Brazilians and 30% of Mexicans say that they are fully satisfied with their looks, only 10% of the Chinese express this feeling of happy complacency (the satisfaction in other ethnic Chinese areas of Hong Kong and Taiwan is even lower). Additionally, it is not surprising that the Chinese are moving their loyalty more and more toward the Korean and Japanese brands, where the demands on beauty seem to be even more exacting (only 4% of Koreans and 2% of Japanese are completely satisfied with their looks) (GfK 2015).

Independent women consumers are driving the growth. The proportion of working-age women who are actually working and earning in China is one of the highest in the world. According to a report by Ogilvy, female earnings in China grew from $350 billion in 2000 to $1.3 trillion in 2010 and are expected to grow further to $4 trillion by 2020. With own money in hand, women have their own means of consumption and do not have to depend upon their male partners to buy them beauty and grooming products. It also enables them to buy more premium and international brands.

Women in the workplace mean that women feel a need to look good every day and right through the day—not just during certain parts of the day when they feel it is important for them to turn on their charms.

In fact, beauty serves a function beyond enhancement of sex appeal—it is also seen to contribute to looking good at work and to be associated with success in the workplace.

Both men and women are marrying later and divorce rates in China increased by 63% in the past decade. This creates a strong need to keep looking (for a partner)—and also keep looking young and attractive.

The Chinese consumers, in general, are driven by rationality and logic and are not bogged down by sentiments of guilt or an over-active conscience. If beauty can be achieved and preserved through action and money, there is no moral compunction which holds them back (a similar rational and simple mindset makes luxury goods a natural choice for them). Consumers in other cultures could be held back by feelings such as—"let me not fight the course of nature", "one should look one's age, why do I need to look younger than I am", "it is the inner beauty which matters", and so on.

The beauty industry has ridden well on the transition to e-commerce in China, and Chinese consumers are now buying these products heavily on the internet. Given the huge range and variety of products, the fair amount of research and recommendation seeking that the consumers go through for this category would mean that beauty products are very compatible with an online purchase. The industry in China has also transitioned with alacrity to the digital world.

It is not just the women—men are also contributing to the growth. The relatively low level of satisfaction on looks in China, Korea, and Japan holds true not just for women but also for men, which is fueling the market for men's grooming products. Additionally, in big Chinese cities, the competition among men to secure a fair and pretty bride (Bai Fu Mei 白富美—fair, rich, and beautiful) is fierce. While the traditional marketing strategy among men has been to position themselves more on their wealth than looks, with increasing competition, many of them are now looking at the last part of their proposition (gao fu shuai of 高富帅—tall, rich, and handsome) and exploring if beauty aids can help them enhance their competitive appeal. As a result, men's beauty market in China is already the largest in the world.

Home and Home Decoration

They say, "an Englishman's house is a castle"—they should look at the importance and reverence attached to a house in China. This is a bit odd given (or perhaps because of) a rather peculiar history of housing in China. Till the late 1990s there were no private houses in China. Under the benevolent socialist regime, where there was no concept of private enterprise, the state or more specifically your danwei or work-unit had the responsibility of providing you with a roof over your head. As a first step toward private ownership of housing, in the 1980s and early 1990s many publicly owned houses were sold to their existing occupants at low prices and with active financial assistance from the work-unit. Finally, in 1998, the Chinese government ended this system of allocation of houses through the employer, paving the way for a development of the huge private sector housing industry in the country. Today China boasts of the largest private housing industry in the world and some of the most jaw-dropping prices in the cities. The industry is believed to constitute 15% of the economy and supports more than 40 other industries.

There Are Several Factors Responsible for the Housing Boom in China

Firstly, as historically housing was provided to the people, the concept of renting is not salient in the Chinese consumers' mind. Renting a house is associated with uncertainty, fear of rising rentals and the hassle of frequent changes. In fact, purchase of a house is seen to offer a degree of stability and certainty in what the Chinese see as a dynamic and changing environment with a high degree of risk (The Economist 2018).

The access of the child to the school is dependent on the ownership of the house. This has led to the concept of Xue qu fang 校区房 or school district house where consumers spend an astronomical amount of money to buy a tiny apartment near a good school so that the child becomes eligible to attend the school (Jingrong 2017).

When the private ownership of housing took off, there was already a high ownership of housing, as a lot of people had bought the house from their work-unit, but the quality of those houses was poor and in comparison, the new private apartments appeared much more attractive.

There has been a huge flux of people from rural areas and smaller cities to the large cities in pursuit of economic opportunities. Hence a lot of people are living in places other than where they had an access to housing, leading them to the purchase.

The young people seldom stay with their parents after marriage, and purchase of an apartment has almost become a pre-condition for marriage. This results in the Chinese consumers buying a house at very early stages of their lives.

An additional factor contributing to early purchase is the fact that consumers have seen the steady and steep increase of price in the past two decades and there is a firm belief that even though the price is high now, it is very likely to become even higher, making it even more unaffordable than now. As most of the under 30s who are moving into matrimony are single children, both the parents help actively to pay the down payment, which makes the acquisition more affordable.

There are few safe investment opportunities available, and the banks offer an extremely low rate of returns for savings. Having experienced the rapid rise of housing prices, the Chinese view it as an attractive and safe investment and multiple house ownership among the middle class and affluent consumers is common.

Is There a Housing Bubble in China?

Most would agree that if there is a bubble, it is rather a tenacious and sturdy one, as people have been talking about it for more than a decade, and it has not burst as yet. In fact, with minor blips, the housing prices have been steadily rising ever since the market was opened up to the consumers, and no buyers or investors have burnt their hands. Prices do soften up temporarily, especially when the government clamps down and attempts to curb the consumer enthusiasm, however, the momentum inevitably picks up again and the long-term trend has always been moving northward. In 2016 the average new home prices in 70 major cities in China grew 12.4%, with cities like Shanghai and Xiamen achieving an over 30% increase. The fact that the purchase is driven by a real and sustainable demand is supported by the evidence that nearly all buyers pay as much as half the price of the property from their own savings. This implies a certain stability, as these consumers are unlikely to dump the property in the market if there is a small decrease in the price.The second reason the bubble has not burst so far, the experts say, is because the housing prices are not a result of the market dynamics of demand and supply, but that the whole system is rigged, and the prices are finally controlled by the central, provincial and the municipal governments. The government is active in introducing policies—mostly those which would dampen the consumer fervor—by various means, including restricting who can buy a house (most large cities do not allow purchase by a non-resident, unless the family has been in the city for a certain number of years) and raising the down payment requirement to as high as 70% of the price of the house, if a buyer already has a couple of apartments under his belt.

Housing and Family Values

One would normally think that housing is linked to a desire to form and nurture a family. It will be surprising to hear that housing is linked to an increase in the divorce rate in China (though normally only a false and temporary divorce) (Fong et al. 2016). This stems from the fact that in many cities the government has tried to rein in the surging prices by restraining one family from buying only one apartment. Many couples, keenly desirous of multiple house ownership, and confident in their relationship forge a plan to go to the marriage bureau to file for a divorce. Once the divorce is obtained, one family turns into two, and both can buy an apartment, and then re-marry to achieve their goal of two houses (there is no rule that when two people who are getting married each have a house, they need to turn in one). While in many cases this works and the couple is happily reunited with two houses, there have been cases of the divorce gaining an unexpected permanent status. A 2016 film by a popular director Feng Xiaogang, starring Fan Bingbing (I am not Madam Bovary) (imdb.com 2016), depicts one such story in which a couple concocts a divorce to buy a second property, but the husband takes this opportunity to marry another sweetheart leaving his ex-wife in a limbo. The interesting twist is that the outraged ex-wife requests the authorities to annul the divorce so that she could then file a proper divorce in a symbolic rejection of her treacherous husband. Another television serial, Woju 蜗居 or snail house depicted the travails of a family as they struggled to buy a house in a city.

The housing industry supports more than 40 other industries. From a consumer point of view, purchase of a house is followed by home decoration, painting, furniture, and household appliance purchase. To take one example, China accounts for 25% of the global consumption of paint in recent years, according to the World Paint and Coatings Industry Association and for 60% of the Asia Pacific market, and multinational decorative paints companies, including AkzoNobel, SACAL, and Nippon Paint, are all prospering. The industry is also transforming itself to a higher value-addition status, by moving away from merely selling paints, to offering solutions. Consumer tastes are also becoming more sophisticated and discerning, as they move from ubiquitous white to a range of 2000 colors offered by Dulux for instance.

The future outlook for the housing industry, as well as those dependent upon it, in the coming years, is positive. The fact that there is a trend toward higher divorce rate and there are increasingly more single-member households is likely to further fuel the demand. The overall market and consumer trends indicate that the Chinese desire for the purchase of a house is unlikely to be softened; they will continue to invest in creating this symbol of safety and security and spend generously on furnishing it to make it a comfortable home.

Entertainment

The Film Industry

It is not surprising that once the Chinese consumers have achieved their goals of acquiring the basic necessities, the attention moves toward consumption of services which enhance the quality of life, and among these entertainment takes the pride of place. According to the consultancy firm PWC, China's entertainment and media industry is forecast to grow at a compound annual growth rate (CAGR) of 8.8% over the coming five years, compared to a global CAGR of 4.4% (PwC 2016).

China was associated with piracy and refusal to pay for movies, television dramas, or music. While piracy still prevails, it is clear that China has become one of the largest entertainment markets in the world. In 2005, the Chinese box office revenue was 2.8% of the size of the American box office. However, from 2005 to 2015, the box office revenue of Chinese films maintained an average growth rate of 30% and the revenue grew to

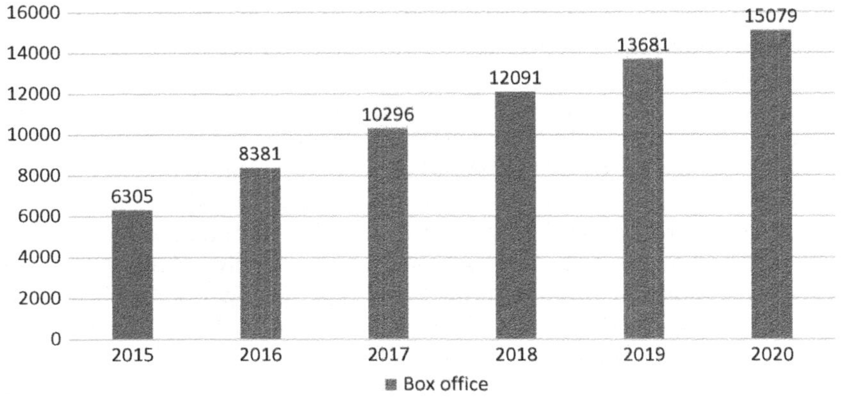

Fig. 5.1 Box office revenue of Chinese films. Source: China entertainment and media outlook 2016–2020, PwC (000 dollars)

49.2 billion yuan making it the second largest market in the world and around two-thirds the size of the American market. The consultancy firm, PWC forecasts that the revenues will overtake the American market in 2020 when it touches the RMB 100 billion mark ($15.08 billion) (Fig. 5.1).

China is the largest market for 3D films, and the 3D box office is already worth $2 billion in 2014—more than three-fourths of screens in China are capable of screening 3D films. The North American entertainment company, IMAX Corp., has 1102 cinemas in 69 countries, and 335 of these are in China. It plans to open 150 new cinemas along with the Chinese entertainment group Wanda (IMAX 2016).

While domestic films are huge beneficiaries of this bounty, the market is substantial for foreign films too, despite the fact that China restricts the number of foreign films that it imports (around 34). In 2015 Hollywood's share of the Chinese box office stood at 38%.

In fact, the Chinese industry is reaching out and investing in the global market—the Wanda group became the largest cinema chain operator in the world when in 2015 it acquired America's AMC Entertainment (China's Wanda to Buy AMC Cinema Chain for $2.6 Billion 2012).

End of the Korean Wave?

Since the early 2000s China has been struck with what was commonly called as "hanliu" or "hallyu" in Korean. Essentially this refers to the extraordinary popularity of Korean pop culture in China. Of course, China is not unique in succumbing to the charms of the Koreans pop stars, most of South East Asia has fallen in love with them. It also helped that the political relations between China and Korea were extremely cordial, the two countries often coming together to complain against the Japanese aggression during the second world war and exploitation of Chinese and Korean women as comfort women or sex slaves. China is perhaps the most important export market for Korean entertainment. Descendants of the Sun, the 2016 intensely popular drama series was released simultaneously in Korea and China (Jung-a 2016).

However, the Korean wave is threatened to come down with a big thud if Korea continues to go ahead with its decision to deploy Terminal High Altitude Area Defense (THAAD) system, which is an American missile-defense system designed to guard against North Korean aggression. Korean businesses are already suffering in China and Lotte, a large Korean conglomerate announced its intention to sell its hypermarkets by the end of 2017.

One Billion Viewers in Search of a Plot

While the Chinese appetite for entertainment is strong, the fare on offer is seldom very appetizing. Cinema plots plod the trite romance and TV drama themes are dominated by China's war with Japan or hackneyed lives of young urban Chinese mostly focusing on office politics.The prudish supervision from the authorities does not allow for anything which is daring or stimulating. A "joint pledge of self-discipline in Professional Ethics" was signed in 2015 by 50 media and entertainment organizations, promising to shun vulgarity, and promote healthy esthetics and socialist core values. The audience has no choice but to chase Hollywood films such as the Fast and Furious and Mission Impossible series. When the US-made Kungfu Panda won much admiration in China, it also elicited much lamentation that even a film about a Chinese icon is made by another country (thanks to the Chinese muscle power, Kungfu Panda 3 was made with Chinese collaboration and was classified as a Chinese made film). Even an odd Indian film like Dangal makes the Chinese audience wonder why they cannot produce films of a higher standard.

The authorities try hard to push films which are supposed to fill the audience's bosom with effusive patriotic fervor and a feeling of immense pride for the country.However, films like the "The Founding of the Republic" or "Founding of the Army" despite their star-studded cast, were unable to enthuse the audience.

A film which did succeed in matching the nationalistic intentions of the authorities and the audience need for simple entertainment was Wolf Warrior II. Starring and directed by the popular star, Wu Jing, the film's plot revolves around the valor and altruism exhibited by Chinese forces in hapless Africa. The Chinese are depicted as rescuing Chinese workers, as well winning African hearts through their sheer goodness.Wolf Warriors II has become the all-time highest box office hit in China, grossing over $600 million in just a month (Laydon 2017).

Clearly, the Chinese entertainment industry, though it has a large and captive audience (also thanks to the limitation of only 34 Hollywood films every year) needs to work harder to try to truly entertain them.

Books

It is would be surprising to some that China is the world's biggest book and magazine publications country. Not only is domestic content thriving, but many international authors find unexpected fame and fortune in China through the popularity of the Chinese translations of their works. The Kite Runner by Khaled Hosseini which has sold 32 million copies worldwide, sold 5 million of those in China. One hundred years of Solitude, by Gabriel Garcia Marquez sold 2.6 million copies in China since the death of the author in 2011. The Chinese have an eclectic taste and books as diverse as

The Ferryman by Claire McFall and M Train by Patti Smith have struck a chord with the Chinese consumers.

As in other areas, the real action in China for books is in e-reading and e-publishing. Like so many other activities, reading books has also made a grand transition to the digital world, and more specifically the mobile world. The Chinese are reading books on their mobile phones, and China's online books industry is valued at over $1 billion. Millions of amateur authors publish online and their works are devoured by numerous online readers. Two of the most popular television serials in China—Empress in the Palace and Scarlet heart—are based on online novels. Most of this works as authors self-publish in installments on certain websites and hope for a positive reader reaction and the dream that the viewers will start making micro-payments for reading. The model is booming and in fact, one company alone, China Literature (of the Tencent Group, owner of the popular Chinese app—WeChat) was listed in the Hong Kong stock market in 2017 and attained a market value of over $10 million, after its shares doubled in trade after its debut.

Online Entertainment: Paying for Content

China was notorious for its disrespect to intellectual property and was a haven for pirated entertainment. While pirated DVDs of the latest releases were and are still available at every street corner, most Chinese did not even pay that $1 for the DVD and just downloaded the movie on the internet. A large number of Chinese continue to enjoy such free content. However, a very significant number has started paying for content. In June 2015, video content provider iQiyi had 5 million paying users, and by December 2015 it had doubled to 10 million. In 2016, iQiyi was expecting the number of paid users to increase to over 60 million, accounting for 10% of all its viewers. iResearch Consumption guesstimate that the number of paying viewers in 2015 ballooned by 2644 to 28.84 million and is expected to reach 54.41 million in 2016. The secret of this transformation as in most other product fields is content. This move to paying mode was triggered by television series such as the Korean love drama "Descendants of the Sun", whose 16 episodes were released simultaneously in Korea and China. In 2015 a similar trigger was provided by the drama series "Grave Robbers' Chronicles", based on a best-selling series of novels, which triggered a paid viewing craze. Good and affordable pricing definitely contributed—iQiyi prices its monthly service only at 19.8 yuan a month or 58 yuan a quarter and 198 yuan per year. Youku Tudou (partly owned by Alibaba), the other major online video site has 4 million paid members today and plans to increase it aggressively through superior and unique content production.

Theme Parks

One of the biggest and most anticipated events in the past few years in China has been the opening of the Disney Park in Shanghai. The anticipation has been matched by an enthusiastic audience reception, and the Park has attracted visitors in hordes. Disney Shanghai is twice the size of the original Disneyland and attracted 11 million visitors in the year one of its operation. Interestingly 57% of the Park is owned by the Shendi Group, which is owned by the Shanghai government.The success can be attributed to several factors, including a fair amount of awareness and exposure to Disney characters, the presence of the Disney Park in Hong Kong next door and sensitive localization efforts of the Shanghai Park, while still retaining its universal, global appeal.

Theme parks were already big business in China and four of the ten largest park operators in the world were Chinese in 2015. Another 21 theme parks opened in 2015 in China and 20 more are under construction. Wanda launched a $3.4 billion project in Nanchang, just before Disney opened in Shanghai in June 2016. Wanda has plans to open another 14 parks across China by 2020. In an attempt to pack attractive content into its parks, which could hope to compete with Disney, Wanda acquired Legendary Entertainment, the US-based film studio, which has produced films like Jurassic World and the Dark Knight. Shimao Property, a Shanghai-based theme park developer, has teamed up with the animation studio, Dreamworks, which owns characters such as Kungfu Panda, to create a theme park to be opened in 2020 in Nanjing.

The Theme Park business is likely to retain its upswing momentum in the coming years because of several reasons:

- The growing affluence and the growing need for entertainment
- Increasing domestic travel and tourism

- Relaxation of the one-child policy, leading to more customers for the park
- Increasing international exposure and growing familiarity with characters from Disney and other studios

Entertainment and Brands

Brand placement in movies and other entertainment programs in China has already been strong, and in fact sometimes overboard. However, a factor which is giving a big fillip to the entertainment industry in China is that brands are beginning to realize that they themselves need to produce content. Hence producing entertainment content is not just within the exclusive purview of the entertainment houses, but every brand which aspires to have strong linkages to the consumers needs to reach consumers through content. This stems from the fact that the traditional vehicle for brands to ingratiate themselves with the consumers, that is, advertising, is no longer able to do the trick (discussed more in Chap. 7—Branding in China). Brands need to *embed* their messages in content, not *insert* their advertising in content. Popular brands like Coke and Pepsi increasingly see themselves as content providers rather than merely sponsors of content through which they reach the audience.

When Pepsi saw that a song called "Xiao Pingguo" (little apple) from the Chopsticks Brothers was a big hit, they asked them to sing another one called "XioaShuiguo" (little fruit) to promote the Master Kong range of fruit drinks in China. Master Kong noodles picked up a television serial called "Love Apartment", which enjoyed a huge popularity among their target audience of students, and produced additional episodes with a prominent role of the brand. The popular smartphone brand, Xiaomi, produced a 20-minute mini-film called "1699 Commencement", portraying four entrepreneurs, who ride a bicycle over 1699 kilometers in China, to prove the idea behind their business. The video touches on themes and concerns such as entrepreneurship, self-exploration, and friendship, encouraging the young people to follow their dreams—something that the company founder Lei Jun did himself in launching Xiaomi.

Given this development, it would seem that learning to entertain the Chinese consumers is something that is of importance not just to the entertainment industry, but for every brand of significant size, which wants to reach out to the consumers.The need for enhancing the quality of the content, that it touches the heart-strings of the consumers is, therefore, a strong imperative for all marketers in China.

Travel and Tourism

International Tourism

According to the data from the World Tourism Organization of the USA, 135 million Chinese traveled to destinations outside China in 2016, an increase of 6% over the previous year. China has been the number one source market for international tourists since 2012. The total spending of the Chinese tourists abroad reached $261 billion, and an increase of 12% over 2015.The spending by the Chinese tourists is more than twice as much as the second largest source market, which is the USA (the outbound tourists spent $122 billion in 2016). The upward trend is likely to continue—Goldman Sachs expects that 100 million more Chinese will acquire a passport between 2015 and 2025 (Kawanao et al. 2015).

Anticipating the growth of the Chinese leisure travelers, Chinese companies had started making strategic investments in global assets and brands which would benefit from the growth of the Chinese tourist. The Fosun Group acquired a small stake of 7.1% in Club Med, the French resort company, in 2011 and ended up buying the company in 2015 (China's Fosun wins bidding for Club Med after two years 2015). China State Shipbuilding Corp and Italy's FincantieriSpA are collaborating to build cruise ships in Shanghai (Fincantieri and China State Shipbuilding Corporation set up JV for Chinese cruise industry 2016) (passenger trips from China registered a 72% year-on-year growth with 4.29 million cruise trips in 2016).

Destination Marketing

Nearly all the top ten destinations of the Chinese tourists are in Asia—including South Korea, Taiwan, Hong Kong, Japan, Thailand and Macau, Malaysia, Vietnam, and Singapore. Outside of Asia the USA, Switzerland, France, Italy, and Germany are favorites (Source: China Tourism Academy, Beijing). The range of destinations is also expanding. Traffic to destinations such as Cambodia, Iceland, and Morocco has been gaining momentum, as more Chinese tourists shun the beaten path and seek newer and more exotic experiences.

Several countries have instituted marketing campaigns in China to woo the huge audience. And these are not just the obvious destinations—places like Alberta have launched campaigns in the Chinese social media (WeChat) to attract the Chinese tourists to its winter wilderness. Malta Tourism Authority has been wooing the Chinese tourists through its Chinese "Visit Malta" website. Just as everything else in China, the popularity of destinations is very sensitive to the inclinations and preferences of the Chinese government. As China launched its "One Belt One Road" initiative (B&R or OBOR), the number of Chinese tourists traveling to the B&R countries increased by 73% in 2016. At the same time, the Chinese tourist pipeline to South Korea dried up, as the Chinese government flexed its muscles and expressed its chagrin at South Korea agreeing to install an anti-missile-defense system on its territory. Surprisingly, Chinese tourist flow to Japan retains a healthy flow, despite a perennial antipathy between the two nations.

From Shopping to Experiences

Traditional Chinese outbound tourism has been driven by packaged tours, with multiple destinations, cheap hotels, Chinese food and Chinese guides, and shopping at the luxury stores. However, as the younger, more educated Chinese start to travel abroad, the obsession with shopping and the insulated mentality is changing. The younger tourists look beyond the stores and are keen to experience the destination in terms of not just its sights and products but also in terms of its culture.

- Chinese tourists are willing to shed the security of packaged tours and venture out on their own. Of course, this is also helped by the fact that the tourists are willing to spend more, and more countries are ready to accept them as individuals rather than just packaged tour travelers.
- While tick mark sight-seeing has been the hallmark of the traditional tourists, the new tourists are happy to go beyond the beaten path and explore new areas.
- They are also packing fewer destinations in one trip, as they now see foreign travel as a regular feature of their lives, and not a once-in-a-lifetime opportunity.
- Consumption of cultural experiences is becoming more important as the Chinese become more familiar with food and drink outside their country.

- Unique and exclusive experiences are favored—whether they are balloon and helicopter rides, extreme or special sports, or unique gastronomical experiences.
- While shopping abroad is still important, it does not have to be the traditional luxury products (the domestic access of such products is much better now, particularly with the popularity of daigou—merchants, mostly on WeChat, who arrange to buy and bring these products for consumers in China, at a nominal fee). The Chinese tourists are now more likely to buy local and culture-specific products that the region is known for.
- Premium holidays to exotic destinations are increasing—Ctrip reported that more than 100 Chinese paid RMB 200,000 each for a holiday to the Antarctica (Chinese warming up to holiday in Antarctica 2017).

However, though a lot is changing, some basics are still important to please the Chinese tourists—a hot water kettle in the room, night slippers, someone who can speak their language, and at least a representation of familiar food still go a long way in making the Chinese tourists feel at home and happy with their holiday.

Domestic Tourism

Apart from international tourism, domestic travel market has also boomed in recent years, owing to the massive increase in infrastructure, including the high-speed railways. According to an estimate by the China National Tourism Administration, 4 billion domestic visits were made by the Chinese travelers in 2015. The domestic tourism gets a special fillip from the two-week-long holidays (one for the spring festival and for the National Day in October) as all from a few other three-day weekends arranged by the government for the core purpose of encouraging traveling and spending. Over 100 million trips were made by rail alone during the National Day holiday in 2017. However, like the international tourism market, the domestic market is also evolving in a similar way. The share of packaged tours is declining, more exotic destinations are being favored, and sports and adventure tourism is on the rise. The Chinese consumers who can afford holidays continue to grow in size and are likely to become more sophisticated. There are huge opportunities for a number of industries which cater to Chinese tourists. The key to exploiting the opportunities is to keep a firm hand on the pulse of Chinese tourists and to continue to change the offer in line with their changing needs.

Pet Care

Given the stereotypical associations with China, it would have been inconceivable to imagine that China will become one of the largest markets for pet food and pet care in the world. However, the country's pet owners spent 130 billion yuan ($19.35 billion) on their pets in 2016, making it the third largest pet care market in the world, after the USA and Japan, with a growth rate of nearly 50% a year (Source: National Bureau of Statistics). Not only are the large multinational companies like Nestle and Mars reaping the benefits of this growth, even the relatively smaller niche players, such as Fish4Dogs of UK (which specializes in using fish as a source of protein in dog foods), are finding a place here (Fish4Dogs takes bite out of growing Chinese market n.d.).

The pet market in China has been growing at a tremendous pace and as for many other high growth markets growing in a fairly chaotic manner. However, the government is trying to regulate the market through licensing and imposing a certain discipline in the care of the pets. Many large cities have imposed a registration fee and also require the owners to clean up after the animal.

Pet Stylists and Hotels

China today has a large industry catering to every need of the pet. Pet care stores offer services ranging from simple shampooing, to styling, to nail painting and swimming. There are stores offering luxury products for pets, and outfits which offer cremation services, including turning the ashes of the beloved pet into diamonds. Wang Sicang, son of the richest man of China, posted pictures of his dog with eight iPhone 7 on his dog's Weibo account and another one with several Apple watches (The son of a Chinese billionaire just bought his dog $9584 worth of iPhones 2016).

VAC Cat Hotel and Spa in Beijing charges $50 a day for a room, including food, beverage, and grooming. In the peak season, when many of the pet owners leave town for holidays and family reunions, the prices go up significantly (Luxury hotels for furry guests boom 2017). During such periods, for instance, the Chinese New Year, the cat would stay at the hotel for around seven to eight days. The rooms are smaller than what the human hotels offer but the service is fine-tuned to satisfy every whim and desire of the cat. More luxurious accommodation may charge as much as $100 a day and may even offer a 24-hour butler service.

Factors Driving the Growth of the Pet Care Industry

To a certain extent, growing pet ownership and increasing spending on pet care is a natural concomitant of increasing incomes and spending power in China. However, there are some special factors in China which are significant contributors to the acceleration of the growth of the market:

- The residents of the most populous nation in the world are actually some of the most lonely. Most children do not have the company of a sibling, and in most cases both parents work out of the home. In smaller cities and villages, children are often left behind in care of grandparents or other relatives, while both parents earn a living as migrant workers in large cities. Additionally, the over-60 population is steadily growing and more of these elderly couples live alone. Seeking companionships from pets, therefore, comes naturally.
- Many Chinese either do not cook at home or cook infrequently. Hence other than in rural areas, the practice of sharing home food—eaten by the family—to feed the pets—while still exists, is on a decline.
- As the ultra-rich spend to indulge themselves, simultaneously indulging pets comes naturally—as pets are being increasingly seen as members of the family
- The growing concern for food safety also extends to concern for food safety for pets—resulting in the purchase of more premium and, what are seen as, "healthy" products.

References

(2016). Retrieved from imdb.com: http://www.imdb.com/title/tt5918090/?ref_=nv_sr_1

Bain & Company; Kantar Worldpanel. (2016). *Dealing with Two-Speed China: China Shopper Report.*

China's Wanda to Buy AMC Cinema Chain for $2.6 Billion. (2012, May 22). Retrieved from bloomberg.com: https://www.bloomberg.com/news/

articles/2012-05-21/china-s-wanda-group-to-buy-amc-cinema-chain-for-2-6-billion

China's Fosun wins bidding for Club Med after two years. (2015, February 11). Retrieved from bbc.co.uk: http://www.bbc.com/news/business-31432322

Chinese warming up to holiday in Antarctica. (2017, 27). Retrieved from chinadaily.com.cn: http://www.chinadaily.com.cn/china/2017-02/07/content_28120180.htm

Fincantieri and China State Shipbuilding Corporation set up JV for Chinese cruise industry. (2016, July 4). Retrieved from reuters.com: https://www.reuters.com/finance/stocks/FCT.MI/key-developments/article/3400000

Fish4Dogs takes bite out of growing Chinese market. (n.d.). Retrieved from globalpets.com: https://globalpets.community/news/fish4dogs-takes-bite-out-of-growing-chinese-market

Fong, D., Qian, J., & Xie, Y. (2016, August 29). *In Shanghai, Couples Rush to Divorce to Buy Property Later.* Retrieved from wsj.com: https://blogs.wsj.com/chinarealtime/2016/08/29/in-shanghai-couples-rush-to-divorce-to-buy-property-later/

GfK. (2015, May 29). *1 in 10 completely satisfied with their looks.* Retrieved from gfk.com: http://www.gfk.com/insights/press-release/1-in-10-completely-satisfied-with-their-looks-1/

He, L. (2017, April 24). *China's cosmetic surgery boom doesn't look pretty when it comes to profits.* Retrieved from scmp.com: http://www.scmp.com/business/markets/article/2090105/chinas-cosmetic-surgery-boom-doesnt-look-pretty-when-it-comes

IMAX. (2016, August 2). *WANDA TO ADD 150 IMAX® THEATRES IN LANDMARK DEAL; LARGEST AGREEMENT IN IMAX HISTORY.* Retrieved from imax.com: https://www.imax.com/content/wanda-add-150-imax-theatres-landmark-deal-largest-agreement-imax-history

Jingrong, L. (2017, March 3). *House prices skyrocket in Beijing's school districts.* Retrievedfromchina.org.cn:http://www.china.org.cn/business/2017-03/03/content_40390802.htm

Jung-a, S. (2016, April 12). *China awash with Korean Wave fever.* Retrieved from ft.com: https://www.ft.com/content/167338ec-fa0b-11e5-8e04-8600cef2ca75

Kawanao, S., Lu, J., Tsang, R., & Liu, J. (2015). *The Chinese Tourist Boom.* Goldman Sachs.

Laydon, J. (2017, August 12). *Film Review: 'Wolf Warrior II'.* Retrieved from yahoo.com: https://www.yahoo.com/entertainment/film-review-wolf-warrior-ii-060837051.html

Luxury hotels for furry guests boom. (2017, January 26). Retrieved from chinadaily.com.cn: http://www.chinadaily.com.cn/travel/2017-01/26/content_28060825.htm

PwC. (2016). *China Entertainment and Media Outlook 2016–2020.* PwC.

The Economist. (2018, February 15). China is trying new ways of skimming housing-market froth. *The Economist.*

The son of a Chinese billionaire just bought his dog $9,584 worth of iPhones. (2016, September 20). Retrieved from businessinsider.com: http://www.businessinsider.com/wang-sicong-coco-chinese-billionaire-dog-iphone-7-photos-2016-9

CHAPTER 6

Luxury with Chinese Characteristics

Luxury in a Communist Nation

"You are so naive, my dear," Xiao Guan is reprimanded by one of her colleagues. Xiao Guan is one of the five female characters in Ode to Joy (Huan Le Song 欢乐颂) ("Ode to Joy"—Chinese "Pride and Prejudice" with 13 Billion Online Views 2016) a popular television drama about five career women from different backgrounds, living in a high-rise apartment building in Shanghai. "You really think people buy famous brands because of their style? Wrong! They buy them for their class," the friends educate the young intern. They go on the assure Xiao Guan that by the time her internship is over she will find it easier to recognize the luxury brands than looking at a business report.

It is ironic that a country which still calls itself a socialist country (though qualified by "Chinese characteristics") has turned into a voracious consumer of luxury goods. In most developed countries, the luxury goods started gaining acceptance with an increase in consumer incomes, in a gradual and progressive manner. However, as in many other ways, China followed a different path. In the late 1990s, while still several hundred million Chinese languished below the poverty line, the metropolitan cities already started seeing the prominent presence of global luxury brands. The boom in the sale of luxury goods started around the turn of the century and has continued to nourish the global luxury manufacturers since then. While the sinking finances of Western consumers prompted them to restrain their indulgences in 2009, the Chinese consumers

A. Sethi, *Chinese Consumers*,
https://doi.org/10.1007/978-981-10-8992-3_6

continued to march ahead on the gilded road of luxury and rewarded the luxury goods industry with a 20% year-on-year growth. The boom has continued since then and large new stores of Louis Vuitton, Coach, and other such brands decorate the shopping streets of Shanghai and socialist China has donned the dubious title of being the largest luxury market in the world, accounting for 27–46% of the global luxury consumption (according to various estimates).

Contributors to the Chinese Luxury Market

Xiao Guan in the television serial mentioned above, a millennial from a lower tier city of China, merely at the start of her career, is receiving lessons on luxury goods from her colleagues. Like many other Chinese consumers, who grew up in families of modest means, her natural upbringing does not expose her to luxury or even premium products. However, the start of the corporate career, exposure to a megacity, quickly sows a seed of desire and such consumers often succumb to the attractions of luxury products despite limited incomes. This relatively young and educated white-collar consumer comprises a unique segment of luxury consumers in China, which is large in number and buys products which are disproportionately more expensive than their modest incomes. These are relatively light buyers of luxury products, though collectively their contribution is substantial, because of the sheer magnitude of their numbers. This group is also fueling the growth of "affordable luxury"—the relatively more modestly priced products, which still have the heritage and aura of luxury albeit at more accessible levels. These consumers are price-conscious and will often buy luxury goods online or on trips abroad, or ask their friends to get them what they want during their overseas travel. Thousands of Chinese students studying abroad serve as carriers of luxury goods (daigou 代购) to pay a part of their expensive education and to make their stay more comfortable during their studies (Shannon 2016).

However, the luxury market in China really took off on the strength of those who took permission from the architect of China's economic reforms, Deng Xiaoping, and "became rich earlier than the others". Through fortuitous business links, lucky connections, gritty entrepreneurship, or merely by virtue of just being at the right place at the right time, they started making more money than they knew what to do with and started buying luxury goods as a relatively efficient way of utilizing the cash. These are the relatively older consumers (older only relatively to the

Western luxury consumers—still around 35–50 years of age and much younger than the luxury consumers in the developed markets) (Buchwald 2015). This group has been the mainstay of the luxury boom in China, buying in larger and larger quantities, to keep pace with more and more money that they made by selling coal, manufacturing undergarments, exporting machine parts, or investing in real estate. These consumers were primarily driven by status initially, though some of them have graduated to a higher level of sophistication and paying for unique experiences. A few have developed a real interest in their acquisitions, which have become a source of personal joy for them, driving them to buy more and more and even start collections. These are relatively heavy buyers of luxury products and often go on an orgiastic shopping spree, particularly on their trips abroad.

This group also contributed significantly to the market through their purchases and use of these products as business tools, to greet their associates, business partners, and those in power, whose benign gaze is necessary for them to continue to make money in a privileged, and the sometimes undeserved, way that they stumbled into. Gifting has been a major contributor to the luxury market in China, though the recent clampdown on corruption has taken the sheen off this segment.

The older among these first-generation rich already have children who are old enough to have aspirations and desires for good things in life on their own. This generation of fuerdai (富二代 or second-generation rich) (Doctrow 2015) and guanerdai (官二代 or offsprings of powerful officials) make up the third segment of luxury buyers in China. These consumers were born with a silver spoon in their mouth (or rather sliver chopsticks) and provided a particularly helping hand to products like luxury automobiles, premium alcohol and food, and expensive entertainment venues, which are an essential part of their lifestyle.

Chinese Culture and Luxury

While rapid economic growth and swelling ranks of the rich are definitely fueling the market, there are also clear cultural and circumstantial factors which make the Chinese more attracted to luxury products than some other markets. The old Chinese saying "yi jin huan xiang" 衣锦还乡 (return home in golden robes) expresses the phenomenon of using visible symbols to reflect your success. Having succeeded, it is important to make sure that your achievement is noticed and applauded. But at the same time traditional Chinese values do not suggest sticking out or drawing undue attention on oneself through conspicuous behavior or consumption ("qiang da chu tou niao" 枪打出头鸟—the bird who sticks out his head gets shot!). The Chinese are torn between these two conflicting pulls to display their success but at the same time try to do it in an inconspicuous manner. Given the success that luxury goods have enjoyed in China, it would seem that the cultural compulsion of announcing success has been the more powerful of these two contradictory forces in China, leading to the Chinese consumers lapping the expensive symbols of luxury. Apart from economic and cultural factors, there are a few other elements serving as psychological fuel for the luxury market in China.

Yes, We Can

Given a common background of poverty just a few decades ago, there is near universality of ambition in China—almost every person dreams of and strives for success. As compared to other societies where there is inherited wealth or "old money", or which are class-based (social or economic), and people feel blessed or cursed by advantages and disadvantages of coming from specific backgrounds or bloodlines, the relatively flat social structure and the fact that all money is "new money" puts everyone on a relatively equal footing. Most Chinese have a clear ambition of moving ahead in life, endeavor for success, and hence have a desire for good things in life.

Markers of Success

In societies with an uninterrupted and long history of money and economic development, the affluent have many ways to distinguish themselves from the hoi polloi. The status is imparted at birth itself and recognition is easy as both the "haves" and the "have-nots" understand the differences. Class or success can be displayed in many diverse ways and manners, which the society associates with sophisticated behavior. Your school, the part of town you come from, your accent and sometimes even your name establishes your position in the societal hierarchy. However, in China, not many symbols of success or achievement are available to display, as the absence of "background" provides little opportunity to display success other than through the symbolism of whatever your new money can buy. Luxury goods provide easily recognizable symbols or markers of having reached milestones of progress and success.

Luxury to Conform

Traditional Chinese beliefs, including Confucianism, stress the importance of conformism, order, and respect to status. Once certain rules are defined, the Chinese have always felt in their interest to conform to these rules, and work their way up according to these rules (as they did it for thousands of years through Imperial examinations to become civil servants to the emperor, and now through gaokao 高考 or the college entrance exam). This phenomenon plays a very interesting and rather unexpected role in encouraging the consumption of luxury in China. In accordance with these rules, acquiring suitable luxury products is now expected as the individuals climb up the ladder of success. Appropriate luxury items serve as markers and indicators to suggest that things are progressing as expected. The Chinese, therefore, buy luxury products not as a wanton display of wealth, but conformist rituals of progress.

The Absence of Price Anchors

Behavioral economics tells us that consumers look for some kind of anchors to evaluate the price of a product. We tend to assess the value of goods and services in relation to certain benchmarks or comparison standards (which sometimes can be quite arbitrary and irrational). When a new product is encountered, often the price that the consumers see for the new product becomes the anchor. In countries like India, which are also booming economies, but where there has been a historic continuity of consumption, the consumers have grown up with products and services which were low priced but still delivered acceptable quality. In relation to these historical anchors it is more difficult for Indian consumers to accept the high prices of luxury goods, but in China where there was a long discontinuity in consumption of quality products, many consumers have no anchor of what a good-quality handbag, watch, or a car should cost—making it easier for them to accept the prices of luxury goods.

Perception of Luxury Goods as Real Quality Products

As discussed elsewhere in this book, the history of branding and availability of quality goods in China is rather short. Over the last 20 years, Chinese consumers have discovered that money generally buys superior quality and hence expect the expensively priced luxury goods to deliver matching value. Chinese attraction to luxury products, therefore, is also driven by an expectation of high quality. The Chinese consumers look at consumers who buy luxury goods as successful people with good taste who want to enjoy life. And qualities consumers are willing to pay for are not just exclusivity and uniqueness but also simple high quality and durability.

As an implication, for luxury goods manufacturers, it is equally important to communicate and deliver product excellence and exquisite craftsmanship, as it is to project a luxurious and exclusive image.

Perception of Luxury Buyers

In China, there is no inverted snobbery or "old money" looking down on the ostentatious behavior of the "new rich" (though in recent years some new rich are scoffed as tuhao 土豪—meaning rustic rich), considering them as wasting money and superficial (Frank 2013). This feeling discourages the use of luxury products in the developed markets and in fact makes it fashionable to appear casual and use moderately priced products. This sentiment restricts the market of luxury goods in developed markets, but because of the relative homogeneity of the society (e.g. all money is new money) does not appear to have a strong restraining effect in China. However, with the emergence of the second-generation rich and tuhao 土豪, this may change over time.

Evolving Needs and Additional Drivers

Luxury is inextricably linked with status. Indeed, as mentioned earlier one of the prime motives of buying luxury is to display one's status. When China' luxury market first took off, status was the key driver of the market. However, over time the consumer needs have evolved and several different segments have emerged. The segments discussed below are often overlapping, with the same consumer driven by different motivations under different circumstances and situations.

Self-reward

Consumers today are as willing to spend to make the right impression as they are willing to splurge to reward themselves and make themselves feel valued and pampered.

Marketers often divide consumer needs into expressive needs and gratification needs. Expressive needs spring from the basic human motivation to express one's feeling in an external, visible manner. This may be driven by a need to win approval, appreciation, or even envy of one's friends, colleagues, and social acquaintances. Gratification needs, on the other hand, are more internal and are driven by a desire to achieve a certain inner feeling of satisfaction, happiness, or peace. The luxury market was largely driven by expressive needs in the initial phase of market development. However, over time as consumers become more experienced and sophisticated, gratification needs are also generating sales of luxury products. One of these needs and a growing segment based on this need is the self-reward segment. This segment largely comprises the relatively more educated, and experienced consumers who are more likely to be corporate executives and professionals. Self-reward indulgence is a means of rewarding oneself for hard work and an instrument of assuaging the tired body and frayed nerves. The way to reward oneself can range from buying an expensive dress or a handbag, but could also encompass treating oneself to a luxury experience.

Experience Luxury

Naturally emanating from the desire to reward oneself is the emerging concept of luxury experiences. With self-reward as the key motivation, an Louis Vuitton (LV) bag not only competes with a Chanel dress, but also with a weekend in an exclusive resort, or an extensive spa retreat. The emergence of luxury experiences is emanating from a saturation of luxury products ownership among a certain segment of consumers, to who buying yet another luxury bag or another pair of shoes does not serve any purpose (as they already have enough to display) or offer any sustainable pleasure. While the purchase still provides short-term excitement, a similar stimulant is offered by special experiences, which sometimes can be more memorable and provide a long-term gratification (Atsmon et al. 2011).

Secondly, a global trend of de-cluttering and simplifying one's life, reducing possessions and ownership, and moving toward just relishing the experiences is also weaning the consumer away from the buying and owning addiction.

Connoisseurship

Another growth segment is that of connoisseurship, where the consumers are driven by a genuine appreciation of the quality and craftsmanship of the product. Here the enjoyment comes as much from cherishing and savoring the ownership of the product as it comes from proudly displaying it. This segment is surely driven by products such as watches, but also by wine, fine furniture, and art.

An additional driver of the connoisseurship segment is likely to prove particularly relevant in China—which is the investment value of the collection. With a sluggish stock market and tightly controlled real estate market, the Chinese investors are hard placed to find suitable avenues for investing their money. Expensive watches and wine may find an additional draw because of their investment value.

Clearly "status" is not going away anywhere and will continue to be the anchor need for a large number of consumers—particularly the relatively new consumers and those from the lower tier cities. However, marketers need to acknowledge all the different segments and ensure that they have products as well as marketing strategies targeted at each of them.

The Digital Catalyst for Luxury in China

The rapid expansion of the internet and its empowering influence is acting as another important catalyst for the luxury market in China. Internet increases the exposure to luxury brands and extends their reach to smaller tier cities, where very few retailers have distribution. Internet as a medium is also specifically suited for providing the kind of in-depth information and detail that the Chinese consumers typically look for in an expensive brand before they decide to invest in it. Almost every potential luxury consumer searches for information on the internet about luxury brands regularly.

Additionally, in this product category, where it is difficult to evaluate and compare products just on the basis of visible and tangible characteristics, consumers often look for recommendations and testimonials, beyond what brands are saying about themselves. The luxury brands were naturally wary of this phenomenon, as they place a lot in store on exercising a tight control of their communication and the brand story, ensuring that the brand is presented in all its glory and heritage. However, consumer-generated information on luxury brands has been particularly effective and was considered more trustworthy than what the brands proclaim. In fact, the phenomenal growth of social media has provided another fillip to the luxury goods market in China, as consumers compare and compete to exhibit their acquisitions.

Not only is the internet serving as a catalyst for the luxury consumption in China, it is also becoming an important channel for the sales of the category. However, this has been achieved after a great deal of reluctance on the part of the manufacturers and skepticism on the part of the consumers. From the point of the view of the consumers, the lack of trust is understandable and luxury brands in China always suffered from the plague of counterfeiting and online websites such as Taobao have been a haven for the purveyors of imitation products. Initial online pioneers such as Coach, which opened a store on Taobao as early as in 2001, hastily withdrew when they sensed the situation and the consumer confusion. However, with the development of Tmall—the official business to business (B-2-B) Alibaba counterpart to its more chaotic consumer to consumer (C-2-C) Taobao—a more credible platform was created for online sales of luxury products, which could offer the assurance of authenticity to the consumers.

The consumers are becoming more open to buying luxury online. Ruder Finn Inc., a global public relations firm, does an annual China Luxury Forecast, supported by a research done by IPSOS, a market research firm. The China Luxury Forecast indicates an increasing consumer confidence in buying luxury products online (IPSOS; Rudder Finn 2015).

In 2016, Christian Dior became the first luxury brand to sell its top-of-the-line bags on WeChat, the most popular messaging and social networking platform in China. The Lady Dior bag offered as a Qixi (Chinese Valentine day) special promotion was a high-end product, priced at 28,000 yuan but was still sold out in two days. Other luxury brands such as Cartier, IWC, Montblanc, and Longchamp have already launched their online sales platforms on WeChat.

Globally, there is an increasing acknowledgment of the fact that the luxury brands have lagged behind the swifter premium brands such as Nike in their embrace of the digital and the social media. It is felt that as the millennials (those born from the 1980s to the beginning of the new millennium) replace the older generations as the key buyers of luxury goods, increasing attention needs to be paid to swerving the strategy to digital. However, in China where the luxury goods buyer is a good ten years younger than their Western counterparts, millennials are already significant contributors to the luxury goods sales, indicating that this change is required even more urgently in China.

Boston Consulting Group (BCG), a consultancy, forecasts that online sales of luxury goods account for around 7% of the global luxury market, but will increase to 12% by 2020 (Abtan et al. 2016). Luxury brands need to dispel their fears about the digital marketplace and embrace the digital opportunity wholeheartedly. While in its earlier stage of development, digital platforms may have offered a threat to the brands, now they offer a huge opportunity to come closer to the consumers, involve them more with the brands, and give them the pampering care and personalized service and product that they demand.

Localization of Luxury Brands in China

There has been a growing sense of nationalism, pride, and cultural renaissance in China. Of course, China has a lot to be proud of—it is not just economic development and prowess, but also an achievement in sports, spectacular staging of the Olympics, and major advancements in science and technology which have made its citizens swell with pride. The Chinese media doggedly promotes and echoes the concept of the "Chinese dream" propounded by President Xi Jinping, which embodies ideas of national pride and rejuvenation. According to a 2014 poll by the Futures Company, 67% of the Chinese say that showing national pride is very important. In contrast, only 48% of the British express the same feeling.

Chinese consumers are also looking back at their own history and culture and rediscovering elements that they are becoming increasingly proud of. Chinese elements in art and design are becoming increasingly prominent. In this context, it is natural to wonder whether the luxury brands need to recognize this and localize their offering and branding.

So far the localization has been scarce and based on the fact that luxury brands such as Chanel, BMW, Rolex, and Gucci are brands, which have an appeal built on cultural origin or the provenance of their founders (e.g. the quality perceptions of Mercedes are underpinned by beliefs about German design and engineering excellence). These brands are nearly always in strong display categories with high aspirational value, embody the best buy in the category, and give status and power.

These brands hence correctly rely on their global heritage—the appeal of the brand is anchored in its origin and the quality perceptions that come with it. Hence despite the cultural renaissance and increasing pride in China, luxury brands need to maintain their international myth and avoid localization.

A Chinese Luxury Brand?

Another question which arises is can we expect to see a Chinese luxury brand in the near future—not just in China but with global appeal and popularity? While there is no Chinese luxury brand as yet, there are premium brands from China, such as Shangxia and Shanghai Tang, which are finding increasing popularity.

However, Chinese brands with their relatively short lives, have not developed to the extent that they could be classified as members of this group. Nor do they have the provenance and the myth to try to enter this elite group. In fact, most successful Chinese brands like Huawei and Lenovo, or Gree which dominates the domestic appliance markets, are all known for offering the consumer a strong value for money proposition. Hence the concept of a Chinese luxury brand, though entirely conceivable, is still a relatively distant idea.

At the same time, with an increasing pride and respect of their own cultural heritage, as well as the growing status and recognition of China in the world, there could be potential for a burgeoning Chinese luxury brands market. However, it is not in all categories that the concept of Chinese luxury brands is acceptable. In categories like alcohol and jewelry, there is an increasing willingness to accept local luxury brands. Chinese white spirits—Maotai and Wuiangye—offer some of the most expensive tipples in the world, though their sale has taken a tumble since President Xi Jinping started tightening the screws on corruption and official banquets.

One attempt at creating a Chinese luxury brand is Shang Xia—a collaboration between a Chinese designer, Jiang QiongEr and Hermes (Shang Xia—Chinese Luxury Fashion Brand with a French Soul 2017). However, the brand keeps away from the traditional product categories associated with luxury brands such as watches, handbags, or expensive apparel. Instead, it focuses on Chinese craftsmanship, heritage, and traditions. Its stores exhibit products such as zitan wood furniture, which could have taken more than 3000 hours to sculpt. The brand targets domestic connoisseurs and pitches its uniqueness on the same aspects that the Western brands proffer—history and heritage—though, for Shang Xia, it is rooted firmly in China and its arts and traditions, an area in which it should enjoy credibility. At the same time, the brand also has ambition for the global market, where there could be a segment of consumers who will pay liberally for Chinese craftsmanship and heritage, just as the Chinese consumers do so for European brands with similar qualities.

Luxury Buying Abroad

It has been mistakenly reported that 120 million Chinese tourists went overseas in 2016. Actually, only around 20 million real *tourists* went abroad, and the remaining 100 million were shoppers in the guise of tourists. The most popular way of buying imported goods remains personal overseas trips, ostensibly for tourism but firmly revolving around the task of securing coveted products that the Chinese are not able to find on the domestic shelves.

Luxury products have been a perennial favorite for purchase on overseas sojourns. Louis Vuitton stores in Paris, Bloomingdales in New York, Selfridges in London and now also the Japanese departmental stores all hire Chinese speaking shop assistants to welcome and service the droves of Chinese shoppers. According to Euromonitor, a research firm, the domestic sales for luxury goods in China was around $22 billion in 2015, and China was at third place after the USA and Japan. However according to different estimates, nearly half of the Chinese luxury purchases take place outside China, and when added to the domestic purchases, clearly make China the largest market for luxury goods in the world.

Is It the End of Luxury Now?

Since 2015 the luxury market in China is showing distinct signs of slowdown. The effect is felt variably by different companies, though most still report a modest growth. According to a November 2015 report from Fortune Character Training, more than 80% of luxury brands, including Gucci, Burberry, and Louis Vuitton have closed down at least one store in 2015. Bain & Company, a consultancy, reported that the domestic market shrank by 2% to 113 billion yuan ($17 billion). Euromonitor, a research firm, actually values the domestic market at $22.5 billion and shows a growth of around 2% over 2014.

The slowdown comes from the fact that the number of people who were able to rapidly accumulate an inordinate amount of wealth in a very short period of time has come down. In the last 30 years, many businesses did well because of a huge unmet demand, and also if they just happened to be at the right place at the right time. Subsequently, the internet boom provides another get-rich-quick opportunity to a lot of businesses as well as the employees of the internet giants like Alibaba, Baidu, and Tencent. However, in today's mature and saturated market, getting rich is becoming more difficult, leading to a slowdown in the luxury consumer growth.

However, on the whole, there are several factors which indicate that though the days of booming sales may be a thing of the past, China will remain a very important market for luxury manufacturers and reward them with higher growth than in the developed markets, if they follow the right strategy.

The first reason for this optimism comes from the fact that the size of the population which can afford luxury goods is still on the rise in China. According to the 2016 China Wealth report from the Industrial Bank Co Ltd and BCG, China is all set to become one of the largest congregation of high net-worth individuals in the world (those with an investable surplus of a million dollars or more), with the number of high net-worth families, rising from 2.1 million in 2015 to 3.9 million by the end of 2020. China's total investable assets will increase from 113 trillion yuan ($17 trillion) to 200 trillion yuan at the compound annual growth rate of 12%—with the assets of the high net-worth individuals accounting for 51% of the total in 2020 (BCG: Chinese HNWIs assets to double by 2021 2017).

Similarly, the white-collar consuming class who are light consumers of luxury goods, but collectively account for a huge proportion of the sales, because of their large numbers, are also likely to increase continuously over the coming years. According to a report from BCG, the number of upper-middle-class and affluent households (with an annual income of $24,000 and above) will double to 100 million and account for 30% of all urban households, compared to only 17% today.

Secondly, the luxury brands in China still have limited physical distribution—mostly restricted to the tier-1 and tier-2 cities on the Eastern coast. While e-commerce compensates for this lack of distribution to some extent, brands would benefit from the selective and strategic expansion of distribution in Central and Western China and smaller affluent cities. Successful luxury brands such as Omega have clear plans to do so.

Thirdly, the growth of e-commerce will continue to increase the reach of luxury products, even though the physical distribution may not spread.

Fourthly, as discussed earlier, there are strong cultural and sociological factors which boost China's consumption of luxury. While China has been modernizing at a furious pace, it is not abandoning its cultural values and traditions. These forces are likely to remain strong and will continue to drive the Chinese consumers toward luxury goods.

Fifthly, though today the Chinese are buying more luxury products out of China than in China, because of differences in price as well as a wider choice of products, these disadvantages for domestic purchase are likely to diminish over time. At the beginning of 2016, China reduced the import tariff on several products including bags, suitcases, and certain items of clothing to just around 8–10%. In fact, duty-free stores are opening in China itself offering imported products to Chinese consumers.

Lastly, new luxury categories are likely to emerge and grow, including newer experiences, as well as a luxury which is more rooted in elements of Chinese culture and art—such as Chinese art, antiques, furniture, jewelry, and fabrics.

On the whole, the luxury marketers should maintain their investments in the Chinese market, keep a strong hand on the pulse of the consumer, and embrace the internet. These investments, strategically made, are likely to continue to provide rich returns in the coming years.

References

"Ode to Joy" – Chinese "Pride and Prejudice" with 13 Billion Online Views. (2016, May 18). Retrieved from cnspoon.com: https://cnspoon.com/2016/05/18/ode-to-joy/

Abtan, O., Barton, C., Pianon, N., & Tsusaka, M. (2016). *Digital or Die: The Choice for Luxury Brands.* Boston Consulting Group.

Atsmon, Y., Dixit, V., & Wu, C. (2011, April). *Tapping China's luxury-goods market.* Retrieved from mckinsey.com: https://www.mckinsey.com/business-functions/marketing-and-sales/our-insights/tapping-chinas-luxury-goods-market

BCG: Chinese HNWIs assets to double by 2021. (2017, May 8). Retrieved from fundselectorasia.com: https://fundselectorasia.com/bcg-chinese-hnwis-assets-double-2021/

Buchwald, B. (2015, July 7). *Eight Surprising Facts About the Chinese Luxury Consumer.* Retrieved from forbes.com: https://www.forbes.com/sites/onmarketing/2015/07/07/eight-surprising-facts-about-the-chinese-luxury-consumer/#61a369db74a5

Doctrow, C. (2015, October 1). *Fuerdai: Paris Hilton with Chinese characteristics.* Retrieved from boingboing.net: https://boingboing.net/2015/10/01/fuerdai-paris-hilton-with-chi.html

Frank, R. (2013, November 15). *China has a word for its crass new rich.* Retrieved from cnbc.com: https://www.cnbc.com/2013/11/15/china-has-a-word-for-its-crass-new-rich.html

IPSOS; Rudder Finn.(2015). *China Luxury Forecast 2015.*

Shang Xia – Chinese Luxury Fashion Brand With a French Soul. (2017, October). Retrieved from martiroll.com: https://martinroll.com/resources/articles/asia/shang-xia-chinese-luxury-fashion-brand-with-a-french-soul/

Shannon, S. (2016, September 27). *On the floor with the daigou, China's overseas shoppers.* Retrieved from ft.com: https://www.ft.com/content/0e0c6a36-330c-11e6-bda0-04585c31b153

CHAPTER 7

Looking into the Chinese Consumer Mind

Chinese Consumer Values

Marketers often debate whether the Chinese have the same fundamental needs as the consumers in the rest of the world. Do they also open their purse strings to the lure of protecting their loved ones, exhibiting their status and the joy of camaraderie? Or is the Chinese consumer a different animal—and is driven by very different needs and desires? Some very erroneous views prevail around the subject—including that the Chinese consumers are not emotional and only go by very tangible product characteristics, or that they are not susceptible to the charm of humor, or that they always display a collectivist tendency making them immune to the glory of individualistic excellence.

Needs are formed by a number of factors—some are specific to a product category and some run across categories and influence all aspects of our behavior. A major contributor to the general needs which apply to all our decisions is our values—fundamental beliefs which shape almost everything that we hold dear and every aspect of our behavior. American politicians swear by family values under the assumption that voters are irresistibly drawn to pictures of beaming families living in apparent bliss. The family is, of course, a strong force in China too and is an important part of the Confucian value systems that the Chinese have inherited. Many experts argue that of late there has been a resurgence of traditional values and Confucianism ideals which were condemned during the Cultural Revolution, but are now being officially embraced again. Chinese cinemas

A. Sethi, *Chinese Consumers*,
https://doi.org/10.1007/978-981-10-8992-3_7

showed a full-length commercial film on Confucius (imdb.com n.d.), with the megastar Chow Yun-fat playing the lead role of the philosopher a few years ago, and hundreds of branches of an organization called Confucius Institute propagate Chinese language and culture all over the world.

Of course, one would also expect China to be governed by socialist values, something that the current government emphasizes a great deal and urges the citizens to abide by. Interestingly, the current socialist values not only stress the expected ideals of equality, justice, and patriotism but also preach striving for prosperity, democracy, and freedom! It would seem that, as far as values are concerned, the Chinese have a wide array to choose from! So the key question is, which values are having the greatest influence on the Chinese consumers—are they driven by Confucian values, the socialist values, or universal values which cut across cultures and societies?

Several organizations have conducted research to understand and measure values across the world. World Values Survey, a network of social scientists, conducts periodic value surveys in over 100 countries, the last wave of which was conducted in 2014. Illuminera, a consumer insights and strategy firm, regularly tracks consumer values for various brands. GfK, a global research firm, conducts an annual study called Consumer Life, which aims to track changes in consumer values and decipher trends across 25 markets in the world, including China. As an important part of the research, the consumers are asked to indicate how important do they consider each of around 50 basic values or beliefs which shape our behavior and attitudes and hence influence our choices (examples of values are protecting the family, freedom, respect for elders, and so on). These research studies provide important insights into the consumer mind in China.

Core Values

It All Starts with the Protection of the Family

As in almost every part of the world, in China concern about the protection and welfare of the family reigns supreme. "Protection of the family" is rated as the most important value among a list of 50 values the consumers are shown in the Consumer Life research from GfK. The importance of this value naturally stems from the love and concern for the family and is accentuated by the fact that the Chinese see a growing number of threats to their family. With the days of starvation and deprivation behind them, the Chinese were beginning to expect a certain degree of security and certainty in their lives. They began to expect that the food that they will eat will not kill them and the air that they breathe will not asphyxiate them. But then came the onslaught of new threats and perils. The milk powder that they fed to their children was contaminated with melamine (an industrial chemical), hundreds of dead pigs were floating in Huangpu River in Shanghai, and tiny but deadly PM2.5 particles were swarming in the air, which embed themselves in their lungs causing respiratory diseases of a life-threatening order. The Chinese consumer is first and foremost a soldier to defend his or her family from the dangers which lurk in every corner (危险潜伏在每一个角落 wei xian qian fu zai mei yi ge jiao luo) as the Chinese idiom goes.

Tragedy Fueled Premiumization

In the autumn of 2008, when China was basking in the glory of Summer Olympics, it was struck by what came to be known as the "melamine" tragedy (China: Inquiry on tainted milk powder 2014), a grim reminder of the hazard of greed overshadowing honesty and ethics. Thousands of children in China were hospitalized as they developed kidney stones as a result of drinking milk which was contaminated with melamine—an industrial chemical which found a new revenue stream as an aid to showing a high protein level reading in the milk sold to the milk plants. The adulteration allowed unscrupulous vendors to sell diluted milk as high protein and high-quality stuff and command a higher price. That year milk powder contaminated with melamine left at least six Chinese infants dead and almost 300,000 with kidney ailments. Sanlu, a household name in the nation's dairy industry and an iconic brand of Hebei-based Sanlu Group Co, one of China's leading sellers of milk powder for 15 years, was implicated as one of the major culprits in the scandal. The company announced bankruptcy about six months later, its assets were auctioned, including the company's four plants.

This tragedy led to one of the largest and swiftest premiumization that any market has seen anywhere in the world, as mothers abandoned domestic infant milk brands and rushed to buy from the more developed parts of the world, where they felt the product will be safer. The most popular ingredient of the daigou (代购 or buying products from overseas) and haitao (海涛 buying products from overseas e-commerce websites) baskets is baby milk formula. In fact, according to a recent survey conducted by PayPal Inc., the US-based payment service provider, Chinese parents, especially those with children under the age of six, have become the largest spenders on overseas online stores. Chinese parents want to only buy foreign goods for their babies, as the domestic producers have lost their trust. Not just the melamine scandal, but intermittent and frequent news for various types of contamination and adulteration has put the parents on the edge and they want to do everything to protect their children.

Chinese behavior of buying foreign goods is driven by certain basic needs. Foremost of them is a desire to buy the safest possible products for themselves and protect their families. Domestic manufacturers need to up their game and try for their products to be seen as defenders and nurturers of the family, rather than threats to it. Consumers are willing to pay a lot of money for the protection of their families.

The Balance Between Duty and Enjoyment

The common perception of the Chinese is that they are slaves to what they see as their duty and obligations, work like a horse, and are scarcely able to find any time for recreation and enjoyment. Data on values suggests that though there is a modicum of truth in this stereotype, the Chinese are well capable of enjoying themselves.

Duty does not figure in the top ten values globally—and it is also declining in importance. But in China, it is the third most important value. But what is this duty toward? To a great extent, the duty is toward your family—or filial duty toward your parents (respecting elders is the 7th most important value in China, but only 18th most globally). Confucian ideals of filial piety hold strong and the Chinese often make important decisions driven by the sense of duty to family. Filial duty also presents a market that many Chinese companies are also riding on. Huan Jin Da Dang and Lao Bai Jin, traditional healthcare products in China, carry special advertisements before the Chinese new year holiday projecting themselves as ideal gifts for the children to take back home to their elders to show filial piety. Buying apartments for parents, holidays with parents are all market opportunities driven by the strong feeling of filial piety. The concept of duty also extends to the country, fueled by a strong feeling of patriotism and nationalism (marriage of Confucian and socialist values).

In fact, it is interesting to observe how the Chinese balance the demands of duty on one side and enjoying life and having fun on the other hand. All these figure in the top 15 values of the Chinese—with duty way above the others. Hence in case of a conflict between duty and enjoyment, duty is expected to take precedence. But they also say that enjoying life and having fun is what makes life worthwhile (though they still lag behind the global average on this aspect).

Furthermore, enjoying life is much more important than having fun—implying that enjoyment in life does not necessarily have to come from a boisterous celebration and that there are many ways to experience the sense of joy in life. In fact, in China, enjoyment needs to be subtle and not overtly pleasurable (pleasure is among the ten least important values of the Chinese) so as not to threaten the sense of propriety and duty which govern the Chinese behavior. Lin Yutang (1935), a Chinese writer, and linguist of the early twentieth century, while describing the Chinese character in his book, My Country, and My People, uses the word "mellowness" and explains it as being suggestive of calm and passive strength, not youthful vigor and romance. These provide important pointers for designing effective marketing communication in China. Brands need to portray themselves as instruments for enhancing the quality of life and enriching it—not as enablers of a transit moment of fun.

Working Hard and Fulfilling Work

Along with duty comes the importance of working hard. This is a value which has always been associated with China. Arthur Henderson Smith in his book on Chinese Characteristics (Smith 1894) mentioned "indifference to comfort and convenience" as one of the defining characteristics of the Chinese. The trait seems to have stuck on as the current data supports the popular belief. This is a value which is held as more important in China than the rest of the world—industry is mentioned as one of the 15 most characteristic traits of the Chinese character by Lin Yutang. "Working hard" is the 12th most important value in China (16th globally). While the rest of the world is stressed out because of financial worries, the Chinese differ, by saying that it is not money that causes them stress, but it is the relentless pressure that they put on themselves that troubles them. In fact, money is not among the top three causes of stress in China—the other two irritants being "not getting enough sleep" and "not having time for the things that they want to do". The "self-caused stress" also seems a strong phenomenon in other developed East Asian countries with Confucian influence, including South Korea and Japan. The relentless strife and pressure to get ahead in life is a reality in several Asian countries and has several sociological and cultural underpinnings. China and other Asian countries have undergone transformational economic development in a very short period of time. In fact, China is still very much in the midst of it and is far from a developed nation economically. In this environment of progress and development, no one wants to be left behind, and the pressure to continue to move ahead is high. Chinese tiger moms are seen ferrying their kids from piano lessons to painting classes, from English coaching to gymnastic training, all in an effort to arm the children to succeed in this competitive environment. Competition is fierce and for the Chinese and excelling in 高考 (gaokao or the college entrance examination) is a must to ensure career progress. The combination of intense competition and a strong desire to move ahead creates enormous pressure both from external sources and of course from within to result in the stress.

So the Chinese are willing to work hard, but do they care what work they do? "Fulfilling work" is the 19th most important value among the Chinese (the same as the global average). On the whole, when it comes to the balance between the material aspects of the job—pay, promotion, and growth versus how interesting and fulfilling is the work—the Chinese tend to tilt to the former. However, it is not the ready cash which is the supreme and irresistible attraction; the Chinese do seem to take a slightly balanced and long-term view and value possibilities of promotion and growth much more.

Looking at the differences between different age groups, it seems that this is something which is likely to change over time. According to a research done by zhaopin.com (a popular jobs website) the Chinese generation Z (or 九零后 Post 90s) consider their liking of the job nearly twice as important as the early post-1980s (八零后)

Ambition

The desire to work hard is normally driven by a sense of ambition. Interestingly and contrary to what one would expect, ambition does not figure in the most important values of the Chinese. This may seem a bit counterintuitive, and makes one wonder what is the purpose of the toil? In fact, the stimulus to work hard is the desire to achieve a sense of material security (which is considered important).

The Chinese often talk about the iron bowl (贴晚饭 tie fan wan) which is a reference to the relatively cushy and secure jobs for life in state-owned enterprises, which may not pay as well as the more glamorous positions in private enterprises and IT firms, but offer a comfortable lifestyle, a secure income and respectable allowances and perks. The number of Chinese who apply to appear in the national civil service exam catapulted from 120,000 in 2004 to 1.12 million in 2014 (chinadaily.com.cn 2013), a nearly tenfold increase in a decade for just around 25,000 jobs. The popularity of such iron bowl jobs seems to reinforce the fact that it is a desire for security that is driving the Chinese to hard work, rather than a strong ambition to charge ahead.

The seductive power of self-employment is restrained at the moment, but definitely on the rise among the younger generations. In 2016, 7.65 million Chinese graduated from University, and a survey by zhaopin.com (a jobs website) suggests that only 3% of them plan to spurn the job offers and set out on an adventure of self-employment.

Take It Easy

A clear indication of slackening of aggressive ambition and acceptance of moderate success was evident during the mood of the Chinese during the Rio Olympics in August 2016. Even the Chinese government pitched in and lowered its expectation and passionate calls for medal success. One of the most endearing figures to emerge from the Rio Olympics was the Chinese swimmer Fan Yuanhui, who expressed pride in a picturesque manner at securing the bronze in women's 100 m breaststroke. "I am so fast, and used 洪荒之力 (hong huang zhi li) or prehistoric powers to do my best", she said in an interview with the media (Light-Hearted Chinese Olympian Becomes Internet Meme 2016). This is a big change from the previous Olympics, in which the disappointment and disapproval of stars such as Li Ning and Liu Xiang, who failed to meet expectations, was overwhelming.

This slackening of single-minded focus on success resonated well with the young Chinese audience, who are also keen to slow down and relax from the relentless pressure to excel.

Friendship and Stable Relationships

Friendship is a universal value and expectedly important in China too. Perhaps there are special factors to make it even more important in China. One of which is the traditional Chinese concept of guanxi (关系) or personal relationships. Guanxi is what gets you ahead in the queue and bestows privileges which would have otherwise been denied to you—such as get your child admission in a prestigious school, get you an important approval to expand your business, or secure an iron bowl job (贴晚饭 or tiewanfan) for your son. In fact, many Chinese believe that it is guanxi which gets you ahead in life and not just hard work. This belief in the people rather than the system is what prompts the Chinese to try to collect as many name cards as possible or scan the QR code in Weixin of new acquaintances that they may come across. "You never know who you are going to need", is the guiding principle.

Another more modern dimension has been added to further strengthen the need and importance of friendship and relationships. Nearly every urban Chinese under the age of 35 is a single child. With the absence of siblings at home and often both parents working, the joy and need for friendship are clearly magnified. While friendship is more important in China than the rest of the world, interestingly stable relationships, while still treasured, are a little less important. The Chinese like to experiment now. Nearly 40% of the couples live together before they tie the knot. Divorce rates in China increased by 63% in the last decade (Mengwei 2016).

China Taiping insurance, betting on the instability of relationships, started offering an insurance policy to unmarried couples. The policy has a one-time cost of 599 yuan ($90) and guarantees a payout of 10,000 yuan if the couple marries in the period of three to ten years after the policy is purchased (Chinese insurer launches marriage insurance 2016).

From a marketing point of view, it would seem while it may be easy to befriend the Chinese consumers, maintaining a stable relationship and winning their loyalty would be a challenge. The data does suggest that the Chinese are some of the most promiscuous consumers in the world, often falling for the temptation of a price-off or a discount. On the positive side, the openness of the consumers facilitates the expansion of products at an extraordinary pace. Two years ago, there were practically no users of online payment systems like Alipay or WeChat money. Now it is difficult to come across anyone under the age of 40 who does not use these services.

Knowledge and Learning

The Chinese have always valued education, starting from ancient times when any scholar who could master the classics could have a go at the Imperial examination (科举 keju), which could land you a coveted job as a state official. Knowledge and learning, normally assumed to be the direct off-shoots of education, are also highly respected. Interestingly they are not respected any more than in the rest of the world. In fact, these values seem to be the hallmark of the middle class and the less privileged everywhere in the world and seen as proven tools for a better life.

But the Chinese seem to worry more than the rest of the world about the quality of education that their children receive. This may be surprising given the recent reports which certify the Chinese students to be one of the best in the Organization for Economic Cooperation and Development (OECD) in important subjects like mathematics, and the numerous testimonies to Chinese teachers' expertise and competence (PISA 2015 key findings for China 2016). But the concern comes from the rather high expectations and demands that Chinese parents have in this area. Education has been a sure short route to social mobility in China, and a superlative performance from the child all through, particularly in that all-important "gaokao" or the college admission test, is widely believed to be what can make or break a child's future. This remains one of the most dominant concerns of the Chinese and shows no sign of dilution.

The Chinese are famous for their Tiger moms, who relentlessly drag their kids around from English classes to tennis coaching and from piano classes to even Confucian classics to provide them with the required knowledge and learning. The question is whether it is real knowledge and learning that the mothers are seeking for their children, or merely equipping the child to fare better in the intensely competitive world. Perhaps it is the latter as while knowledge and learning are considered very important, the value of curiosity and imagination is less appreciated.

In fact, this is an oft-sighted lament in China, that the Chinese education does not prepare the child for the changing world, where the emphasis is shifting from technical expertise and tasks (a lot of which is likely to be taken over by machines) to creativity and imagination. The changing economic environment will perhaps see this value increase in importance.

One in Five College Students in the World Is in China

2900 colleges and universities in China harbor and nourish the minds of 37 million students. One in five college students worldwide is in China, according to a report released by the Chinese Ministry of Education in April 2016. These colleges produced 7.65 million graduates in 2016—160,000 more than in 2015. Additionally, the ratio of Chinese who went abroad and who came back dropped from 3.15-to-1 in 2006 to 1.28-to-1 last year, leading to a large number of educated youth in China who have had the benefit of exposure to the West.

Stifling Creativity?

It is widely believed that the Chinese education system is based on the strict foundation of rote learning and stifles creativity. As an evidence, it is sited that the Chinese excel in copying or repetitive manufacturing but have failed to show much of original creation. While there is definitely true that China tends to follow the more traditional pedagogic techniques, which do rely on memorizing and information absorption, this traditional pedagogy is not unique to China, but is adhered to in nearly all of the developing world, where so far just reaching everyone with some kind of education itself was a challenge. Despite the baggage of traditional teaching practices, theoretically, innovation is thriving in China, particularly if indicators such as the number of patents are considered. Secondly, China may not have come up with an iPhone, it has definitively come up WeChat (微信 or Weixin) an extremely innovative social media platform, nothing like which exists anywhere else in the rest of the world. The huge size of the Chinese market, the demanding but relatively less prosperous customers, large supply of talent—both homegrown and foreign returned—coupled with the Chinese governments' recognition of the need for innovation is driving the country forward on the road to innovation. Even if the education system currently falls short of offering the required support to the innovation challenge, it would evolve in line with the changing demands.

Faith

Traditionally the Chinese have been ardent believers and worshippers. Belief in mystical powers and superstitions has pervaded the Chinese lives. Strong religious and moralistic beliefs, including Confucianism, Taoism, and Buddhism, have had a strong influence on the people. The rationalist and atheist Marxist tried to free the Chinese from the traditional power of religion and superstition and the ostensible results have been impressive. In fact, communism itself became a kind of religion as it provided a clear sense of direction and a guideline to what is right and what is wrong. Cultural Revolution further destroyed the traditions of religious beliefs and customs and thrust the populace into a fervent cult of Mao worship.

After the opening up and economic reforms, the physical needs of the Chinese are increasingly being met, but they are plagued by questions of conscience and absence of moral compass. It is not surprising, therefore, that more and more turn to spirituality in search of answers. The importance of "faith" as a guiding principle in life, though still relatively low, has been increasing among the Chinese.

This increasing importance is reflected in overt terms as witnessed by an ever-growing number of practitioners. The Church today has nearly 100 million followers in China. However, the real driver of this change is an increasing desire among the Chinese to rediscover a moral compass, which can give a meaning to their lives. An incident in Foshan city of Guangdong province of Southern China, brought this concern under magnification when a two-year-old girl called Xiao Yueyue, was run over by a van and in the following seven minutes, 18 people passed by without lifting a finger to help her or even raise an alarm or ask for help (FlorCruz, China soul-searching after toddler's death 2011). The incident caught the consciousness of the nation and the Chinese widely bemoaned the lack of trust prevailing in the contemporary society. This lack of trust was in fact blamed on another incident five years before this one, in which a young man named Peng Yu helped an old woman who had fallen down, who after the incident accused him of causing her injuries, and secured significant damages against him. It was reported in the media that the online payments firm, Alipay, is offering an insurance, which covers any good samaritan against any false claims from the people they extend a helping hand to.

The Chinese today are looking for something more than an insurance policy—they are in search of faith and a moral compass, which they feel is required to guide them to the right path. From a marketing point of view, it is useful to remember this concern for lack of trust and growing importance of faith, which means that the brands need to portray themselves in a manner which is consonant with these values.

Equality

It is perhaps not surprising that "equality" figures among the top 10 most cherished values in socialist China, while globally it is only among the top 20 most important values. However, what is surprising is the co-existence of this value in relation to one of the most unequal societies in the world. When Deng Xiaoping said, "let some people become rich first", perhaps he did not anticipate the extent to which his permission would be adopted and the enormity of the rich-poor gap it will generate. China's Gini coefficient (a quantitative indicator economists use to evaluate the distribution of wealth in a country or society—where 1 stands for 1 person has all the wealth, and 0 stands for evenly distributed riches) increased from 0.3 in 1980 to 0.46 in 2015, which is higher than most affluent countries in the world (China's dirty little secret: its growing wealth gap 2017).

Needless to say that this economic disparity is met with a fair amount of disapproval and resentment from the Chinese and has become a major concern for the Chinese government as they worry that this may foment social strife and unrest. The younger generations, particularly the post-1990s are more indignant about it, as they feel that the "get rich quick" means that the previous generations had access to, have now basically dried up. They see nothing but endless toil to move ahead in life or even to afford a house in the large city, whose price may well equal their 20–30 years' salary. This is definitely an area of disgruntlement and brands need to portray aspirational products with caution and care, so as not to alienate the consumers with the portrayal of wanton and ultra-elitist consumption.

Status and Face

No discussion on Chinese values can be considered complete without an analysis of the importance of "face". Arthur H. Smith, an American missionary who spent over 20 years in China, started his nineteenth century book, called the Chinese Characteristics (Smith 1894), with a chapter on "face". To quote from the book " … the word 'face' does not in China signify simply the front part of the head, but is literally a compound noun of multitude, with more meanings than we shall be able to describe, or perhaps to comprehend". The booming luxury market definitely gives fodder to the belief that the Chinese are obsessed with face or status and are spending large amounts of money is projecting their success in an attempt to save or project face. In fact some experts would argue—that is the key role of brands in China—to help consumers gain or retain face among their friends and peers. Maintaining face implies that one's deportment, bearing, dress, and possessions are in line with what would be expected of one—it should not be below the expectation but at the same time it cannot be beyond and in contradiction to the expectation. Products need to be bought as they befit one's status and position in life. Hence a successful businessman cannot be without an Audi or a BMW—not having one, and traveling in a Volkswagen will lead to loss of face. At the same time seeing to driving a Lamborghini or Ferrari for a moderately successful businessman will be seen as out of place. In any case, the incremental benefit of excessive display is nil, when something more modest can help establish face. Excessive display needs to be supported by extraordinary success. The equation changes a bit among the second-generation rich, (富二代 or fuerdai) where youthful competition and pride in relation to the parents' success may lead to excess.

In general more Chinese believe that maintaining face is essentially a protective activity, and not a status projecting one, implying that consumption needs to be modest and not stand out. Excessive and out of place consumption will in fact again lead to loss of face.

In will be prudent to add that there are two sides to the importance of face in China—the physical and the figurative. Scholars have normally spent an enormous amount of effort commenting and explaining the importance of the figurative face—why it is so important for the Chinese to look respectable, honest, well-off, superior (one could add a lot of adjectives to this list) in the eyes of their peers, friends, and the general world. But the importance of the physical face cannot be underestimated, in fact it is so important for the Chinese to look good, and they have such exacting standards for what is good looks, that it has given a really strong fillip to the face-care and skin-care industry, not to mention the cosmetic surgery business in China. In fact, not to sport an attractive physical face is to lose face—hence an enormous amount of expense and effort needs to go into maintaining the physical face (discussed in Chap. 4—Key Industries).

The Money Matters

Thrift and Wealth

Economists often complain that the Chinese consumers do not spend enough and are not giving the global economy the boost that it needs after the American consumers were forced to tighten their purse strings as their wealth plunged with the declining housing values after the financial crisis in 2009. It is also well established that the Chinese save a much higher proportion of their earnings than the consumers in the developed markets (China Gross Savings Rate 2018). Hence it is surprising that as a value, "thrift" does not figure among the most important values of the Chinese (nor does it figure among the most important values globally).

Many will argue that there is enough evidence to suggest that actually the economists are wrong and there is enough evidence of the Chinese indulgence and profligacy as seen from the number of luxury cars on the road and, on the more modest side, the penetration of iPhones. The issue of thrift versus luxurious indulgence in China, like most others is a complex one. The Chinese are thrifty and indulgent at the same time.

A huge change in the Chinese values in the past ten years is the decline in the importance accorded to wealth—and even material security. However, economic worries are not altogether out of the consumer mind—40% are worried about not having enough money to pay all their bills and nearly an equal proportion is worried about inflation. Clearly, as the Chinese incomes have been increasing, the concern for material security has been decreasing (it was the 3rd most important value in 2008 but has declined to the 20th position in 2015). This was to be expected, as not only the Chinese incomes have been steadily increasing, they have also been able to shed the fear that the global financial crisis put in their minds. Today the Chinese show more resilience and confidence on this aspect and evince a higher concern for higher-order values.

Not only that, as the Chinese have acquired wealth (a whole lot of it through housing—which is one of the most expensive in the world), the desire for wealth has attenuated. However, the anxiety about having enough money personally is still significant. This can perhaps be explained by the expanding consumer needs and desires. It is well established that the consumers are not only consuming more but also consuming better quality and more premium products, increasing the demands on their resources. In this context, the Chinese consumers show frustration about how much more difficult it is now to make money as compared to when China just opened-up and a lot of people struck gold, just because they happened to be at the right place at the right time. Very few avenues of "get rich quick" seem to exist now and often when they seem that they could bring home the bacon, the promise is found to be misleading and leads to disaster.

Are the Chinese Price Sensitive?

An oft-debated subject is whether the Chinese show a higher level of price sensitivity as compared to consumers in the rest of the world, particularly the developed world. This is a complex question to answer and perhaps has no single answer which can apply to all segments of Chinese consumers and all product categories. The first thing we need to keep in mind while addressing this issue is that China is still a nation with a very modest income. The per capita disposable income in even urban China is only RMB 31195 per annum (less than US$5000 per annum) as compared to the US$40,000 in USA. Secondly, there is no single answer to this question, as the situation depends on the product category, the available choices, and the differences the consumers see among them and who will be the end consumer for the product. So when it comes to selecting a baby milk formula, the Chinese mothers show little price sensitivity and will easily pay five times for an imported brand that they see as safe as compared to a domestic alternative toward whose quality they harbor some doubts. But when it comes to selecting a floor cleaner, they may switch to a brand which has an offer of "RMB 2 off", as long as they feel that it will not endanger their health. They are willing to pay more than their one month's salary for the new iPhone, as they relish the admiring glances from onlookers and feel that it is the price of entry to be a part of a social group that they want to belong to.

While it is futile to attempt to answer this question in a generalizable way, what can be said with certainty is that the Chinese love to bargain and secure a deal. The idea here is not to save money or buy something cheaper but to assure themselves that they have won the contest through their skill and expertise. Hence bargaining is not confined to the purchase of fruits and vegetables, but equally prevalent when purchasing a BMW. Unlike other cultures, where the affluent may consider it to be infra-dig to ask for a few bucks off on a luxury purchase, the Chinese are happy to spend several thousands of dollars, but only after assuring themselves that it could not be bought for even a few dollars cheaper.

Ponzi Schemes

Chinese banks pay an abysmal interest rate. The stock market provided a dream run ten years ago when the Shanghai composite index crossed 6000 but has now been languishing at less than 3000 in the past several years. In this context, enter private peer-to-peer lenders, who promise the Chinese a decent return for their savings. At the same time, they offer a financing solution to small and medium enterprises who often get rebuffed from the giant state-owned banks. Nearly 4000 peer-to-peer outfits started courting investors. Ezubao, one such peer-to-peer lender emerged on the scene in 2014 and promised a return on savings which was several times what any bank offered. Nearly a million investors willingly parted with their hard-earned money, happy that finally, they can get a decent income on their savings. However, Ezubao lacked in ability to actually make the money grow and ended up as a giant Ponzi scheme, paying new deposits as returns for the older ones, and Zhang Min, the President of the parent company became the Chinese Bernie Madoff (Leader of China's $9 billion Ezubao online scam gets life; 26 jailed 2017).

Home: The Source and Detractor of Wealth

In China, a home is your identity. If you have no home, you have no hope. The desire for home starts early, almost simultaneously with the sexual awakening. In the Western societies and many parts of Asia too, people graduate to home ownership after renting for many years, and saving enough money for a down payment. In China, if you take this path you are a loser (屌丝 or diaosi as it is more graphically referred to) (China's disaffected Diaosi tribe 2015). In a poll conducted among mothers of young unmarried women in Shanghai, 70% said that they would not even dream of giving away their daughter to a diaosi who does not own an apartment. When the competition for brides is severe, as men belong to the much more numerous gender, thanks to a parental preference for the masculine, men need to seduce the bride with the lure of an owned apartment—rental accommodation cannot house the marital bed.

This obsession with houses creates an extraordinary effect on the personal finances of the Chinese consumers, as home needs to be bought, bought as early in one's life as possible but is murderously expensive.

Dollar to dollar, the per square meter price of an apartment in Shanghai or Beijing is higher than most cities in the USA and Europe. A young lad who is purchasing a house at the age of around 30, basically has to pledge 20 years income and accept the burden of large mortgage payments for the next 30 years, which at least in the initial stages may be more than half his income. Even if the parents help with the down payments, the mortgage itself is crippling enough to earn the couple the moniker of house slaves (房奴 or fangnu) (FlorCruz, Chinese 'house slaves' grow in booming economy 2010). Economists argue that with such an inordinately large proportion of income going toward the house, the disposable income available for other discretionary spending is significantly reduced. It may well be that obsession with buying a house is curtailing the growth rate of other product categories of discretionary spending.

Health, Fitness, and Beauty

Health and Fitness

With a history of famine, starvation, and disease, good health is something the Chinese have not enjoyed till recently. Of course, it has changed totally with increasing availability of quality healthcare and increasing cash in the hands of the Chinese consumers to spend on it. At least by conventional yardsticks such as life expectancy, China is doing well (a Chinese born today can hope to live up to 75 years, and in large cities like Shanghai and Beijing over 80 years). But while ill-health from inadequate food and major infectious diseases has nearly totally disappeared, the Chinese now see that they face new perils which threaten their health—with increasing incidence of cancer, diabetes, and hypertension. It is not surprising, therefore, that out of a set of 50 values, health and fitness is rated to be the sixth most important value in China. Of course, this is of importance globally, and consumers in every country consider this as among their most important values—but the importance in China is clearly higher than in the rest of the world.

While this is definitely driven culturally, there are also very strong modern day reasons for this. Some of the top television advertisers in China are health-care products. Pharmaceuticals is the largest advertised category on television, with a spend of $3.3 billion in 2015, and a growth of 39% over 2014 (Source: Group M).

Several new product categories have sprung up or have received a big boost in China in the past decade or so, almost entirely on the basis of health claims. These include ready to drink (RTD) tea, yogurt, and red wine. According to the China beverage association, the share of RTD tea in the beverages market has increased from 20% in 2005 to 25% in 2015. Correspondingly the share of carbonated beverages has declined from 19% to 17%.

The fitness industry is booming and so are Nike and Adidas who equip the consumers for participation in fitness activities. Nike China registered a turnover of over $3 billion in 2015, more than doubling its volume in six years. According to a recent study by GfK, 45% of urban Chinese adults, who are internet users, monitor their health and fitness via an online or mobile application or a fitness band or smartwatch. The figure for the USA is only 29%.

Chinese Government and Health

In October 2016, the Chinese government released a blueprint for a plan to achieve ambitious improvements in the Chinese citizens' health and achieve parity with the developed nations on key indicators such as life expectancy and infant and child mortality and morbidity rates. Specifically, the target for life expectancy is to reach a figure of 79.

Obesity

The Chinese are not a people that you would associate with obesity. Most women in China's large cities sport a svelte figure, and it a rare sight to see men with, what the Chinese call a General's belly. However, as they say, appearances can be deceptive, and obesity has already become a weighty issue in China. In 1975, still suffering from the extreme food deprivation brought about by the misguided policies of the Cultural Revolution, there were only 2.4 million obese in China—1.7 million of whom were women. They accounted for less than 2.5% of the global obese population. While the Chinese were relieved to be rid of the excruciating period of food scarcity and starvation, prosperity brought its own problems and the number of Chinese obese rose to 89.6 million by 2014, nearly half of these being men. Now China leads the obese brigade, housing 12.4% of the global well-endowed. From 2002 to 2012, the number of obese in China rose from 7.1% to 12%.

Along with the increase in weight comes the increase infliction of diseases like diabetes and now the World Health Organization estimates that 110 million people suffer from diabetes in China (Rate of diabetes in China "explosive" 2016). Clearly, the market for pharmaceutical and health products is likely to continue to exhibit spectacular growth in the coming years.

Beauty

It is commonly believed that the Chinese have a very high concern about beauty and place a lot of importance on appearance. The industry data does support this hypothesis with China being one of the largest beauty markets in the world. According to a research done by research firm Mintel two-thirds (65%) of Chinese consumers spent more on facial skin care in 2015 than they did in 2014, and driven by this growing consumption, China's beauty retail market is expected to be worth 338 billion yuan (US$50 billion) by 2020. Not only that, skin care and makeup are two of the important product categories, where Chinese consumers are moving to use more premium products.

To what extent is this size and growth driven by the importance of beauty in China? The data suggests that the overall value that the consumers place on beauty in China is not very different from elsewhere in the world. Hence unlike the common perception, the Chinese do not spend more on beauty and grooming because they care more about their beauty—beauty is equally desired and sought everywhere in the world. The key reason, in fact, is that they have higher standards of beauty which leads them to fuss a lot more about their appearance and also spend a lot more to take care of it.

Natural Products

Whether it is health products or beauty aids, the Chinese consumers seem to favor the natural over the man-made. Traditional Chinese Medicine (TCM) which favors natural products, and natural therapies over chemicals and invasive procedures, is the first choice of therapy for many Chinese, particularly when the condition does not appear to be life-threatening. The beauty products market is similarly influenced by the fondness of the natural. One of the most popular traditional health and beauty products in China is "ejiao" or donkey skin gelatin. The product has a history of over 300 years and is believed to improve blood circulation and boost energy levels. It is believed that this was one of the products that Marco Polo took back with him after visiting China and it is now a major export earner for China. Dong'e Ejiao, a leading manufacturer of the product located in Dong'e county of Shandong province, claims to sell over 10 billion of the stuff. The popularity of the product has actually increased over time, to the extent that China is now believed to have a severe shortage of donkeys (E Jiao (Colla Corii Asini, Donkey-Hide Gelatin) n.d.).

The Conscientious Chinese

Concern for the Environment

"Preserving the environment" as a value is as important in China as in the rest of the world. However, it is well known that one of the biggest bugbears of the Chinese is environmental pollution—hence overall the concern for the environment in China exceeds the rest of the world—but not because the Chinese care more about the environment, but because they care more about the effect it is having on their health.

It was not so—till the American Embassy roof-top air quality monitor readings found their way into the Chinese social media, and increased the vocabulary and the concern of the Chinese people with terms such as PM2.5—the tiny particles which can embed themselves deep in the lungs and cause serious damage to health."Under the Dome", a powerful documentary about the hazards of breathing in China by the journalist and environmental activist, Chai Jing, received over 150 million views on the

Chinese video sharing websites in 2015, before it was pulled out by the authorities. The data suggests that this concern dominates the urban Chinese mind much more than the rest of the world. Sixty percent of the Chinese consumers mention this as one of their key problems today—more than any other issue keeping them awake at night. While globally too, this is one of the key consumer concerns, in the rest of the world it competes closely with financial worries including fears about inflation and high prices.

Secondly, this is a concern which is acquiring larger and larger significance in the Chinese consumer mind. In 2009, just after the global economic crisis, worries about recession and unemployment plagued the Chinese consumers—much more than the environment. However stable economic growth and low unemployment rates in China since 2009 have been instrumental in displacing economic worries with environmental pollution. It remains to be seen if the recent economic slowdown will still keep environmental pollution ahead of financial worries or the post-recession scenario of 2009 will make a come-back.

Concern for the environment also manifests itself in relation to brand choices—consumers not only avidly proclaim a strong environmental conscience, they also demand responsible behavior from companies. Chinese consumers say that they are plagued by guilt when they indulge in an environmentally unfriendly manner. Their demand from brands and companies is even more exacting—80% of them feel that brands and companies need to be environmentally responsible. Here again, the Chinese consumers are ahead of most developed countries in their standards.

Will the Consumers Pay for an Environmentally Friendly Product?
The key question, of course, is will the Chinese consumers pay a premium for an environmentally friendly product? On this, the results in the market so far have been disappointing and there is no evidence of consumers paying a premium for environmentally friendly products—as we see them paying for a safe product. Chinese mothers are buying infant milk formula and other baby products from all over the world at the highest prices. However, they do not seem to reflect a similar enthusiasm for products which are less of a strain on the environment. Tesla, the premium fully electric car, which has become an environmental badge in the US seems to have

had limited traction on the Chinese roads so far. Even in terms of common environmentally friendly practices such as shunning plastic shopping bags or buying products with reusable or light packaging the Chinese consumers are not holding a beacon to the rest of the world.

What do marketers and policymakers need to bridge this gap between espoused values and actual behavior? The key to achieving this is to link the desired positive behavior to a clear consumer benefit. Consumers seldom pay to assuage their conscience, but invariably do when they see a clear and meaningful benefit. Less pollution and safer environment are clear candidate benefits that can be dangled in front of the consumers. Benefits do not just need to be functional or tangible—emotional benefits could also hold a powerful sway. The related emotional payoff, in this case, could be potent—particularly if it relates to the long-term protection and health of children. Chinese consumers will pay if they feel that the premium that they pay today will create a better and safer world for their children tomorrow. The key to a more desirable behavior and premium for environmentally friendly products lies in converting the guilty conscience into a powerful emotional benefit that the Chinese consumers can identify with.

One category of green products which is thriving in China is the new energy vehicles—though it is difficult to say to what extent its growing acceptance is driven by an environmental conscience and to what extent by the financial incentives that the Chinese government offers to anyone who chooses a new—energy vehicle in preference to the conventional petrol consuming car. The incentives are strong—to the extent, that in some cities while the consumers need to wait for an uncertain amount of time for a number plate, based on a lottery, they can drive away immediately in their car if they choose one which runs on batteries.

The Guiding hand of the Conscience

A popular campaign in the Chinese media depicts celebrities like Li Bingbing, biting their nails and proclaiming that "Rhino horn has nothing your own nails don't have." (Knott 2016) Chinese are known to be avid and shameless buyers of the forbidden, the illegal, and the unsavory ranging from rhino's horn to tiger's penis and African elephant ivory. Huge quantities of shark fin soup continue to be served in wedding banquets, along with birds' nests and abalone. However, the wind of change is also touching the Chinese hearts and behaviors. Now the Chinese consumers, like everywhere else in the world, reflect a consumption pattern that is governed by their beliefs, values, and ideals. In a research conducted by GfK in 23 countries, 72% of the Chinese consumers claim that they only buy those products which match their values, beliefs, and ideals. In fact, the ardor of this expression is one of the highest in the world and the Chinese consumers seem to surpass the consumers in most developed countries in the intensity of their expressed emotion.

On social conscience and helpfulness, it is interesting that the Chinese often blame themselves and many stories of apathy and failure to help others have surfaced and get talked about in social media. The most well known of these is the story of Xiao Yueyue mentioned earlier, who was run over by a van in the city of Foshan. The incident led to a lot of soul-searching in China, with the people asking whether they have lost this basic humanness that they, traditionally, prided themselves with. Many blame this apathy to pengci'r (a person who blames you for breaking a piece of porcelain which is already damaged) based of the story of some good samaritans who got into hot water by extending a helping hand guided by their conscience (A Chinese Woman Does A Really Bad Job Pretending To Be Hit By A Car 2016).

The Philanthropic Chinese: Led by Ma & Ma

In April 2016, Ponny Ma (Ma Huateng), the chairman of Tencent Holdings Ltd., donated 100 million shares of the Hong Kong-listed company to create a charity fund. In 2014 Jack Ma, co-founder of Alibaba, an e-commerce company, created a philanthropic trust. There have been other calls for the Chinese billionaires to open their pockets and Bill Gates and Warren Buffet even hosted dinners in China for its richest to persuade them to emulate their US-style generosity and sign the "giving pledge".

According to a report by the Tsinghua University's School of Philanthropy, a total of 357 foundations raised 1.9 billion Yuan ($294.7 million) in the three-year period after the Ya'an earthquake in Sichuan province in 2013. Total charitable donations in China is estimated at $16 billion, from $4 billion in 2007. In comparison to other countries though China's philanthropic contributions seem limited.

Philanthropy in China has not been untouched by scandal and in 2011 a young and attractive lady called Guo Meimei, claiming to be associated with the Red Cross, made a lavish display of her luxury handbags and cars on social media. In 2014, One Foundation, China's first private charitable fundraiser, was accused of embezzlement and misappropriation, but later explained credibly the reasons for the rather slow spending of the donations they had collected. Government's suspicious attitude has also been a restraining factor. However, the attitudes are changing, and especially the younger Chinese are driven by a feeling of conscientiousness and come outpouring their hearts in droves in case of a natural disaster. Similarly, they expect the corporations to behave with a conscience and generosity.

References

(2013, November 25). Retrieved from chinadaily.com.cn: http://usa.chinadaily.com.cn/china/2013-11/25/content_17127868.htm

A Chinese Woman Does a Really Bad Job Pretending to Be Hit By a Car. (2016, December 28). Retrieved from npr.org: https://www.npr.org/sections/goatsandsoda/2016/12/28/507245116/a-chinese-lady-does-a-really-bad-job-pretending-to-be-hit-by-a-car

China Gross Savings Rate. (2018). Retrieved from ceicdata.com: https://www.ceicdata.com/en/indicator/china/gross-savings-rate

China: Inquiry on tainted milk powder. (2014, January 11). Retrieved from nytimes.com: https://www.nytimes.com/2011/01/15/world/asia/15briefs-Milk.html?rref=collection%2Ftimestopic%2FMelamine&action=click&contentCollection=timestopics&region=stream&module=stream_unit&version=latest&contentPlacement=8&pgtype=collection

China's dirty little secret: its growing wealth gap. (2017, July 13). Retrieved from scmp.com: http://www.scmp.com/news/china/economy/article/2101775/chinas-rich-grabbing-bigger-slice-pie-ever

China's disaffected Diaosi tribe. (2015, February 3). Retrieved from gbtimes.com: https://gbtimes.com/chinas-disaffected-diaosi-tribe

Chinese insurer launches marriage insurance. (2016, August 10). Retrieved from insurancebusinessmag.com: https://www.insurancebusinessmag.com/asia/news/breaking-news/chinese-insurer-launches-marriage-insurance-49661.aspx

E Jiao (Colla Corii Asini, Donkey-Hide Gelatin). (n.d.). Retrieved from chineseherbshealing.com: http://www.chineseherbshealing.com/e-jiao/

FlorCruz, J. (2010, January 20). *Chinese 'house slaves' grow in booming economy*. Retrieved from cnn.com: http://www.cnn.com/2010/BUSINESS/01/20/china.gdp.narrow.dwelling/index.html

FlorCruz, J. (2011, October 22). *China soul-searching after toddler's death*. Retrieved from cnn.com: https://edition.cnn.com/2011/10/22/world/asia/china-toddler-reaction/index.html

imdb.com. (n.d.). Retrieved from http://www.imdb.com/title/tt1397498/

Knott, K. (2016, January 13). *Chinese celebrities chew their nails for campaign against rhino horn trade*. Retrieved from scmp.com: http://www.scmp.com/lifestyle/arts-entertainment/article/1900650/chinese-celebrities-chew-their-nails-campaign-against

Leader of China's $9 billion Ezubao online scam gets life; 26 jailed. (2017, September 12). Retrieved from reuters.com: https://www.reuters.com/article/us-china-fraud/leader-of-chinas-9-billion-ezubao-online-scam-gets-life-26-jailed-idUSKCN1BN0J6

Light-Hearted Chinese Olympian Becomes Internet Meme. (2016, August 9). Retrieved from womenofchna.cn: http://www.womenofchina.cn/womenofchina/html1/people/sportswomen/1608/1103-1.htm

Mengwei, C. (2016, July 13). *Divorces up 63% in past decade*. Retrieved from chinadaily.com.cn: http://www.chinadaily.com.cn/china/2016-07/13/content_26067806.htm

PISA 2015 key findings for China. (2016). Retrieved from oecd.org: http://www.oecd.org/pisa/pisa-2015-china.htm

Rate of diabetes in China "explosive". (2016, April 6). Retrieved from who.int: http://www.wpro.who.int/china/mediacentre/releases/2016/20160406/en/

Smith, A. A. (1894). *Chinese Characteristics*. EastBridge.

Yutang, L. (1935). *My Country, My People*. Hesperides Press.

CHAPTER 8

Branding in China

Role of Branding in China

Marketers sometimes debate whether branding plays the same role in developing markets like China as it does in the developed markets (though some in the same breath contend that China is not a developing market anymore). China is in a relatively unique position here, as it shares some characteristics with the developing markets, but in some ways, it is not only ahead of the curve from developing markets but also leads the developed markets.

To start with, research, in fact, has often indicated that consumers in markets like China, like consumers in other emerging Asian countries, place a lot of importance on brands. Brands are surrogates of quality and brands imply trust. That is why in surveys more Chinese and Indian consumers agree to statements like—it is better to buy well-known brands as you can rely on quality—than anywhere else in the world. These consumers aver that they only buy products from a trusted brand. While in the developed world branding is a "value addition", in the developing world branding is a "value assurance".

Consumers need this value assurance as they have burnt their fingers with myriad products of dubious quality. Scandals on contamination and suspicious ingredients in food products are rife in markets like China and India, driving consumers to undertake a tougher scrutiny of brands. The consumers in the developed markets, on the other hand, normally enjoy safe and reliable products, and hence the branding serves as a tool of value

A. Sethi, *Chinese Consumers*,
https://doi.org/10.1007/978-981-10-8992-3_8

addition. In the world of fiercely increasing competition, this value addition is often in the intangible area of brand image and personality rather than the basic product attributes.

Numerous studies also show that while brands are considered important, historically consumers have been less loyal in China as compared to the rest of the world. This had, to a great extent, to do with the fact that the history of branding and marketing in China is relatively short. Thirty years ago there were hardly any brands in China. Brands have not enjoyed the same kind of long-lasting affinity with consumers as they have in other societies where consumers have grown with brands. That is the reason marketers have often placed more importance on tactical measures such as price and promotions than brand building.

However, this is rapidly changing. Today while brand loyalty is declining in the developed world, it is actually increasing in China. Consumers today are realizing that all that comes with attractive packaging and seductive advertising is not necessarily good or even safe. Hence they are now more selective in their embrace of brands and more loyal once they find satisfaction. It is time for marketers to increase or at least maintain their investments in brand building in China and try to forge a strong and long-lasting bond with the consumers. While it is clear that it is time for marketers to increase their investments, the rather special nature of markets like China indicates that the traditional approaches to brand building will be inadequate. So the key question really is how should marketers go about the onerous and challenging task of endearing their brands with the Chinese consumers.

It Is All About the Consumer Needs

The answer to this needs to start by first ascertaining whether there are very specific and special factors which make the task of creating and nurturing powerful brands in China very different from the task in the rest of the world. To start with there is possibly one thing that the experts will agree on—branding needs to be based on consumer insights. The process of creating a super brand in China, therefore, clearly needs to be based on the process of deriving perceptive and penetrative insights about the Chinese consumers. Hence branding for China should be different if our insights tell us that the Chinese consumers are different from the consumers in the rest of the world—if they value different elements in products and brands and have different criteria or processes for evaluating and selecting from the different options. Here the answer is clear—there are many basic similarities between the consumers in China and the rest of the world, but there are also many important differences. Quite often the similarities are large enough to imply that the core values of the brand can be the same as in the rest of the world. Apple, Coca-Cola, and McDonald's offer the same brand values that appeal to consumers across the world.

Branding in China, I would therefore argue, is not any different than branding in Norway or Mali. Brands need to find a set of important needs to satisfy in a relatively unique and captivating manner. In doing so they would need to make sure that the ways in which they satisfy the needs are specific to the local environment. But in the end if it is the same brand, the consumer needs to be left behind with the same feeling of satisfaction and gratification which is at the core of the brand—otherwise, of course, it is not the same brand.

The Key Differences

While we need to accept the commonality of the framework, we also need to acknowledge a few unique characteristics of China, which make the task of branding a bit different. Firstly, we need to recognize that 1.3 billion Chinese differ vastly in terms of their income and lifestyle and live in over 31 diverse provinces, in a land area which stretches over 5000 kilometers over extremely different climatic zones. This heterogeneity raises an important question—whether the brand should be tailored to the different needs of this heterogeneous body of consumers. Here again, I feel that the core values of the brand need to be common—but their expressions can be local.

Secondly, marketers need to appreciate that the whole phenomenon of branding is relatively new in China. Unlike the developed markets, where consumers grow up in a familiar milieu of brands and advertising jingles, the Chinese consumers started experiencing brand communication only in the last few decades. This has shaped many aspects of their interaction and perception of brands, including a strong desire to learn about the brands. Unlike the consumers in the developed markets, who are jaded because of excessive communication from brands, the Chinese consumers are still receptive to brands. It is important for a brand to ensure that they are able to satisfy the consumer appetite for detailed brand information—both offline and now more importantly online.

From "Me" to "We"

Thirdly, the digital age has descended on the Chinese in rather an abrupt manner and many young Chinese grew up with "digital", just as their counterparts in the developed markets. As consumers become more selective, they are quick to share their evaluations of brands through online ratings and reviews—a phenomenon which is more prevalent in China than in the rest of the world. The fact that for many the preferred way to connect is the mobile phone and not the PC makes it easier to share as well as to seek reviews and recommendations. This offers both an opportunity and also a challenge to brands in China, as they need to closely monitor and in fact lead the online buzz and conversation. At the same time, they have the ability to tap the enormous pool of consumer creativity which the Chinese youth are keen to unleash online. If unheeded, this creativity can devilishly disfigure the brand, but if nurtured it can be channelized to strengthen the brand and spread its values. Brand image or positioning in China is not just owned by the marketer—but co-owned by the marketer and the consumer. A clear strategy is required to make sure that the consumers are not only listened to but even encouraged to co-create with the marketer (Illuminera 2017).

Consumers are expressing themselves, and brands need to stretch to accommodate the growing voice and the growing heterogeneity of the consumers. Hence though the consumers in China are becoming more individualistic, or moving from "we" to "me", brands need to move from "me" to "we". This will make sure that the consumers can identify with the brands and see their own reflection in the brands. That is the challenge for the brands in China—how they can retain their core values, while still reflecting the emotions of the consumers, and letting them get a strong feeling of co-ownership.

Foreign Brands Dominate the Consumer Mind

In 1773, King George III dispatched Lord McCartney as his ambassador to China to present himself at the court of the Qing Emperor, Qianlong. Emperor Qianlong, widely considered as an enlightened ruler, dismissed the ambassador by saying, "As your ambassador has seen for himself, we possess all things. I set no value in objects strange and ingenious and have no use for your manufactures". It is not without reason that the Chinese name of the country means the "middle country". Chinese have traditionally considered their place right at the center of the universe and historians and commentators often ascribe to the Chinese the attribute of an enormous self-pride, bordering on xenophobia. However, if there is one attribute which a modern historian will ascribe to China, it is "change". China has changed beyond recognition since Deng Xiao Ping opened its doors to the external world, while at the same time proclaiming that "to be rich is glorious". The change is not only evident in gleaming new highways and sky caressing towers, but also in the people's minds. Today, in China, as in many other developing countries, products of international origin command a certain degree of respect and are often favored over their domestic rivals. The most loved brands are international. Nine of the top ten brands in terms of consumer attachment are international brands, as seen from a study of Asia's top 1000 brands from Campaign Asia, a magazine (Asia's Top 1000 brands 2017) (Table 8.1).

However, the actual balance of local versus foreign brands in China varies across different product categories. In many areas, China has been protective of the local companies (many of them state-owned) and markets in telecom, banking, and finance are fully dominated by state-owned companies. On the other hand, in the automobiles category, foreign brands (all manufactured in China normally with a 50:50 joint collaboration with local state-owned companies) totally dominate the landscape—though local brands are slowly inching forward, and even making international forays.

It is interesting to look at the FMCG category, where there have not been any strong protective policies, technology is not very critical but

Table 8.1 China's best brands of 2016

China's best brands 2016	
1.	Samsung
2.	Nestle
3.	Chanel
4.	Apple
5.	Sony
6.	Nike
7.	Tong ren tang
8.	Starbucks
9.	Adidas
10.	Panasonic

Source: Campaign Asia.www.campaignasia.com/Top1000Brands/

brand strength and marketing prowess plays a big role. The picture is quite diverse. In some categories, the answer is expected—chocolates, carbonated soft drinks, and chewing gum are foreign products, relatively new to the Chinese market and hence foreign brands dominate. On the other end of the spectrum, instant noodles and ready to drink (RTD) tea are Chinese in origin and the Chinese companies rule the roost.

In food and drinks such as biscuits, candy, beer, and juice, where local tastes and preferences are important, and strong local distribution is an asset, including in the traditional trade, local brands seem to have an upper hand (Bain & Company: Kantar Worldpanel 2016).

For the other categories, the division of spoils seems to be linked to the global marketing prowess of the multinational companies and the strength of the domestic companies. No foreign player, for example, has been able to make any headway in the yogurt market. In categories like shampoo, the marketing strength of global giants like Proctor & Gamble seems to help foreign brands secure an advantage. Interestingly the same might does not seem to help to that extent in the oral care, personal wash, and fabric detergent categories and kitchen cleansers (Table 8.2).

Domestic Brands Catching Up

The general trend in the FMCG category is definitely a move toward domestic brands. In 2015, according to the data from Kantar Worldpanel, in 16 out of the 23 categories analyzed by them, domestic brands gained share at the expense of the foreign brands. Skin-care, diapers, toothpaste, hair conditioners, and shampoo were some of the big share loss categories for foreign brands. On the other hand, the biggest gain for foreign brands was in the infant milk formula market (already from a very high level), a category where, for historical reasons, the consumers do not trust domestic brands.

These are the categories where there is no intrinsic advantage seen by consumers for a domestic brand or a foreign brand. In fact, many are not very clear about which are local brands and which are international brands. The battle here is fought on the strength of marketing proficiency and muscle. In general, the local companies are far behind the multinationals in this area. However, large Chinese companies such as Yili (a milk producer) are aggressively recruiting marketing talent from multinationals and using the same professional advice and services that the global companies use. The marketing expertise gap between the local firms and the

Table 8.2 The Share of foreign brands 2015

Chewing gum	Infant formula	Chocolate	Carbonated soft drinks	Diapers	Shampoo	Hair conditioner	Personal wash	Make-up
92%	80%	77%	77%	84%	71%	51%	44%	38%
Toothpaste	Biscuit	Toothbrush	Fabric detergent	Candy	Facial tissue	Beer	Skin-care	Juice
33%	33%	31%	25%	35%	22%	21%	29%	19%
Toilet tissue	Instant noodles	Packaged water	Kitchen cleanser	Yogurt	Milk	RTD tea		
11%	11%	8%	8%	5%	3%	2%		

Source: China Shopper Report 2016, Vol. 1, Bain & Company & Kantar Worldpanel

multinationals is bound to narrow in the coming years, and local brands likely to grow further.

Graeme Pitkeethly, CFO of Unilever, noted in his statement, releasing the quarterly results in April 2016, that consumers are increasingly being drawn to brands that align with their cultural identity and lifestyle (Driest et al. 2016). However this does not necessarily mean a disadvantage for foreign brands in China—it just implies a need for more localization and dilution of central control on brand identities and profiles.

The Rise of the Smaller Niche Brands

Globally the large consumer multinationals are feeling a squeeze. According to a study by Boston Consulting Group, a consultancy, and IRI, a sales data provider, from 2011 to 2015, large consumer product companies (CPGs) lost nearly three percentage points of market share in the USA. In the developed markets much of the loss is to newer niche players who offer more interesting and cheaper products. Internet and social media allow the newer entrants to quickly and cheaply create small franchises of loyal consumers. In China, this is especially true in retail, where small and specialized stores on WeChat offer personalized advice and service to customers on products such as wine or health and organic products.

Importance of Being "Foreign": Global, Local, or Glocal?

Multinational companies in China often wonder the extent to which they should emphasize their foreign origin to the consumers as against demonstrating roots and strength in the local market. The reasons for this are not difficult to fathom—including frequent disastrous experiences that consumers have had with some miscreant local players. However, given the ascending star of China on the global stage and the emergence of a strong streak of national pride, one could also be forgiven to assume that emphasizing local roots is of paramount importance.

Like many marketing riddles in China, this is a complex question and the answer depends upon many factors. First of these factors is whether the product category in question is a premium product or an inexpensive product for daily use. At one end of the spectrum are luxury product categories. In these categories, only international brands have been able to register their prowess with the consumers so far. Consumers use such products for their exclusivity, as status symbols and as markers of success in their climb up the ladder of success. Brands are valued for their high quality, craftsmanship, and heritage. Brands are often strongly associated with a country and derive their image from the perception of the country (as in case of Luxury automobiles from Germany, a country known for its craftsmanship and engineering skills, or perfumes from France, associated with romance and chic). Clearly establishing your international origin is of critical importance in this category. Such brands normally do not need to (in fact are not advised to) adopt their core offer and brand essence to the local markets.

At the other end of the spectrum are daily use products whose usage is in the private space. Whether you use an expensive premium product or a cheap one may have a significant effect on how well does your bathroom floor shine, but not in terms of how are you seen by your friends and compatriots. The consumer choice of such products is based on price and basic functionality, and consumers show little concern about the origin or provenance of the brand. In fact, often the consumers are not able to correctly classify such FMCG as local or foreign. In a research among consumers in second-tier cities of China, when consumers were being asked about the origin of various brands, many consumers mentioned Johnson & Johnson as coming from Shanghai!

For products which fall somewhere in between the continuum of luxury and pedestrian, the issue is a bit more involved and establishing the international origin can be a plus though not necessarily so. While being foreign may be associated with better quality, being nimble and having a strong pulse of the market and the consumers can be even more important. Marketers have to carefully decide the relative emphasis they need to place on their international origin and local roots. For high technology products, consumer experience suggests that international brands bring in a quality and panache that local brands struggle to achieve. On the other hand, for some categories such as skin-care or apparel, understanding of local tastes and preferences can act as a plus. In this middle territory, local brands often try to disguise themselves as international by choosing names such as Metersbonwe (a popular apparel brand in China) with varying degrees of success (Chinese fashion group has global designs 2012).

The third factor guiding the brand's strategy is specific to the brand. For brands like Coca-Cola and Nike, which through clever and consistent marketing investments, have built a unique narrative and aura for themselves, which has stood the test of time as well the test of geographical diversity, it makes sense to exploit their universal value in all markets. For other brands, which though still international, lack that strong narrative, localization and amassing local strength may be a more logical choice. Even when such brands choose to retain their global aura and persona, localization of communication themes and styles is necessary—the absence of which often leads to alienation.

Lastly, while such preferences and attitudes do determine the importance of being “foreign”, certain events can suddenly change the equation. The most notable of which has been the milk contamination scandal (China: Inquiry on tainted milk powder 2014), which drove mothers to imported milk powder in an attempt to ensure the safety of their children. In a short period of time, the share of imported milk powders rose to unimaginable levels. International marketers need to be on the lookout for such sudden “change of wind”, which can make their provenance and heritage more valued by the consumers.

The Importance of Being Chinese

It also needs to be recognized that the ascent of the Chinese star in the global stage has resulted in an enormous degree of pride, which manifests itself in trends such as the revival of traditional thoughts, motifs, and designs. Linked to that is a kind of cultural renaissance (China Focus: China’s cultural renaissance inspires lawmakers 2017) that we are seeing in China—where the Chinese are increasingly attracted to Chinese art, design, and culture. There is even a revival of Confucian thought and young Chinese parents are sending their children to special schools which emphasize traditional learning.

On the whole the Chinese show a balanced view of the world looking at each country on its merit—knowing where they have strengths.

However, when it comes to matters of taste and food preferences, some of the most successful brands in China are those which have totally transformed themselves to cater to the local needs and preferences. KFC perhaps is a strong example, whose menu of dough sticks and congee bears little resemblance to the options displayed in their store in Milwaukee (Bell and Shelman 2011). Similarly, the range of flavors offered by Lay’s potato chips in China and India have almost no overlap—while hotpot and spicy meat flavors dominate in China, magic masala and mint mischief titillate the taste buds of the Indian consumers. However, the question is not really whether the product is the same, but whether the brand has the same core characteristics and hooks which are clearly at play despite the apparent differences in the product. KFC offers tasty, convenient, and value meals in a clean and comfortable environment in every country—it is merely the definitions of these benefits that need to find local expression.

Country of Origin

The preference of brands by country of origin remains tainted by political undertones. A recent casualty of the political differences has been Korean brands, when China took askance to the erection of the Terminal High Altitude Area Defense (THAAD), an anti-missile system in Korea. Despite Korea and the USA asserting that THAAD is merely a defense against North Korea's nuclear threat, China sees it as an undermining of its own defense capability. The first brand to suffer was Lotte, whose land is being used in Korea to install the defense system. Most of the Lotte mart superstores in China were closed due to the sudden discovery of problems in their operations, including fire and safety hazards (Hancock and Xueqiao n.d.).

The number of Chinese tourists, which constitute around half the tourists in South Korea, decreased by nearly 50% in the first seven months of 2017. Businesses in Seoul's Dongdaemun district have been reported exhibiting signs saying, "THAAD retaliation shock! Going out of business sale!". Lotte Duty-Free, the country's biggest duty-free operator, suffered its first quarterly loss since the 1980s this year.

Apart from these political hiccups, the Chinese display the expected stereotypical associations with different countries. On the whole, Germany and America are the two countries admired the most for their products. In the field of computer hardware and software, USA is the clear leader—with no other country anywhere near it (India a distant second in software). In general, American products have a perception of being technologically advanced, innovative, and modern. Germans are admired for their automobiles and machinery and their products are seen as having good craftsmanship, good detailing, and a long life. But when it comes to perfumes and luxury products, no country can match the allure of France—a perception which extends to personal products in general and in fact also garments (though the Chinese feel they themselves make pretty good garments).

America is seen to combine the best of science and art and is not only seen as a center of technological excellence but also as a fashion leader and a trendsetter. The USA is far ahead of anyone else in producing good popular music and good movies and drama. The Chinese express their appreciation of this by lapping up the pirated DVDs and downloading from free file share sites—though not as the USA would like them to express—by paying the full price that the Americans normally pay (though that is also changing with increasing box-office success of American movies in China).

Not only science, technology, and art, the Chinese recognize American excellence in education and sports. American Universities are considered as the best, with the UK not far behind.

While in pop art, the USA reigns supreme, when it comes to serious art and culture, it is France which takes the place of pride, and specifically on the quality of museums, UK takes the top spot. As a country with rich culture and traditions, the Chinese are proud of their own place—India and UK are a distant second (TNS 2008).

Changing Affinities

In some categories such as beauty and skin-care, the Chinese preferences are shifting from Europe and America to South Korea and Japan. According to a report by Mintel, South Korean brands accounted for 47% of the global beauty and personal care products bought by the Chinese consumers, and Japanese products made up another 24% (Zhuoqiong 2016). South Korean beauty purveyors have made big strides in China, with companies like Innisfree offering more than 2000 products in its Chinese stores. South Korean companies also aggressively target Chinese tourists and international travelers. The products offered by Korean firms are more diverse and often contain exotic ingredients that the Chinese are fond of—creams made of snail slime and sea-kelp face masks. However, the gravy train of South Korean brands is at least temporarily derailed because of political differences between the two countries.

Chinese Digital and Tech Brands

If there is one product field where the local brands really dominate, it is the field of digital services. Of course, the base of this local dominance is solidly built on the helping hand of the Chinese government who made it difficult for Google to continue to operate here, or for Facebook to be the dominant social media platform despite Mark Zuckerberg's regular wooing of the Chinese decision makers, including a creditable effort in learning Chinese.

However, it needs to be acknowledged that while Google, Facebook, and Twitter do not operate in China, WhatsApp, eBay, and Amazon continue to do so. But in those areas also the dominant players are Chinese—Alibaba (with its Taobao and Tmall) and Tencent with its extraordinarily popular WeChat (微信 or Weixin in Chinese). Uber, after a valiant couple of years of aggressive expansion and generous subsidizing of both the drivers and the passengers, decided to sell out to the local dominant player Didi Chuxing (Uber to sell to rival Didi and create new business in China 2016). The triumvirate of dominant brands in China is often referred to as BAT (Baidu, Alibaba, and Tencent) or acknowledging the power of Sina's Weibo (the Chinese Twitter), as BATS (S added for Sina).

Clearly, then the Chinese brands in this area are not built entirely on the foundation of protectionism but have actually and truly been able to attract the consumers through more attractive features and a better offer. Both exceptional product innovation and clever marketing have played a significant role in ensuring these domestic wins. No product is as full of innovation and has demonstrated as rapid an enrichment of itself as WeChat—which started as a WhatsApp knock-off but has today become a combination of Facebook, Amazon, and Whatsapp—all put together. By mid-2016, 700 million Chinese used WeChat. In fact more than a third of the time spent by the Chinese on mobile internet is on WeChat. There are many factors that have been responsible for the phenomenal growth of WeChat—and a very fundamental of these is accurate realization that the Chinese internet will be the mobile internet, and that WeChat built and developed itself for the mobile phone.

The most recent achievement of the platform has been to convert itself into an online payment and e-commerce platform. Having persuaded over half of its users to link their bank cards to their account, WeChat Pay has become the next most popular method of payment after Alipay. Millions of small entrepreneurs as well as large companies have opened their official accounts on WeChat, which they have subsequently linked to e-commerce. WeChat made its transition to payment through building on its advantage of the network of friends and relations, exchanging small sums of money or red packets with whom is a common practice during the Chinese new year (We Chat About WeChat #5: Red Packets—WeChat's Secret Weapon in Payments 2016). Alipay was already a much more established payment platform but WeChat had a network of friends readily associated with the users' account. The innovations of WeChat, hence, are both product and marketing innovations—as were those of Alibaba, several years ago, when it managed to reduce eBay to a practical non-entity in China.

WeChat has made significant progress outside of China too, despite the strong presence of WhatsApp and Vibe. Other Chinese apps such as Meitu, a photo-editing software, is loved by the selfie-crazed Indians and Brazilians.

On the hardware front, Lenovo, a Chinese brand (which acquired the Thinkpad brand and business of IBM a few years ago) dominates the market not just in China, but globally. Chinese mobile phone brands—Xiaomi, VIVO, OPPO, and Huawei—dominate the Indian market, with a share of more than 50% (Chinese Mobile Phones Dethrone Samsung from Top Position in India 2018). In many other developing markets, the Chinese brands are major players.The largest drone manufacturer in the world is DJI—a Chinese company based in Shenzhen.

It is through these product fields, where China has a genuine advantage, has been investing and innovating heavily, and made efforts in brand creation, that we can expect to see more progress in the creation and development of global Chinese brands.

References

Asia's Top 1000 brands. (2017). Retrieved from campaignasia.com: https://www.campaignasia.com/Top1000Brands/CountryRanking/China

Bain & Company: Kantar Worldpanel. (2016). *China Shopper Report 2016, Vol. 1.* Bain & Company & Kantar Worldpanel.

Bell, D., & Shelman, M. L. (2011). KFC's Radical Approach to China. *Harvard Business Review.*

China Focus: China's cultural renaissance inspires lawmakers, a. (2017, March 6). Retrieved from xinhuanet.com: http://www.xinhuanet.com/english/2017-03/06/c_136107384.htm

China: Inquiry on tainted milk powder. (2014, January 11). Retrieved from nytimes.com: https://www.nytimes.com/2011/01/15/world/asia/15briefs-Milk.html?rref=collection%2Ftimestopic%2FMelamine&action=click&contentCollection=timestopics&region=stream&module=stream_unit&version=latest&contentPlacement=8&pgtype=collection

Chinese fashion group has global designs. (2012, May 25). Retrieved from ft.com: https://www.ft.com/content/dba6d4fc-a4c9-11e1-9a94-00144feabdc0

Chinese Mobile Phones Dethrone Samsung from Top Position in India. (2018, February 14). Retrieved from sputniknews.com: https://sputniknews.com/science/201802141061649592-chinese-smart-phones-india/

Driest, F. V., Sthanunathan, S., & Weed, K. (2016). Building an Insights Engine: How Unilever got to know its customers. *Harvard Business Review*.

Hancock, T., & Xueqiao, W. (n.d.). *South Korean consumer groups bear brunt of China's Thaad ire*. Retrieved from ft.com: https://www.ft.com/content/f3c78afe-821d-11e7-94e2-c5b903247afd

Illuminera. (2017). *China's Digital Transformation*. Illuminera Institute.

TNS. (2008). *The China Source Book*. TNS.

Uber to sell to rival Didi and create new business in China. (2016, August 1). Retrieved from nytimes.com: https://www.nytimes.com/2016/08/02/business/dealbook/china-uber-didi-chuxing.html

We Chat About WeChat #5: Red Packets – WeChat's Secret Weapon in Payments. (2016, January 27). Retrieved from wechat.com: http://blog.wechat.com/2016/01/27/we-chat-about-wechat-5-red-packets-wechats-secret-weapon-in-payments/

Zhuoqiong, W. (2016, January 26). *Imports of S. Korean cosmetic products doubled in 2015*. Retrieved from chinadaily.com.cn: http://www.chinadaily.com.cn/business/2016-01/26/content_23244140.htm

CHAPTER 9

The Changing Marketing Game

Digital Leapfrog

The developed world has a long and rich history of marketing, in which marketing strategy, advertising management, segmentation, and positioning play a central role. Marketers in China have also been rapidly acquiring this marketing knowledge and trying to grow their brands in the country. However, China will go down in history as the country with the briefest exposure to marketing as the world has known marketing so far. At the end of the Cultural Revolution in 1977, there were practically no brands in China, nor were there any consumers with money to buy them. In the 40 years since the opening up of the economy and flourishing of the private sector and market economy, China has transformed itself into one of the most competitive and crowded markets in the world. The hypermarkets (and now the online markets) are heaving with super loaded shelves, and hundreds of television stations, publications, and outdoor billboards and signs are proclaiming the merits of myriads of brands from all over the world. However, the digital age threatens to bring an abrupt end to this 40-year period of conventional marketing in China. China has leapfrogged into the mobile-driven digital age—and now marketers face a huge challenge to take the same leapfrog.

A. Sethi, *Chinese Consumers*,
https://doi.org/10.1007/978-981-10-8992-3_9

Digital: Not Just Another Channel

The response of the marketers so far to this phenomenal change has been highly inadequate. Marketers have hastened to move their advertising spends online and based on this alone congratulate themselves for having rapidly evolved a digital strategy. The advertising industry responded to the challenge by introducing a digital offer along with the traditional services, and many new agencies cropped up offering specialized digital expertise. However, with 710 million internet users, the need of the hour was not to develop a digital strategy, but to comprehensively overhaul the strategy with digital at the core of it, not just an addendum to it. The Chinese consumer is already spending more time on digital channels than the time spent glued to the television. The average Chinese spends six hours and six minutes consuming media in various forms, and out of this three hours and five minutes is devoted to the partaking of social media and digital content.

GroupM, a part of the WPP group, estimates that online advertising expenditure in China was 277 billion yuan in 2016, an increase of 30% over the previous year (GroupM 2017). This growth trajectory is likely to be maintained in the coming year and the online ad spend is expected to nearly double in 2019 to 543 million yuan from the 2016 figure. This comes at the cost of traditional media advertising, which declined by 2% in 2016 (after seeing a growth of 1% in each of the preceding years).

However, for most advertisers, this has merely translated into a change in media channel—the same TV commercial has been moved from TV (television) to OTV (online television) or other digital channels (61 billion yuan out of the total online spend of 277 billion yuan was on OTV) (GroupM 2017).

This is an unfortunate mistake as this often harms the brand rather than promoting it. The research shows that even the Chinese consumers, who in general show a high level of tolerance for brand messages, feel that the TV ad seen on OTV is unacceptably intrusive. The reason for this lies in the fact that the consumption of digital and non-digital media is in different contexts and states of mind.

China is now the world's largest market for anything digital—software or hardware. Its citizens have embraced the digital lifestyle with such gusto and enthusiasm that it leaves marketers with no choice but to embrace digital as *the core of their strategy*, not just as another channel to reach their customers. The SODA+Forrester Global Digital Outlook proclaims that one of the trends they see is "The death (and rebirth) of the digital agency" (SODA+Forrester 2017). As the report explains, "What was once an area of specialized differentiation may become dead weight for agencies and marketers who think too myopically about digital as a distinctive channel or capability and fail to open their aperture to the wider role technology now plays in connecting marketing activities to a more fundamental and integrated human experience."

Hence it is time to stop talking about digital channels and digital strategy, but really explore how to devise impactful communication to woo the consumers in the digital world—regardless of whether you are reaching them through a digital or a non-digital channel.

Eroding Role of Advertising

For more than a hundred years, advertising has served an important role in the lives of the consumers as well as businesses. The first and foremost of which has been to connect the businesses and the consumers by informing the consumers of what is available, including information on price and distribution. However, in the digital age, manufacturers can connect directly to consumers without using advertising—for example, by opening a store on Taobao, having a WeChat account or through online word-of-mouth. Similarly, consumers have many more ways than advertising to learn about products, especially through social media. In fact advertising as a source of information about products is now the least credible of all the different sources available to the consumers.

Secondly, advertising has played a role in stimulating the economy by encouraging consumption. While this role is still relevant, the economy is not as dependent on advertising as before. As product information can be conveyed through ways other than advertising, there are other ways to encourage and facilitate consumption.

Thirdly, advertising has been a significant cultural influence by reflecting the cultural mores and magnifying the popular memes of the society. However, in the digital age, all these roles of advertising are under question. In fact, cultures and subcultures develop on the internet without any role from brands or advertising. Like-minded people with even the narrowest of interests can now easily connect with each other, bypassing geographical and other barriers, fomenting new ideas and memes at a rapid speed.

Apart from these factors which point toward a *reduced role* of advertising, there are also several others which have resulted in a *reduced effectiveness* of advertising—both in the traditional media, as also in the digital media (particularly if the use of digital media is purely a transfer of offline advertising to online media) (Illuminera 2017). One of the key reasons for the reduced effectiveness is the clutter. The amount of messages that the consumer is exposed to had gone well past the limit of their abilities to understand or even notice these messages. Consumers are dealing with this deluge by filtering out most of the messages they are exposed to. Even for the messages on products they are interested in, they have developed filtering and processing methods, which will make most advertising fairly ineffective. This problem of clutter and overload was even true for the traditional media but has become even more amplified in the always-on digital media.

While there have always been questions about the effectiveness of all ad spend (traditional or digital) the questions about the effectiveness of digital investments are even bigger. In fact, many suspect significant advertising fraud and question whether much of digital display advertising is seen by a human at all. Though digital media should actually offer objective ways of data based evaluation, either advertisers have not adopted these methods or problems of data access and fragmentation prevent them from achieving an accurate and objective evaluation.

Fragmented Life, Social Media

Clearly, the appropriate strategy for the digital times needs to hinge on the understanding of consumer behavior and attitudes in relation to consumption of digital media. The biggest impact of mobile digital on the consumer life is fragmentation (Illuminera 2017). In the pre-digital era, the consumers had a relatively fixed schedule for work, entertainment, news, social interaction, and shopping. However mobile has enabled the consumer to indulge in any of these activities any time of the day. Consumers have adopted this opportunity and the consumer life now is characterized by flitting from one activity to another, right through the day and multiple times in the day. But while the consumer life is fragmented and the consumer flits from one activity to another, the experiences are getting more unified— mostly under the umbrella of social, facilitated by WeChat but now being rapidly adopted by Alibaba. Shopping merges into social, as consumers click on the links shared by their friends, work merges into pleasure as colleagues connect on WeChat, and content which is shared straddles personal as well as pleasure. This social character of the web along with the fragmentation creates a unique environment, as well as unique consumer state of mind. For brands to get their messages across in this environment is a challenging task and a different game altogether.

We also need to acknowledge several other key differences in the manner in which digital and non-digital media is consumed by the consumers. Consumption of traditional media like television is normally passive, depends on the schedule of broadcast (not controlled by the consumers), and can only be interrupted through scheduled breaks from the broadcaster—not from the viewer. In this situation, interruptions or breaks are expected and natural, as is the appearance of advertising in these breaks. The online media is consumed in an entirely different way and with a totally different frame of mind, as compared to the offline media. While offline media's fixed-schedule content, over which consumers do not have control, is naturally amenable to interruptions (where advertising can make an appearance) in the consumption of online content, on the other hand, the schedule is controlled by the consumers, and there are no natural interruptions for advertising. The interruptions are engineered by the consumers, and for a specific purpose that they have in mind—not to consume advertising. The consumer state of mind wants to control and focus on their mission, whether it is to snatch a piece of entertainment or seek information for a report. Hence marketers who attempt to insert their ads in the digital media in the same manner in which they insert them on television, do not receive a positive consumer reaction.

Second difference emanates from the fact that a large proportion of digital media consumption in China is on the mobile phone. The small screen offers little scope for the inserted banner and video advertising.

Micro-content

Before we look at the implication this change has on marketing and the ways brands convey their messages to the consumers, we first need to see what impact has it had on the media content itself. Here the change is evident—fragmentation, and the limited amount of time that consumers spend at one point of time of the internet (mostly on their mobile) has meant that the entertainment content also needed to transform itself to suit the changing consumer habit. Essentially. this has resulted in growing popularity of what is referred to as micro-content, which can provide short moments of entertainment to the consumers in the brief interludes they steal for themselves right through the day. Absorbtion of news has also changed from the traditional perusal of a newspaper from page to page, or a systematic browsing of a website, to consumption of individual news-bites or social media, or through frequent reference to apps like Jnri Toutiao (今日头条), which serves algorithmically selected, personalized, bite-sized content to suit the individual preferences of the readers (A Saucy App Knows China's Taste in News 2018).

Embed Not Insert

In this context of bite-sized media consumption, the scope of the conventional 30-second ad is greatly reduced. The consumer is naturally unwilling to watch a 30-second commercial when the media consumption itself it only for a few minutes. The marketers and the advertisers hence have to learn how to *embed* the message in the content, not *insert* it, which implies that the only practical way to reach the consumer with your message is through content.

If marketers are compelled to communicate through content, clearly it shakes the foundation of advertising the way we understand it now. The principles of advertising are all based on rationally and emotionally appealing to the consumer in a 30-second commercial, for which it is assumed that the consumers offer at least some degree of attention. The digital content environment is entirely different and the consumers' acceptance of direct claims about product features and unique attributes is likely to be low as such messages are bound to compete with content. The messages need to be subtly integrated into the content possibly through demonstration of the features and qualities rather than loud proclamations. A product which wants to establish its taste needs to demonstrate through users licking their lips over it, and the company which wishes to demonstrate its social responsibility has to put up stories which embody these activities at its core.

Information Overload

Not only has the exposure to media content been transformed from discrete long stretches to brief but near-continuous exposure, so has the exposure to brand communication. The key question here is that has it led to an information overload and is the consumer resentful of this barrage of exposure? Information overload is a term which has been used even before the internet and there is no doubt that the digital age has further exacerbated the excess. It is natural to fear that the consumer is drowning in the deluge of information. Right from the time she wakes up and reaches out to open her WeChat account, to the end of the day when she reluctantly places the mobile phone on the bedside table to catch some sleep, the Chinese consumer is a recipient of information and stimuli of all nature, including myriad of messages from brands in innumerable forms and manners. Is the Chinese consumer drowning and suffocating under a barrage of information?

Research conducted by Illuminera, a consumer insights, and marketing consultancy firm, indicates that despite the overdose of information, the Chinese consumers are not overwhelmed. In fact, they revel in the immersion and many even feel that the internet relieves stress through the amusements and entertainments it offers. Different consumers have developed different mechanisms to cope with and make sense of the volume so that they are able to extract, take benefit from and enjoy the part that they feel is relevant to them (Illuminera 2017).

However, the consumers are still anxious and there is a sense of not being fully in control. The anxiety, strangely enough, emanates from the concern that they may miss out on some information which is relevant for them (e.g. a great sale which offered everything that they need on a huge discount!). Brands do not need to withhold information and control their communication. On the contrary, brands need to populate the net with all the information that they feel a consumer may need. But brands need to pass the map and the key to access that information to the consumers—so that the choice of the extent of depth the consumers want to plumb is left to them. As also is the choice of when and where they want to dig the information.

Brand Entertainment

Hence brands need to do the same as what the content does—entertain and reduce consumer anxiety. Unless brands do this, their content will be still seen as advertising and filtered out through the mental ad-blockers. The overall guidelines are clear—brands need to communicate through native content, preferably micro-content which has to appeal to the consumers and reflect the consumer culture in an entertaining way. The appeal, in fact, has to be strong enough for them to not only enjoy the content themselves but also share it with their friends on social media, creating a viral stream that marketers dream about. Clearly, it is easier said than done, and in general the brands, not just in China but all over the world, are finding it extremely challenging to produce the content which gets the kind of exposure the brands hope for.

Perhaps the brand that comes to everyone's mind when thinking about social media promotions in China is Durex (from the British consumer-products company, Reckitt-Benckiser). Durex achieved a threefold increase in sales and achieved a 10% market share in the crowded Chinese condom market primarily through effectively reaching out the consumers on Chinese social media. Durex created an account on Weibo (one of China's Twitter clones) which attracted a reasonably large following. But the turning point was in 2012 when Durex started to make references to and link their product to current events. One of the first posts to go viral was when Durex's online representation, Dudu, posted, "Rainfall is flooding Beijing today. Lucky me—I have two Durex in my pocket!" And accompanied it with a visual of a pair of sneakers sheathed in two condoms. The key pillar of Durex online strategy has consistently been to shun aggressive brand promotion, and to endear itself with the consumers through light-hearted, humorous, and entertaining posts.

Quantity was another hallmark of Durex social media promotion. Durex seized at every opportunity to juxtapose itself in the context of current events in a light-hearted, humorous way—whether it is the launch of a new iPhone, a change of season, or an upcoming festival (Going Social: Durex in China 2014).

Creativity: Do We Still Need It?

The television commercials attracted the best creative talents and advertisements won many awards for their ingenuity in conveying the required messages to the consumers. While the 30-second commercial may be struggling to attract the Chinese consumers' attention in the digital environment, it is certainly not an indication to abandon the creative process in reaching and appealing to the consumer. If anything, creativity is even more critical. In the days of television, the advertisers paid the same amount for a great ad as they did for a dud one. The television stations did not charge based on the effectiveness of the ad. While the digital publishers too do not charge according to the impact created by the ad, in the age of social media, great content is cheaper to spread than poor content. If the content gets a response from the users, social media will show it more, the users will share it more, the consumers will click it more—all going to reduce the cost. The ability of social media to give us real-time feedback imparts more power in the hands of the marketers, as well enhances the value of creative power.

In fact, creativity in marketing needs to be expanded from a mere choice of clever words and visuals to convey the story in the advertisement to a broader conceptualization of how the brand can devise ways to improve its salience and image in the consumer mind. While the conventional advertising heavily relies on celebrities for testimonials, the social media promotions also cleverly leverage celebrities and Key Opinion Leaders (KOL).

One of the earliest success achieved in KOL marketing in China was for Tourism New Zealand, which recruited the services of Yao Chen, one of the most successful microbloggers in China, who in 2011 had over 40 million followers on Weibo (Micro-blogging Queen Yao Chen the face of campaign shoot 2012). Yao Chen went on a holiday to New Zealand and tweeted all the way through her trip. She also wedded in a New Zealand resort town, and her photos and comments generated significant enthusiasm among the potential Chinese tourists for the country. At the end of 2012, China became the source of the largest number of tourists to New Zealand. While this success story is based on the recruitment of a celebrity KOL, brands do not necessarily need to recruit a "blogging queen" to promote their brand. KOLs', also referred to as Wanghong (网红), abound on the social media and the key to leveraging their popularity is to identify the ones, who have both reach and credibility in the product category. Wanghong or cyber celebrities tend to attract a certain group of people through some specific talent or expertise or credibility. Wang Hong use their social media connections to hawk products and services and often carry a credibility and give a feeling of authenticity which is missing from mass media. Wanghong offers brands in China an opportunity to hitch themselves to figures of credibility and utilize the most powerful influencer of consumer choice—word-of-mouth.

From Segmentation to Personalization

One of the most important strategic tools marketers have employed is segmentation. Segmentation purports to divide the consumers into a few "manageable" number of groups (normally four to eight) so that consumers within a group are homogenous and across groups are heterogeneous. Marketers then go about selecting the segments they want to appeal to and position different brands for different segments and communicate unique benefits that are more likely to appeal to consumers in that segment as compared to any other. It was important that the number of segments be manageable as it is difficult to create unique brands or offers and devise strategies for more than a handful of segments.

Digital has created a new meaning to segmentation, and now we are in an age of super-segmentation in which each consumer is in his or her unique segment. Digital marketers like to refer to this as segmentation of 1 or personalization. Taobao, JD.com, and all other e-commerce platforms present the consumers with a unique array of products based on their past purchases and browsing history. It is not just behavioral information that guides the marketers, but Chinese marketers are also acquiring the capability to serve advertisements based on what the consumers say or post on their social media accounts.

The digital environment not only frees marketers of the constraint of using a handful of segments, it also rids them of the need to use one static segmentation for all marketing activities. Today marketers can use different consumer characteristics (or tags) for different marketing activities—interests and preferences for the nature and tone of the advertising, purchase history and price paid for targeting of price promotions, or quantity bought for targeting the pack sizes.

Programmatic Marketing

Is this leading us to the era, where machines will do most of the marketing as we know it? According to eMarketer, programmatic ad spending in China was $16.69 billion in 2017, a 48.6% increase over 2016 (Programmatic Advertising in China: eMarketer's Updated Forecast and Estimates 2018). Programmatic ad spending or buying is a subset of the wider phenomenon of programmatic marketing, where programs and machines rather than humans make marketing decisions. Programmatic buying specifically refers to the process of choosing the media options or slots to display advertising. According to Adage, "The advertising industry is on a march toward automation (10 THINGS YOU NEED TO KNOW NOW ABOUT PROGRAMMATIC BUYING 2015). Plenty of advertisers today are buying digital ads without speaking to a single human at a media company". Quotes, price-lists, and negotiations are being replaced by decisions arrived through programs and automated bidding.

One of the key features and advantages of programmatic buying is that it is dynamic and self-correcting. Gone are the days when you made a media plan for a quarter (or even longer) and locked the plan in the safe. Programmatic buying changes from day to day, hour to hour and learns on the basis of the effectiveness of previous decisions.

Essentially programmatic buying so far has been restricted to deciding where and when the ad will be served to the consumers, and not concerned itself with what will be served (perhaps with the exception of deciding on a few simple pre-decided options).Hence the decision pertains to when and where the marketing stimulus is exposed, not to what marketing stimulus is exposed. Dynamic pricing is perhaps one exception to this, in which the pricing is decided in real-time, including Uber's surge pricing. Or the display options by companies like Taobao and Amazon, where the past browsing history of the consumer determines what products are displayed.

The Holy Grail

The holy grail of programmatic marketing is the to expose the brand to the right consumer, as he or she moves through various potential touch points in a way that is likely to maximize the cumulative probability of conversion. The message, the price and promotion, the packaging could all vary by the consumer, by the touch point, by the day and time, by the competitive environment and any other parameter that could affect the probability of conversion. Are we likely to achieve this anytime soon?

This is inevitable as well as desirable. The marketing job of the future is better done by a machine than a human. The humans are required to program the machine and feed it the options to work with. Like in many other things digital, China will lead the way, rather than follow the trails of the marketers in the developed markets.

References

10 THINGS YOU NEED TO KNOW NOW ABOUT PROGRAMMATIC BUYING. (2015, June 1). Retrieved from adage.com: http://adage.com/article/print-edition/10-things-programmatic-buying/298811/

A Saucy App Knows China's Taste in News. (2018, January 2). Retrieved from nytimes.com: https://www.nytimes.com/2018/01/02/business/china-toutiao-censorship.html

Going Social: Durex in China. (2014). *Harvard Business Review*.

GroupM. (2017). *China Media Market Summary*. GroupM.

Illuminera. (2017). *China's Digital Transformation*. Illuminera Institute.

Micro-blogging Queen Yao Chen the face of campaign shoot. (2012, November 21). Retrieved from tourismnewzealand.com: https://www.tourismnewzealand.com/news/micro-blogging-queen-yao-chen-the-face-of-campaign-shoot/

Programmatic Advertising in China: eMarketer's Updated Forecast and Estimates. (2018, January 22). Retrieved from emarketeter.com: https://www.emarketer.com/Report/Programmatic-Advertising-China-eMarketers-Updated-Forecast-Estimates/2002186

SODA+Forrester. (2017). *Global Digital Outlook*. SODA+Forrester.

CHAPTER 10

Looking Ahead

Predicting they say is difficult, especially if it is for the future. All predictions rely on history, deciphering what has happened, sifting long-term trends from short-term blips, and painting a course for the future. Given the fact that China has such a short history of consumption and marketing, and that history is also being re-written by the digital juggernaut, does not really bolster confidence for future predictions—as there are no precedents to learn from the past—either in China or any other country. However, based on an interpretation of historical trends as well as the digital forces sweeping across the Chinese landscape, I am ready to take the risk of extending my neck and making some calls for the future.

More Sharing

"Nothing is yours. It is to use. It is to share. If you will not share it, you cannot use it," said Ursula K. Le Guin in The Dispossessed (Guin 2009), a novel depicting a Utopian society, where no one has any possessions and all goods are held in common. Though past attempts at creating Utopian societies in China have not really hit the mark, the Chinese seem to have taken this particular Utopian idea to their heart. Several recent reports portray a very rosy picture of the future of sharing economy in China—according to the China Sharing Economy Development Report, sharing economy transactions were worth 3.45 trillion yuan in 2016 and sharing economy is expected to account for 10% of China's GDP by 2020, with an

A. Sethi, *Chinese Consumers*,
https://doi.org/10.1007/978-981-10-8992-3_10

annual expected growth rate of 40% per annum (China's "sharing economy" up 103 pct in 2016: report 2017).

Why are the Chinese showing a special predilection for "sharing"? Are there any factors which make the Chinese more favorably disposed to the concept of "sharing" than other cultures and groups? I can list at least eight of these, which are rooted in Chinese socio-economic and cultural peculiarities.

- *Sharing makes financial sense.* While China may be the largest economy in the world, it still ranks somewhere around 90th in terms of GDP per capita. The latest data from the National Bureau of Statistics suggests that the per capita disposable income in urban China in 2017 was around $5800 per annum. With relatively modest incomes but high aspirations, the Chinese consumers love a good bargain, even when they are shopping for luxury products or going abroad on holidays. Airbnb (and china's own Tujia) surely offer cheaper accommodation than similar quality hotel fare, making the Chinese naturally more predisposed to these.
- *Chinese are innately entrepreneurial.* When the floodgates of entrepreneurial opportunity opened after decades of suppression, the Chinese took to business as fish takes to water. If there was money to be made by spinning a venture, investing in the stock market, or moonlighting by opening a shop on Taobao, the opportunity was embraced. Hence when tourists are rushing to China, and the Chinese landlords see a potential for making some money on the side, they are easily seduced. Why not give the apartment for rent for the weekend, when you are leaving town to visit your parents? Or why not let someone drive your car (even if it is your treasured BMW) or take it for a spin yourself and make an extra buck by ferrying some people to and from the airport?
- *China still has low penetration of many things that people want to own or use.* While the automobile market in China has been having a dream run that has never been seen before (except for cooling down to 3% growth in 2017) there are still around only 170 million cars for 1.3 billion people (China's car ownership reaches 172 million 2016). Surely the over one billion car-less Chinese also have aspirations to ride in comfort and if sharing makes their desire easier to fulfill, sharing has a definite role.

- *Sharing is social.* They said a man is a social animal much before the Chinese started demonstrating it with unprecedented gusto. While in the rest of the world, only a part of the internet is referred to as "social media", in China all internet merges together as social media. Sharing offers opportunities for social interaction with other users, as well as owners, who are common people and not commercial purveyors of goods and services. This has intrinsic appeal to the Chinese and tilts their preference to sharing.
- *China's aging population will make it more predisposed to sharing.* 241 million Chinese are 60 years of age or older (Statistical Communique of the People's Republic of China on the 2017 National Economic and Social Develoment 2018). China's cities and villages are full of empty nests, with single children flown away to make their fortunes in other corners of the country or the world. This leads to empty spaces in the house as well as more spare time for the owners of the house. Both of these are highly conducive to offering sharing services.
- *China's ease with digital makes sharing easier.* China has more internet users than the total population of the developed world. These users' heavy reliance and deep bonding with the internet is well known. Not only that, Chinese netizens use mobile phones to access the internet and are deeply into social media. This ability to tap into the digital world, anywhere anytime with the mobile phone, offers a perfect tool for them to participate in the sharing economy.
- *China has many empty houses bought as an investment.* Lack of lucrative investment options and high appreciation of property prices has resulted in many urban Chinese buying multiple apartments, which offer low rentals (China—Ghost Cities. 64 Million Empty Apartments in China 2015). Attracting visiting tourists to these apartments is an obvious route to increase the return on property.
- *Chinese government and environment support this.* Sharing economy is considered as a part of Premier Li Keqiang's, "Internet Plus" strategy, which attempts to bring more traditional businesses to benefit under the powerful impact of the internet.

These factors collectively mean that China will be at the forefront of the "sharing" revolution, through which its citizens can find ways to fulfill their aspirations and lead a richer life. This also means that "sharing" in China will go beyond the traditional areas of transportation and tourism.

It is rumored that some Chinese women were advertising their "spare husbands" on Taobao (the largest Chinese online e-commerce platform) for sharing during the Chinese New year holiday, for young unmarried women to take home in the guise of boyfriends, and assuage parental concerns about their daughters' marital prospects and plans. It is also not surprising that Apple decided to put down a billion dollars and hitch a ride in the Chinese taxi sharing company—Didi Chuxing.

Mobike offers distinctive orange colored bikes with solid wheels that come with a digital lock and a GPS unit. Through an App on their phone, the customers can locate the nearest bike and unlock it by scanning a QR code or even reserve it 15 minutes in advance. In fact, bike-sharing is touted by some as one of the four great new inventions—the other three being high-speed railways, mobile payments, and e-commerce (China's 'four great new inventions' in modern times 2017). The bike-sharing industry has managed to pull in a huge amount of capital. On the face of it, with a combination of right technologies (mobile payment, GPS positioning, and smart lock) bike-sharing seems to have found a well-tailored solution to commuters' last mile problem. If it can encourage people to move from personal to public transport, its environmental contribution itself will be significant. However excessive capital, aggressive expansion, and low prices raise questions about its sustainable profitability.

Perhaps no new industry has been received with as much enthusiasm, albeit tinged with controversy than the bike-sharing industry. While the relevance and benefits of the industry are widely acknowledged, the controversy arises from the clutter on the sidewalks from a deluge of bikes, as well as the relatively insensitive treatment of the bikes by some users. In Shanghai, there is one shared bike for every 16 people, and such an excessive supply causes havoc with the sidewalks and many other places including bus shelters, and even the roads where bikes tend to inevitably spill over to. The unsupervised bikes sometimes incur the wrath of various groups of people, ranging from nearby residents, complaining about lack of a place to walk, and unauthorized rickshaw drivers, whose business is adversely affected due to the shared bikes. But the key issue is the consumer apathy to the treatment of public or shared property. Some of the social media discussions blame the Chinese consumers' behavior on low (suzhi) 素质 or quality, which leads to a poor public responsibility and conduct. Leading bike-sharing companies are now experimenting with various incentive schemes to reward good behavior, and discourage poor behavior, like leaving the bike at an inappropriate place or vandalizing.

Almost every industry feels that it can benefit from the booming sharing economy. Four square meter boxes with a treadmill and some other exercise equipment surfaced in Beijing in August 2017, as shared mini-gyms. The cubicle is fitted with an air-conditioner, an air purifier, and a television screen. The user scans a QR code on the door with a smartphone, unlocking the mini-gym and pays around 0.2 yuan every minute. The facility appeals to the casual users, who value the convenience of location more than anything else and do not wish to commit themselves to a large annual fee which most gyms try to extract from the users in advance. Doubar, the company which pioneered this concept, plans to put 1000 mini-gyms into the market by the end of 2017. Other examples of sharing include umbrella sharing (Brolly bad show: Chinese sharing startup loses 300,000 umbrellas 2017) at metro stations in Shanghai and sleep capsule sharing for a quick restful nap for sleep-deprived office workers, located in commercial buildings.

As has been with several other areas of the digital services, Chinese clones of the global leaders try their best to provide additional value and service. Just as WeChat has left WhatsApp way behind in terms of the value it provides to the users, Shenzhen-based Zhubaijia.com wants to go beyond the core offer of Airbnb and is trying to lure the customers through value additions such as airport pickups, car rentals, and tickets to local places of sight-seeing.

More New Energy

A few years ago, China assumed the dubious crown of being the biggest greenhouse gas emitter in the world. Four decades of heady growth has been made through industrial expansion, using fossil fuels and neglect of the environment. However, China wants to change this course of development is clear from the fact, that unlike the USA, China remains firmly committed to the Paris agreement on climate change and has clear goals to reduce its carbon dependence. During the 12th Five-year plan (2011–2015) China reduced its carbon dioxide emission per unit of GDP by 20% (Climate Action Tracker 2017). China plans to increase its use of non-fossil energy to 15% by 2020. Carbon emission targets set for the 13th Five-Year Plan (2016–2020). The Chinese Present Xi Jinping mentioned the environment 89 times in his three-and-a-half hour speech to the delegates of the 19th CPC conference in 2017. China's economy was mentioned only 70 times (Tough Tasks for China's New Environment Ministry 2018).

The move to new energy is undoubtedly driven by the Chinese consumers' concern for the environment and a strong need to offer a cleaner and safer air for themselves and the next generation. As a result, the Chinese consumers express extremely positive attitudes toward the need to protect the environment and also their willingness to contribute to the effort.

China has become the largest automobile market in the world, with over a 170 million cars on the roads. This makes automobiles a natural target for change to more environmentally friendly options. Not surprisingly, one area where China is taking a clear lead is new energy vehicles. The Chinese government proactively supports the new energy vehicles (NEV) market both to stimulate demand as well as to encourage production. A key instrument to encourage demand is preferential licensing. In cities like Beijing which allot the car license plates based on a lottery, there is a separate quota for NEVs with a higher chance of success. Consumers sometimes choose an NEV just because they failed to win the lottery for a license plate of a regular vehicle. In fact, regulatory restrictions are a key contributor to the sale of NEVs and have propelled the Chinese NEV market to become the largest in the world. Nearly half of the world's NEVs are running in China.

In 2017 China announced that it is planning to draw up a timetable to ban fossil fuel cars. The government further announced its plan to implement a dual credit system that puts caps on car-makers fossil fuel consumption and also imposes minimum sales quotas for NEVs starting from April 2018. Under the program, all manufacturers or importers, who sell or import 30,000 vehicles a year or more, are required to achieve sales of NEVs equivalent to 10% of their sales of traditional vehicles in 2019 and 12% in 2020 (China sets 2019 NEV sales quota for automakers at 10 pct of annual sales 2017).

More than 200 Chinese companies, with backers such as Terry Go, Ma Huateng, Jack Ma, and Jia Yueting are developing 4000 models of new energy vehicles. The Chinese government has committed to boosting of NEVs by a factor of ten in the next decade with a target of 3 million by 2025. In 2015 domestic NEVs sold 331,092 units (247,482 pure electric and 83,610 plug-in hybrids), according to the China Association of Automobile Manufacturers. In 2016 the figure increased to 520,000 vehicles, but the total automobile sale was 28 million. According to the Boston Consulting Group (BCG), NEVs will represent 7% of new vehicle sales by 2020.

The Chinese company BYD is the largest producer of NEV's in the world, selling 114,315 vehicles in 2016. Nine Chinese brands are ranked among the top 20 in the world, according to a report by Fitch (Daye 2017). Several indicators point to the continuation of the rapid movement of the country in this direction:

- Continued government support and nudging
- Strong consumer concern for the environment
- China's competitive advantage in manufacturing NEV vehicles, where the requisite areas of expertise are in things like battery technology, digital and data, rather than internal combustion engine, where its technology lags behind the Westerns and Japanese manufacturers
- Continuous improvement in the quality of NEVs (poor perceived quality is a current deterrent for the purchase of NEVs).

More Autonomous

China has one of the worst traffic accident records in the world. That itself is reason enough for China to move to autonomous driving ("it is easier to teach machines to drive than it is to teach the Chinese car owners," the cynics espouse). In several other product fields China has leapfrogged from nothing to the most advanced form of technology (e.g. moved from no phone straight to mobile phone, bypassing the landline phone altogether, or from no camera to digital camera, bypassing the film camera). With a population of over 1.3 billion, despite selling nearly 25 million cars a year, the penetration of cars is relatively low. With a relatively low penetration of cars in the country, there is no reason why Chinese consumers cannot leapfrog from no cars to autonomous cars (along with using rather than owning).

According to a 2016 survey by BCG and the World Economic Forum (WEF) with 5000 consumers in ten countries, 81% of the Chinese are willing to try a fully autonomous car. In contrast, only 41% of the Germans are willing to let go of the steering wheel and entrust the vehicle to drive itself. Even the Americans, the home of Google and Tesla, which are pioneering the self-driving movement, only 48% agreed to be driven by an autonomous vehicle (Fulco 2016).

The Chinese consumers' enthusiasm for self-driving vehicles (SDVs) is apparently matched by the Chinese industry which is focusing its efforts on perfecting this technology. Interestingly it is the digital members of the industry, led by Baidu, who are pushing ahead ambitiously. Baidu expects that the idea will be fully commercialized by 2018, and it may be running around on the Chinese roads in another two years after that. In April 2016, two cars manufactured by Changan Automobiles from Chongqing traveled 1900 kilometers from Chongqing to Beijing over five days. Baidu will test its SDVs in Wuhu city and Wu'zhen in 2016.

The BCG and WEF report says that SDVs and self-drive robo-taxis could result in 60% drop in the number of cars on city roads, an 80% or greater decrease in tailpipe emissions, and 90% fewer road accidents. According to Accenture, 56% of the vehicles sold worldwide will be "connected cars" in 2020, which will increase further to 77% by 2025. Car companies are offering free 4G in the vehicle to ensure that the vehicle is always connected.

A similar study by PricewaterhouseCoopers, which interviewed 3000 car buyers on the mainland China and in Hong Kong, also concluded that the Chinese customers are among the world's early adopters of in-car technologies, including better connectivity and autonomous driving functions. BCG projects that China would be the largest market for autonomous cars, with 5.2 million partially autonomous cars and 3.4 million fully autonomous cars by 2035.

The adoption and acceleration of autonomous vehicles in China will be driven by:

- Chinese consumers' openness to trying and adopting new technology
- Chinese consumers' lack of strong emotional attachment to cars and the joy of driving (which would be a deterrent in the developed markets)
- China's advantage and lead in the relevant technologies including big data and artificial intelligence (AI)

- Significant number of new first time buyers likely to come into the market in the coming years, who do not have any past experience with cars, and hence no attachment to the current technology and no resistance to new technology
- Chinese government and industry's aggressive push in this area (just like in NEVs, this is seen as an opportunity to get rid of the technological dominance of companies from developed markets)

More AI

Perhaps one of the most salient topics in the media recently has been the AI race. If China is interested in areas such as autonomous driving, it cannot afford not to invest in AI. And investing in it has secured full support from the government. China has produced 76% more papers on the study of AI than the USA in 2016 and 2017 and also has a higher citation rate. China also holds the world record in big data computing speed since 2014. The Chinese President, Xi Jinping, specifically mentioned AI (along with internet and big data) as one of the industries for promoting investment and innovation.

At the core of any AI application is data and the machine's ability to learn based on the data. Here China already possesses several strong advantages:

- The profusion of data with over 800 million internet users, with heavy usage of social media, e-commerce, and online payments. Didi, China's Uber, produces and harnesses data on 9 billion routes driven per day
- Enormous resources of China's large technology firms (particularly the BAT—Baidu, Alibaba, and Tencent). Baidu has opened two research labs on AI in Silicon Valley. Alibaba is already testing a facial recognition payment system and investing heavily in developing it further. Tencent has developed its own version of AlphaGo called Jueyi (Huang 2017).
- The profusion of data Fast computing power. With the backing of the Chinese government, the fastest supercomputers to crunch the data are in China (202 of the 500 fastest computers in the world are in China—as compared to 144 in the USA).

However, the real driver of AI in China will be the enormous benefit that it will bring to the economy and the consumers:

- One of the important applications of AI is in the area of robotics—and with a reducing working population the number of people in the age group of 15–59 decreased to 911 million in 2015, from 925 million in 2011 and is expected to shrink to 830 million in 2030). China needs robots if it wants to grow or even sustain its current level of industrial activity.
- Facial recognition will bring enormous convenience to the consumers as they are already big users of activities which require authorization (such as online payments).
- China's future economic growth hinges heavily on its ability to further develop the service sector. Providing excellence in service to a population as large and diverse as China's is fraught with difficulties. Bots and AI will play a major role in ensuring a high level of service.
- An aging population and increasing number of single households will need more services which could be provided through AI.
- With a large population and relatively underdeveloped primary health care (only 7% of China's doctors are in primary health care), AI driven smart health care products will play a major role in early diagnosis and self-monitoring.

Though already discussed in Chap. 8 (the Changing Face of Marketing) it is possibly worth mentioning here again that AI will also be marketer's best friend in reaching the right consumers, at the right time, with the right message. This marketing task has acquired such a level of complexity that its conventional tools of marketing are ill-fitted to meet the challenge. Operational delivery of marketing can only be done programmatically, and of course, AI will play a major role in delivering this.

References

Brolly bad show: Chinese sharing startup loses 300,000 umbrellas. (2017, July 11). Retrieved from theguardian.com: https://www.theguardian.com/world/2017/jul/11/brolly-bad-show-chinese-sharing-startup-loses-300000-umbrellas

China – Ghost Cities. 64 Million Empty Apartments in China. (2015, September 30). Retrieved from globalresearch.ca: https://www.globalresearch.ca/china-ghost-cities/5421229

China sets 2019 NEV sales quota for automakers at 10 pct of annual sales. (2017, September 28). Retrieved from reuters.com: https://www.reuters.com/article/autos-china-electric/china-sets-2019-nev-sales-quota-for-automakers-at-10-pct-of-annual-sales-idUSB9N1LU02P

China's 'four great new inventions' in modern times. (2017, December 17). Retrieved from english.gov.cn: http://english.gov.cn/news/photos/2017/12/19/content_281475982414739.htm

China's "sharing economy" up 103 pct in 2016: report. (2017, March 5). Retrieved from xinhuanet.com: http://www.xinhuanet.com/english/2017-03/05/c_136104460.htm

China's car ownership reaches 172 million. (2016, January 26). Retrieved from chinadaily.comcn:http://www.chinadaily.com.cn/business/motoring/2016-01/26/content_23253925.htm

Climate Action Tracker. (2017, November 6). Retrieved from climateactiontracker.org: http://climateactiontracker.org/countries/china.html

Daye, C. (2017, October 10). *Chinese NEV firms feeling bullish.* Retrieved from globaltimes.cn: http://www.globaltimes.cn/content/1069667.shtml

Fulco, M. (2016, November 21). *Hands off: self-driving cars in China.* Retrieved from knowledge.ckgsb.edu.cn: http://knowledge.ckgsb.edu.cn/2016/11/21/technology/self-driving-cars-china/

Guin, U. K. (2009). *The Dispossessed.* Harper Collins Publishers.

Huang, Z. (2017, March 20). *Google's Alpha Go now has a serious game-playing rival from Tencent.* Retrieved from qz.com: https://qz.com/936654/googles-alpha-go-now-has-a-serious-game-playing-rival-with-tencents-jueyi-or-fineart/

(2018). *Statistical Communique of the People's Republic of China on the 2017 National Economic and Social Development.* National Bureau of Statistics of China.

Tough Tasks for China's New Environment Ministry. (2018, March 17). Retrieved from thediplomat.com: https://thediplomat.com/2018/03/tough-tasks-for-chinas-new-environment-ministry/

CHAPTER 11

Illustrative Consumer Portraits

In this chapter, I offer more intimate and holistic portraits of Chinese consumers from different segments. The purpose of these portraits is to create a more graphic picture of the consumers, describing their lifestyles, motives, aspirations, and worries. I hope these portraits will create useful and vivid pictures of the consumers, enhance the marketers' understanding and help in thinking about the possibilities and strategies of marketing to these segments of consumers.

Moving Up

Li Qiang and Wang Li have known each other for nearly all their lives. They grew up together in Hubei province, passed the college entrance exam and entered a well-known university in the provincial capital, Wuhan. Born in the 1980s after China implemented its one-child policy, both were supposed to be the only lights in their respective parents' lives, but Wang Li's parents, having started their own factory in the wake of China's economic liberalization and reforms, were reasonably well-off, went ahead and had the boy that the society demanded from them, and paid the required penalty. Wang Li grew up in the company of a much-pampered younger brother but recalls

This portrait of Li Qiang and Wang Li has been earlier published by the author in "China's Evolving Consumers—Eight Intimate Portraits", edited by Tom Nunlist. Earnshaw Books Ltd. ISBN-13:978-988-8422-90-6

A. Sethi, *Chinese Consumers*,
https://doi.org/10.1007/978-981-10-8992-3_11

the play and companionship of her childhood with more fondness than Li Qiang does. After their undergraduate degree, Wang Li came to Shanghai to do her Master's. Li Qiang was less keen to pursue further studies at that time as he did not want to be a further drain on his parents' modest income, but nevertheless accompanied Wang Li to Shanghai and joined the ranks of the white-collared workers in the megacity. Life in Shanghai was not easy with his modest income, but the city was enchanting, its charms many, and they slowly settled down in the metropolis with a feeling that this is where they will like to seek their fortune and build a family. Li Qiang was intelligent and dedicated, his employer appreciated his work and rewarded him well, but he soon found an even better-paying employment in a multinational company, and discovered that for the first time in his life he had money to spend on most, if not all the things, that he desired. Wang Li acquired her Master's degree and settled down in a more comfortable but interesting job in the university department that she was studying in.

Li Qiang feels that perhaps one of the best financial decisions that he took was to somehow scrape together the money to make the down payment on a 130 square meters apartment near the university that Wang Li worked. Though a good one-and-half hour's commute from his place of work, the apartment was modern, well-built, and very close to his wife's university. Both sets of parents generously chipped in to fund the purchase. They were smart enough to invest in an apartment in Shanghai when they were still kind of affordable and often congratulate themselves for having the wisdom to do that. They see many of their contemporaries still desiring to buy a place of their own, but slowly seeing the dream slipping out of their reach, or having to consider compromising in terms of the size of the apartment and location that they never thought they would accept. It does pinch a bit when they see that they will pay back the mortgage of RMB 15,000 a month for nearly the rest of their working life, making them feel like fang nu 房奴 (or house slaves). In the initial years, the going was not easy and a large proportion of their salary went to the bank. But in the consistently growing economy and healthy business environment, Li Qiang's salary more than doubled since they bought the apartment, and now they are in a better position to enjoy the good things of life and the joys that Shanghai's supermarkets and malls have to offer.

Qiang and Li set a lot in store on education and self-development. They get this from their parents, who always encouraged them to study hard and go to the university. They led their lives by this principle, and have extended it to their daughter when she brightened up their lives. Qiang went on to acquire a Master's degree in Data Analytics while still working, a subject that he became more and more interested and a skill which was also prized in his line of work. Li is more interested in arts and often tries to acquire new skills or knowledge to enrich her life. With the birth of the child, Niuniu, the focus on development shifted from self to the child. Li does not like to call herself a “tiger mom”, but diligently shepherds her daughter from piano classes to English classes, to museum visits, and tries to make sure that every moment of their interaction has an element of education. As they are preparing for their daughter’s entry to a primary school, they try to make sure that she can already recognize over 500 Chinese characters that the school expects her to, even before she begins her formal education.

It is not just Niuniu’s mental development that worries them, they are also concerned about her physical health. One of the first things the couple checks on their phone in the morning (after the mandatory WeChat updates) is the state of the air on the Air Quality app. Niuniu’s schedule for the day (and to some extent their own) hinges on the reading of the air quality index (AQI). They also worry about contamination of food and drink, of which there are shocking examples often reported in the media, which puts them on the edge.

Li Qiang and Wang like to put away at least 20% of what they earn for the future, and the rest they spend, now more and more on the internet shopping—particularly for their daughter. In fact, rummaging for products which are safe and beneficial for Niuniu is a favorite pass-time of Wang Li. This started even before she was born as they went to great lengths to buy a German infant milk formula directly from a German store, trying to minimize the chances of ending up with a spurious or poor quality product. Niuniu’s perambulator, toys, and even many of her clothes are all bought online, often as a result of the discussions and recommendations from other mothers’ in the WeChat group that she is enrolled in. Wang Li feels that she will be quite lost without this group, as her own mother brought her up in a totally different world, and really has little to offer in terms of advice and guidance. But their online purchases are not just restricted to children’s products. Wang Li is keen to use the best skin-care products, as she sees the inevitable signs of aging skin, and often buys imported and luxury skin-care products, sometimes brought in by WeChat “daigou” (代购), who source or personally bring these products from overseas. Both the husband and the wife buy apparel and shoes online, but Wang Li more so, and more often than not these are stylish and fashionable, but not from luxury brands. The couple is also not able to understand the frenzied behavior that some of their richer friends exhibit when it comes to acquiring handbags and watches. Li Qiang did present his wife with a Coach handbag on her birthday, and Wang Li gifted a Tag Heuer to her husband on their tenth wedding anniversary, but apart from these they shun these symbols of ostentatious wealth that they feel are more in line with the tastes and preferences of newly rich "tuhao" (土豪) rather than educated urban professionals like themselves.

However, they do find themselves spending increasingly more on fresh foods, fruits, yogurt, nutritional supplements, sports goods, and even red wine. "This is the only life we have and I want to lead it as long and as healthily as possible" as Li Qiang often likes to say and feels guilty if he is not able to do a couple of rounds of jogging in the park every day. Wang Li prefers Yoga and meditation for her health.

The extent to which they have begun to rely on the internet, and particularly their phones, for all their shopping, their search for safe and healthy products, for recommendations and advice from friends and experts even amazes them. When they were in the university, there was no Weibo, no WeChat, and even Taobao. It was only during the working lives that they slowly found themselves adopting a digital lifestyle, and not nearly all key aspects of their lives—their entertainment, social interaction, information seeking and of course shopping—are all digital. They feel it has enriched their lives—and feel confident that they can handle the deluge of information as well as protect their privacy from those who could exploit it to their advantage.

Tourism and particularly overseas travel is a special indulgence, for which they do wish they had more money than they have now. They first set out across the seas just a year before Niuniu was born. Wang Li's parents also accompanied them. This holiday to Europe exposed them to a new kind of joy, and an even a new kind of life, where the air is clean, and the life is unhurried and where they can bond together and relax in a way they struggle to do when they are in Shanghai. After Niuniu came along they took short holidays with her to Phuket and Bali, which were also enjoyable, more so as they were delighted by the little joys their Niuniu showed as she splashed around in the waves in the sea and tried to build sand castles. They would like to go abroad more often and if there is one thing that they would like more money for, is to travel more often abroad.

Once a while the thought of just selling the house and moving abroad lock stock and barrel does cross their mind. This is particularly so on days when the city is shrouded in smog, or another scandal of food contamination is doing the rounds on Weibo and Weixin, or worries of the future of the country or the intense competition that Niuniu will face in gaokao (university entrance exam) and myriad other worries about their lives are clouding their minds. But then they shrug these off and feel that they should just brave on, as they are invested too much right here—not just financially, but in relationships and emotionally.

As they go about their daily life, relishing its comfort and simple joys, they sometimes wonder about the big questions of life and the meaning of it all. But then the spiritual thoughts are pushed aside by the day to day challenges and the joy of looking after their daughter as well as the more practical concerns about her safety and her future. They wonder if they are bringing her up well and whether she will be able to have a secure and good life, and devote themselves to the daily business of remaining safe and healthy, and enjoying the comforts and indulgences that their parents never had access to, and they never imagined that they themselves will benefit from.

A Digital Native's First Love

As his parents were reasonably well-off, one could say that Wang Lei was born with a silver spoon (or rather silver chopsticks) in his mouth. But more often it was said that he was born with a mobile phone in his hand. When he started school, mobile phones were already ubiquitous in China. His parents, running a successful business, always had the phone glued to their ears. From an early age, Wang Lei had a keen desire to get his hands on their parents' phones to amuse himself with playing games.

He acquired his own mobile phone when he entered high school. He really wanted an iPhone but had to settle for a Chinese android phone, as he could not persuade his parents that he really needed such an expensive phone. The school did not allow the use of mobile phone on the premises, but he made good use of it to play games and to chat with his friends. Being a single child had its advantages and disadvantages. He never had to compete for his parents' attention, in fact often felt that he got much more of it than he really wanted. But he was happy to be their only target for pampering and the sole beneficiary of their resources. When he passed gaokao (高考 or the university entrance exam), he did get his iPhone as well as the latest MacPro.

He discovered online gaming when he entered the university, and soon was an enthusiastic player. In fact, playing online games and downloading music and videos were the primary personal demands he made on his MacPro. Of course, he made good use of the computer to do his assignments and research and he secured his first job through an online job website that he registered with on his computer. As a student, online browsing was of high interest to him—both for personal and study related reasons. Of special interests were websites such as Zhihu, Douban, and Weibo.

His parents often worried about his "digital addiction", as whenever he came home, his phone was always glued to his hands—unlike his parents whose phones were glued to their ears. Even when he sat down with them for dinner, his fingers were always dancing on his phone. When he watched television, he was more likely to watch it on his computer than the big screen. He grew up in a generation where the television was a boring box that his parents sat in front of most of the time. He really wonders why anyone will wait for something interesting to show up on the dumb box, when you can scan through all the goodies and choose whatever fancies you, anytime and anywhere on your mobile phone or the computer. Wang Lei himself did not feel he was addicted and shrugged off their concerns. The parents too did not try to push him as his academic performance was satisfactory and he had landed himself a decent job.

Having just started his first job and going through the grind and coping up with long commutes, Wang Lei found much solace in his mobile phone. The subway journey is not so much a strain, as he is able to catch up on news and listen to music—while continuously chatting with his friends, and catching a review of the new Bluetooth handset. Back at home he sometimes uses the MacPro to watch videos or catch up on his work. But his primary connection to the digital world is through his iPhone, and WeChat is his main tool for being connected. Through his mobile phone he is connected all the time—with his friends, his girlfriend, even his colleagues and his boss. WeChat on his mobile phone is where Wang Lei's world lies, and it has become a single point of access to all the social interaction that he desires, the news that he seeks, the advice that he seeks about what career leads to the highest pay with the least amount of work, and what limited edition sports shoes are worth looking at. He has not let his parents on his WeChat account as yet, but wonders whether he can keep them away for long.

Wang Lei has not known life without a mobile phone. For him, it is an extension of his body, and it goes with him wherever he goes, even to the washroom. The question of life without a mobile phone is difficult for him to comprehend and moreover he wonders why would anyone want to contemplate such a scenario. Most mornings, the phone is already in his hand while he is still in bed, and he has already got a good lowdown on who is dating whom and who is attending the music concert this weekend.

Wang Lei, as a single child, should have been lonely, but loneliness is not a concept that he is familiar with as through his phone he can be in touch with every friend that he ever had. In the mobile phone age, it is more difficult to unfriend someone than to friend.

At work, the use of digital for networking and collaboration comes naturally to Wang Lei. The company that he joined uses several tools of online collaboration and virtual teams, and Wang Lei has taken to them like fish to water.

Wang Lei's interaction with brick and mortar stores is restricted to buying a quick snack or a drink from convenience stores or window shopping in some fancy malls. The actual purchases are almost all online. He used to buy a lot on Taobao, but of late has shifted more to specialist retailers on WeChat, some of whom are "dai-gou" (代购). Crazy about sneakers, he has built a nice collection and is always looking to add to it. He likes to hear about products and brands from experts on WeChat, who often explain the benefits in a nice and simple manner and even help in buying the product that he needs. In fact, these people on WeChat have become his advisors and sellers. It is reassuring to him that many of his friends also use them.

His newest value addition in life, he feels, is through the sharing economy—particularly the shared bikes that are dotted around the city. This makes traveling so much more convenient and he is not thinking of buying a personal vehicle in the near future. Online meals delivery is another service that he has taken enthusiastically to and feels really happy about being able to enjoy a large variety of foods without having to budge from home or office.

When Wang Lei hears about the digital media and the digital economy, he wonders what is the fuss about. His life has been revolving around his phone and his PC for as long as he can remember, and imagining a life without these is akin to imagining a life without a part of the body. He also does not feel drowned in the data and information on the net, as he feels he is in control and can easily filter or ignore whatever is not relevant. What he really cannot stand is when the advertisers come in the way of him and what he is trying to do—whether it is to watch a video or search for a product. He cannot stand the pre-roll ads on iQiyi and Youku and sometimes downloads pirated copies even when they are legitimately available. In fact, in products of his interest—such as sneakers—he would like even more information if he can get his hands on it.

He seldom worries about the privacy of his data or the digital trail he leaves behind as he goes about living his digital life. In fact, if it helps him to access more relevant information, more pertinent products, or saves him time, he welcomes it. When he recently heard about some applicants to Harvard, who were refused admission as they were found to have left offensive comments on Facebook, he did feel a bit concerned and resolved to be careful about what he says in his online posts.

Success Is Having a Choice

Lin Shu was born in a small town in Jiangxi province. He grew up in poverty in a family with four other siblings. His father, who was a teacher instilled the love of study and learning, and Lin Shu cleared the gaokao (高考) with flying colors and ended up at the Zhongshan University (one of the best Universities in China) in Guangzhou with a major in social sciences. With an excellent academic performance, it was not difficult for him to secure a position for postgraduate studies in a reputed US university and after graduation a well-paying job in data analysis. Unlike most Chinese of his generation, who decided to take root in the USA after having secured an opportunity to go there for education, Lin Shu decided to come back to China to seek his fortune as a haigui 海龟 or sea turtle (term used for returning educated Chinese). The booming economy, the burgeoning seeds of liberalization and opening up, as well as the love of Chinese food and the familiar comfort of home were all strong pulls to come back home.

So Lin Shu, the haigui 海龟 or sea turtle came back to China to find his fortune—and he did find it soon enough, first through working in senior positions in a few multinational companies, and then starting his own consultancy firm. Lin Shu's is a rags-to-riches story—but so are stories of most successful people in China. Lin Shu was able to gradually transform his lifestyle from relative frugality when he returned to China to measured indulgence after the successful establishment of his firm. But his consumption and preference differ sharply from those of the tuhao 土豪, who represent another genre of the rags-to- riches story, where consumption is the centerpiece of the plot.

Lin Shu's consumption, on the other hand, is modest but sophisticated. His friends describe him as a connoisseur and "a man of substance". He bought an apartment a few years after his return to China and well in time before the buying frenzy and Chinese consumers' insatiable appetite for housing sent the prices in a tizzy. His apartment is spacious but modest, and his home is comfortable but not a palace. It is equipped with the latest appliances and good quality furniture. The taps in his bathroom are not gold-plated but are among the best functional devices available in the market. His clothes are well-fitting, comfortable and roughly in line with the latest fashions. But he does not sport luxury brands and is reluctant to spend a $1000 on an Armani suit. His choices are practical and he exhibits a good taste of an educated professional. His style and choice of colors is understated and unobtrusive.

In areas that he is keenly interested in, he is willing to buy the best—or nearly the best. A keen audiophile, he invested more than $4000 in a pair of speakers and some high-end audio equipment. Photography is another of his passion, and he is always searching for lenses and filters for his cameras. Also an infrequent but interested wine drinker, he does not scrimp on the drink and often spends more than $50 dollars on a bottle. His latest passion is golf—the trigonometry and aerodynamic of the game, as well as the unique challenge interest him, he says. He has acquired several iPhone apps and a few gadgets to help him analyze and improve his game.

He has been a direct witness to the genesis and growth of the internet in the USA. He was already using the internet as a work tool, and email was an important part of his life when he came back to China. In fact, it was through internet that he located and applied for his first position in China. However, it was only after he came back to China that he really witnessed the explosive growth of the internet and the rise of Chinese internet giants like Alibaba and Tencent. Today he is as enthusiastic a user of WeChat as is his daughter—and is happily paying for coffee and lunch through Alipay. However, his activities on the platform are mostly work related and revolve around interaction with clients and colleagues. But he also uses WeChat for information on his passions and interests—including buying wine and learning about the latest options in audio equipment and photography.

A frequent international tourist, Lin Shu's most frequent destination is the USA and his last visit to the country was focused on a university tour for his daughter. He shuns the usual tourist destinations in Europe and South East Asia, and looks for places of special interest to him. It is either a desire for cultural richness or photography opportunities that draw him out. He also avoids loading his bags with duty-free luxury products and prefers to spend on interesting experiences such as a visit to the theater or a well-known restaurant to savor the local cuisine. He is seriously considering a trip to the Antarctica, though the hefty price-tag deters him—it is not that he cannot afford it, but more that he shuns the excessive in all areas of life.

Not much of a shopper, Lin Shu delegates most of his shopping to his wife. But he did make the effort to book the latest iPhone online and is now a proud and satisfied owner of an iPhone X. Apart from that he occasionally purchases wine from his WeChat vendor and sometimes browses for photography and audio equipment.

Like most of his compatriots, Lin Shu keeps a disdainful distance from politics. But he cannot help thinking about what is happening around him and what impact will it have on the country. He often wonders about the future and the reflection leaves him with a feeling of uncertainty and even unease. He likes the way the economy has developed in the last few decades and realizes that he has been a great beneficiary of this transformation. But he worries about the cost at which this has been achieved. It is not just the political cost that bothers him but also the impact on the environment and the pollution in the cities. These things sometimes bother him, and he feels less than certain that the future will remain the way it is now. But he feels fortunate that, unlike his parents, he has choices and options about deciding what he wants to do, where and how he wants his daughter to study and seek her future and happiness.

Li Yue's Love Hotel

A young mother's lot in China is fulfilling but exhausting. Li Yue, who achieved motherhood a few months ago in Shanghai, was thankful for the fact that she received a longish paid leave of absence from her company. Thanks to Chinese benevolent policies, she was able to secure a longer maternity leave than what an average mother is eligible for, as she was over 30 years and delivered the baby through a caesarian. She was also thankful for the fact that China is one of the few countries where it is possible and affordable to move into a post-delivery hotel (called Yuezi zhongxin 月子中心) where all your needs are taken care of and you have 24 hours access to medical care. She and her husband jokingly refer to the hotel as their "love hotel"—it was here that they experienced the joy and tenderness of their first experience to look after their baby.

Li Yue married Hong Tao two years ago, after knowing each other for a few years before that. Both are from provinces outside Shanghai and met through some informal introductions from friends. They hit off well and found that though their interests were quite different they had a lot in common in terms of outlook towards life. They enjoyed two years of rich companionship and love and were happy to let things go on as they were. But wanting to have a child was one of the key motivations to tie the knot and formalize the relationship. Like many other mothers-in-law, Li Yue's mother refused to let her daughter marry till the groom had an apartment. Both of them being dushengzinv 独生子女 (single child) both sets of parents were generous with helping them with the requisite funds to buy the apartment. Once married and moved into the IKEA decorated apartment, they got down to the serious business of building a family, and when Li Yue announced that she was all set to become a mother, she was greeted with cries of joy and happiness from the husband, as well as both sets of parents, who felt that they will now have a mission and someone to play with and care for in their lonely years of retirement.

Li Yue, rather devoted to the job at a consultancy firm, kept working right till the last week before the baby was due to arrive, and rather than asking her parents (or Hong Tao's parents) to come and lend a helping hand after the child is born, decided to check-in into the post-natal care center, for the first month of the baby's life.

Before the child was born, both Li Yue and Hong Tao were active online shoppers, and their entire wardrobe was sourced from online shopping websites. Their love for online shopping is not changed after the birth of their child—just the focus of shopping is now single-mindedly on baby products and their own needs take a secondary place. The other thing which has changed is that now they buy more on Kaola and Amazon which provide better access to overseas products than Taobao and JD.com. Since the milk powder adulteration scandal in 2008, the couple finds it difficult to trust any Chinese product for their child. Not just the milk powder, almost all products they buy for the baby are from overseas—including some of the clothes, products for skin care and even some of the toys.

Li Yue is a member of several WeChat groups of mothers. She is an enthusiastic participant and feels that she gains a lot of tips on child-care and children's products from the groups. In fact, some of her purchases are within WeChat itself. When she sees that the recommendations are coming from other mothers like her, she feels that he can trust them more. Even the words of those entirely unknown to her carry more credibility than the claims of the manufacturers.

After Li Yue went back to full-time work, they had no choice but to ask her mother to come and help look after the child. The help was offered whole-heartedly and with a great deal of enthusiasm. While appreciative of the help, Li Yue is not sure if her mother has all the contemporary knowledge about how best to care for the child. Both she and her husband themselves are actively involved in all decisions about child-care, often over-ruling the mother's advice. With loads of information on the internet, and many other like-minded parents to seek advice from, Li Yue feels confident that she can take good care of her child—not just now, but also in the future. She often talks to her husband about what kind of future life they will like to have for their child. There are many things that they do not quite agree on—but one thing unites their thinking—they hope that their child will be able to grow up being a happy child, enjoying and relishing her learning and experiences, and not just a rote machine to enter gaokao 高考, graduate from a good university and become a cog in the wheel of business and money making.

The Best Is Yet To Be

Wang Xiu Lan and her husband lead a life of quiet retirement in Shanghai. They are in good company, as 30% of Shanghai's population is over 60 years of age. Often referred to as belonging to the "lost generation" people of this generation endured much hardship and were deprived of education due to the chaos of the Cultural Revolution. Wang Xiu and her husband, nevertheless, managed to build a comfortable home for their daughter, and give her all the opportunities that they themselves could not benefit from. Now they see the world through their daughter who is constantly exposing them to new joys and experiences, trying to make sure that they are comfortable to make the most out of the remaining years of their lives.

A few years ago, her daughter brought her a mobile phone and her social life took a new and vibrant dimension. After her retirement from the factory, her thoughts often went back to her school days and she wondered what happened to the friends whose companionship was such a joy to her in those tumultuous times. She slowly started digging out the telephone numbers of friends she had lost touch with. Many of them had moved to other cities, and some even abroad. She enthusiastically got in touch with them and relished the experience of refreshing her ties with them. She used the phone just to make calls and seldom used SMS, as she found it that the task of typing on the small phone was not so easy or enjoyable.

In her past life, Wang Xiu Lan's relationship with the telephone was a rather distant one. In the long years when her husband and she worked in different cities, the weekly rationed calls involved quick conversations on the public phone while several other claimants to the service waited in the queue. Her family never had a land-line phone at home. She did feel a need for one when her children left home but it was not very easy to get one. Her children acquired mobile phones when they left home to work in bigger cities but seldom called as she and her husband did not have a ready access to the phone.

One of the most important part of her daily routine is the visit to the local wet market—in fact often twice a day. The superiority of fresh food is strongly etched in her mind, and she likes to buy only as many vegetables, meat and fish as is required for one particular meal. She is really happy that now she can pay the vendors with her mobile phone through the Alipay account that her daughter helped her set up.

Internet was something that she only had a vague idea about. When her children came home to visit her, she often found them using their laptops and mobile phones and looking very busy. It is something that you really need if you work in an office nowadays, she reckoned. But last year, after her daughter gave her a new kind of phone, which had a large screen, on which you could see pictures, videos, she also got connected and in fact hooked. Initially, she found the instrument quite daunting, and it irritated her when the screen locked itself or it asked her questions and she did not really know how to answer them. She even told her daughter to take it away and replace it with something which could just make calls. But then she slowly discovered the joys that the little box had hidden in it. The nicest of these pleasures was that during her calls to her daughter and other children, she could even see them. She could see their pictures and videos when not talking to them. Slowly a kind of understanding and then friendship developed between Wang Xiu Lan and the new smartphone and now she finds it a window to the world.

Earlier, she often worried about the children and the grandchildren. Even when she had acquired a mobile phone, it was not so convenient so often for the children to take her calls, and the long distance calls were not really cheap. Now she can send them a WeChat message whenever she wants and keep up with the latest antics of her grandchildren through WeChat Moments. Her daughter often asked her to come and stay with her in Shanghai. And the thought of being able to play with her grandson every day was a strong temptation. But she was too used to her life in the county and too independent to live with someone else. With WeChat on her mobile phone, she felt that she was almost living with them, but free to switch them off and focus on her own life when she wanted. The frequent video calls where she can see her grandchildren is a source of delight.

Through the digital access on the mobile phone, she rekindled her interest in Kunqu opera. She did try to catch up with her interest sometimes on radio, or on the CD player, but it was so much simpler on the mobile phone. Not only was she able to listen to the opera when she wanted, she could read about the singers, the performances, everything she always wanted to know was available at her fingertips. She was a member of several WeChat groups where all the members shared the same passion. She felt that she is now able to indulge in her passion more fervently than she ever did before.

WeChat on her mobile phone is where Wang Xiu Lan's world lies now. It has become for her a single point of access to all the social interaction that she desires, the news that she seeks, the advice that she seeks about what food is best for her arthritis, and what shoes will make her more comfortable this winter. She always keeps the mobile phone within reach, even when she is cooking or watching the television in the evening. She does not want to miss out on the what is happening in the world of the people she loves.

Wang Xiu Lan has not really taken to e-commerce as yet. Though her daughter has transferred money to her WeChat account and showed her how she can buy online. She still prefers to go shopping every day for fresh foods, and a few times a week for the other daily necessities. But she does amuse herself with browsing on Taobao to do some "screen shopping" and compare prices with what she buys in the store. If once in a while there is something that catches her fancy, or if she finds that the price is irresistible, she finds it easier to tell her daughter to buy for her, rather than go through the process herself. In fact it is her daughter rather than herself who is the real decision maker on what brands she buys. She grew up in a time when there were no brands and feels a bit overawed by the bewildering choices before her. She leaves it to the more knowledgeable judgment of her daughter to decide what make the choices.

Though initially skeptical about the use of mobile phone, she now feels that her life is enriched by the way it has connected her digitally to rest of the world. She feels more knowledgeable, more connected, and more in control. After using an Android phone for a year, she is now eyeing her daughter's iPhone, which she knows will come to her, when her daughter buys the new iPhone.

Her daughter has warned her of accepting invitations on WeChat from people that she does not know. Initially, she enthusiastically accepted every invitation that she got, but came to realize later that some of the new "friends" were more interested in her savings than her. Or were keen to sell her medicines and tea, which will rejuvenate her or some rare herbs which will cure her joint pain. But her daughter noticed this in time and cautioned her of the dangers and perils of the digital world. Wang Xiu Lan now treads cautiously and often checks with her daughter when she comes across something that she does not know or has never seen before.

Explanation of the Chinese Terms Used in the Book

白富美 bai fu mei—fair, rich, and beautiful—is the profile of the woman that every Chinese man desires.

八零后 ba ling hou—or post-1980s refers to those born in the 1980s.

暴发户 bao fa hu—instantly rich. In the early stages of China's economic development there were many opportunities to become instantly rich, merely by being at the right place at the right time. However, as the economy has matured, such opportunities of overnight wealth acquisition are becoming increasingly difficult to find, and the young have to slog their way to move ahead economically—something which is widely resented by them.

拆二代 chai er dai—demolition rich, refers to erstwhile occupants of old residential buildings, which the government decided to demolish to make room for modern high-rise structures. While there are many disputes between the occupants and the builders, in general the occupants are well compensated, and hence become rich through the demolition of their houses.

单位 dan wei means the work-unit or the place of work. While the term is still used, it has lost the import it enjoyed in the pre-liberalization socialist era, where an individual's identity was completely linked to the danwei, and the individual entirely depended upon it for practically everything in life—including the place to live in (as there was no private housing at that

A. Sethi, *Chinese Consumers*,
https://doi.org/10.1007/978-981-10-8992-3

time, the danwei had to provide a roof over the head) and permission to marry.

屌丝 diao si literally means pubic hair, loosely meaning a loser in English, is a popular term to describe the average Chinese youth, with no connections, inherited wealth, or privileges. This derogatory term of obscene origin became surprisingly popular among the Chinese youth and many of them comically described themselves as diaosi.

地沟油 di gou you or swill oil refers to the used oil from restaurants, which was retrieved and recycled by some unscrupulous elements and sold for cooking again. This was one of the many scandals about food safety which continue to raise their head periodically (most recent being the disguising of low priced meat as highly priced donkey meat).

改革开放 gai ge kai fang or reform and opening-up refers to the program of economic reform initiated in 1978 by the Communist Party led by Deng Xiaoping. This laid the foundation for development of the market economy, private enterprise and ownership.

高富帅 gao fu shuai—tall, rich, and handsome—is the kind of man that a Chinese woman will like to marry (the male counterpart of 白富美 baifumei).

关系 guan xi—perhaps the term most popularly associated with Chinese culture, meaning relationship. The Chinese put a lot in store on developing and maintaining relationships, particularly with people in powerful positions, so that these relationships can be exploited to secure privileges and favors, which may not fall in one's lap in the natural course of things. When there are too many children competing for a place in a popular kindergarten, or too many patients waiting to see a senior doctor, Guanxi can help your secure a place.

光棍 guang gun meaning bare branches is a term used to refer to the leftover men who have failed to secure the hand of a women by a reasonable age. This group is likely to increase in size, as thanks to the one-child policy and a strong gender skew, there are many more men of marriageable age than women.

海龟 hai gui or sea turtle is a term used for the Chinese students who choose to return home after completing their education abroad. They were much sought after a while ago, but now with hundreds of thousands returning home every year, and over 8 million graduating from local universities, the haigui have lost their premium.

韩流 han liu—Korean wave. Since many years now China has been experiencing a Korean wave in popular culture and entertainment, with the lapping up Korean drama and films and swaying to the music of Korean crooners. The government recently has been trying to stem the tide as political relations between the two countries have not been as cordial as before, as Korea colluded with the USA and installed the Terminal High Altitude Area Defense (THAAD), an anti-missile system.

洪荒之力 hong huang zhi li—meaning prehistoric power and implying doing your best. Quoted by Chinese swimmer Fu Yuanhui, expressing pride and satisfaction on her effort, after securing the bronze medal in the women's 100 m backstroke competition at the Rio Olympics. Yuanhui was widely applauded by the Chinese netizens, because of her cheerfulness, positive attitude, and delight in spite of merely securing a bronze medal.

欢乐颂 huan le song or Ode to Joy in English is a popular television drama (now in Season 2) which portrays the trials, tribulations, and joys of five female friends in Shanghai. The series is widely praised for its realistic portrayals and representing women's point of view, but panned for its blatant depiction of materialism.

户口 hu kou—household registration system, which ties a citizen to a place—normally the place of birth. Outside the place of hukou, the citizens do not enjoy many of the important and basic rights, benefits, and facilities—including sending the child to a public school.

九零后 jiu ling hou or post-1990s refers to the cohort born in the 1990s.

科举 ke ju—imperial civil service examination system was used in Imperial China to select members of the State bureaucracy. This was prevalent from as early as the Han dynasty, and remained in force right till the early part of the twentieth century. These exams provided a ticket to upward mobility and prosperity to anyone who had the determination to study hard and master the Confucian classics and other traditional texts. The modern 高考 gaokao or college entrance exam is sometimes compared to Keju, in terms of the intensity of competition as well as the universality of opportunity it offers anyone to access higher education and pave the way to a decent career.

空巢青年 kong chao qing nian—refers to young people, who live away from home in large cities, struggling to get ahead in life and facing problems of loneliness.

老炮儿 lao pao er or Mr. Six is one of the most popular Chinese films of the past two years, with Feng Xiaogang in the lead role.

留守儿童 liu shou er tong literally means "children who are left to guard" refers to the children of migrant workers from villages who have been left in the villages and are working as migrant workers in the cities. The migrant workers do not do it out of choice, but are forced to do so as the restrictive practice of hukou 户口 prevents them from enjoying the basic benefits which the urban residents are entitled to—including access to the public schools. The children are left in the care of the grandparents, and sometimes even entirely alone.

裸婚 luo hun or naked wedding, refers to a frugal wedding without the usual expected paraphernalia of an apartment, a car, or a lavish wedding party. Luohun is highly undesirable, but is increasingly being adopted by force of circumstance of modest income and wealth of the bride and the groom.

面子 mian zi meaning the face, is the quintessential Chinese phrase meaning a sense of dignity. The Chinese will do anything to maintain face and also give face (give others an opportunity to maintain their dignity), at whatever cost.

枪打出头鸟 " qiang da chu tou niao"—the bird who sticks out his head gets shot!—refers to the Chinese belief of keeping a low profile. This became a popular sentiment when several on China's rich list ran into trouble with the authorities and people started dreading the thought of their name appearing on that list or any public place.

七夕节 qi xi jie is what the Chinese consider as their equivalent of the Valentine's day. This falls on the seventh day of the seventh month by the lunar calendar and celebrates the legend of Zhinu (織女) who fell in love with a young cowherd named Niulang (牛郎) but were domed to live separately, and only be united on this one day of the year.

剩女 sheng nv or leftover women is a derogatory term used to describe women, who are considered to have passed a respectable age of marriage (normally around 27 years) but are still single. The term is widely resented by women and others who defend women's right and freedom to remain single as long as they want (even for ever).

素质 su zhi refers to the quality (of a person). The Chinese sometimes attribute irresponsible or crude public behavior to absence of suzhi in a person. Most recently the term was used in relation to those who borrow a bike from the bike-sharing companies, but leave them or abandon them in inappropriate places.

铁碗饭 tie wan fan means an iron bowl. The term is used for lifelong employment with China's state-owned enterprises, which ensured that you have an iron-clad assurance of food for the family. However this is no longer so, as the country has been forced to lay off or retire workers in many state-owned enterprises which lost their relevance in the process of rapid economic development.

土豪 tu hao—local tyrant is now used to refer to the nouveau riche, who have acquired wealth but not the manner and refinement which should go with it.

网红 wang hong is the Chinese term to describe an internet personality. Wanghongs, also called key opinion leaders (KOLs), acquire and display expertise and faculty in a certain field, so that the netizens look upto them, hang on their every word, and lap up the products that they endorse. Wanghong marketing refers to the marketing practice of recruiting the services of influential wanghongs to promote a brand.

危险潜伏在每一个角落 wei xian qian fu zai mei yi ge jiao luo—means that danger lurks in every corner. The Chinese often used this phrase in relation to the numerous dangers to their health in terms of pollution and food contamination.

微博 Wei bo is the Chinese equivalent of Twitter. The platform used to reign supreme till it was ousted from its throne by WeChat, but still remains popular among the youth, who are in search of wider content than what their "friends" can provide on WeChat.

微信 Wei xin known as WeChat in English, the phenomenally popular and versatile app from Tencent, which has become the lifeline of the Chinese and relied on for everything from messaging, to shopping to consumption of news.

蜗居 wo ju or snail house is the name of a popular television drama from 2008 (English name—Dwelling Narrowness), about the struggles of young people in a large modern city to secure affordable housing.

小苹果 xiao ping guo (little apple) popular contemporary song from the Chopsticks Brothers.

学区房 xue qu fang means school district apartment. In most cities, the children are required to go to the school in the district of their residence. The parents who do not reside near a school with a good reputation sometimes adopt a desperate measure of purchasing a tiny but extremely expensive apartment near a good school, which would entitle their child to secure an admission in that school.

衣锦还乡 yi jin huan xiang (return home in golden robes). The term is used to describe those who leave their home to seek their fortune and return home triumphant and successful, sporting expensive clothes and possessions to clearly demonstrate their success and wealth.

中国 Zhong guo is what the Chinese use to refer to their country. Zhongguo literally means the middle country and has its historical origins from the Han dynasty. However, the name was commonly adopted only after the overthrow of the monarchy and establishment of the Republic of China in 1918.

重男轻女 zhong nan qing nu refers to the traditional attitude of gender preference (literally valuing men and belittling women). China has made enormous strides in improving the status of women and achieving gender equality, but like in many other countries, the traditional attitudes die hard.

References

(n.d.). Retrieved from worldbank.org: https://data.worldbank.org/indicator/NY.GDP.PCAP.CD?name_desc=false&view=chart

(n.d.). Retrieved from azquotes.com: http://www.azquotes.com/quote/324531

"Ode to Joy" – Chinese "Pride and Prejudice" with 13 Billion Online Views. (2016, May 18). Retrieved from cnspoon.com: https://cnspoon.com/2016/05/18/ode-to-joy/

10 THINGS YOU NEED TO KNOW NOW ABOUT PROGRAMMATIC BUYING. (2015, June 1). Retrieved from adage.com: http://adage.com/article/print-edition/10-things-programmatic-buying/298811/

(2013, November 25). Retrieved from chinadaily.com.cn: http://usa.chinadaily.com.cn/china/2013-11/25/content_17127868.htm

(2015, January 10). Retrieved from statisticstimes.com: http://statisticstimes.com/economy/united-states-vs-china-gdp.php

(2016, March 26). Retrieved from economist.com: https://www.economist.com/news/china/21695556-ambitious-plan-social-change-has-run-trouble-reformu2019s-big-taboo

(2016). Retrieved from imdb.com: http://www.imdb.com/title/tt5918090/?ref_=nv_sr_1

(2017, April 16). Retrieved from emarketer.com: http://www.emarketer.com/Chart/Average-Daily-Time-Spent-on-WeChat-According-WeChat-Users-China-2015-2016-of-respondents/207293

(2018, February 28). Retrieved from stats.gov.cn: http://www.stats.gov.cn/english/PressRelease/201802/t20180228_1585666.html

(2018, January 18). Retrieved from morningstar.com: https://www.morningstar.com/news/pr-news-wire/PRNews_20180118CN91509/china-labor-market-index-hits-record-high-in-the-fourth-quarter-of-2017.print.html

A. Sethi, *Chinese Consumers*,
https://doi.org/10.1007/978-981-10-8992-3

A Chinese Woman Does a Really Bad Job Pretending to Be Hit By a Car. (2016, December 28). Retrieved from npr.org: https://www.npr.org/sections/goatsandsoda/2016/12/28/507245116/a-chinese-lady-does-a-really-bad-job-pretending-to-be-hit-by-a-car

A Saucy App Knows China's Taste in News. (2018, January 2). Retrieved from nytimes.com: https://www.nytimes.com/2018/01/02/business/china-toutiao-censorship.html

Abtan, O., Barton, C., Pianon, N., & Tsusaka, M. (2016). *Digital or Die: The Choice for Luxury Brands*. Boston Consulting Group.

Amaro, S. (2017, June 28). *China's debt surpasses 300 percent of GDP, IIF says, raising doubts over Yellen's crisis remarks*. Retrieved from cnbc.com: https://www.cnbc.com/2017/06/28/chinas-debt-surpasses-300-percent-of-gdp-iif-says-raising-doubts-over-yellens-crisis-remarks.html

Ariely, D., & Kriesler, J. (2017). *Dollars and Sense: Money Mishaps and How to Avoid Them*. Pan Macmillan.

Asia's Top 1000 brands. (2017). Retrieved from campaignasia.com: https://www.campaignasia.com/Top1000Brands/CountryRanking/China

Atsmon, Y., Dixit, V., & Wu, C. (2011, April). *Tapping China's luxury-goods market*. Retrieved from mckinsey.com: https://www.mckinsey.com/business-functions/marketing-and-sales/our-insights/tapping-chinas-luxury-goods-market

Bain & Company: Kantar Worldpanel. (2016). *China Shopper Report 2016, Vol. 1*. Bain & Company & Kantar Worldpanel.

Bain & Company; China Merchants Bank. (2017). *China Private Wealth Report*.

Bain & Company; Kantar Worldpanel. (2016). *Dealing with Two-Speed China: China Shopper Report*.

Barboza, D. (2008, July 16). *China Surpasses U.S. in Number of Internet Users*. Retrieved from nytimes.com: http://www.nytimes.com/2008/07/26/business/worldbusiness/26internet.html

Barton, D., Chen, Y., & Jin, A. (2013). Mapping China's Middle Class. *McKinsey Quarterly*.

BCG. (2016, November 2). *Capitalizing on Asia's Booming Upper Middle Class*. Retrieved from bcg.com: https://www.bcg.com/publications/2016/globalization-growth-capitalizing-asias-booming-upper-middle-class.aspx

BCG: Chinese HNWIs assets to double by 2021. (2017, May 8). Retrieved from fundselectorasia.com: https://fundselectorasia.com/bcg-chinese-hnwis-assets-double-2021/

Bell, D., & Shelman, M. L. (2011). KFC's Radical Approach to China. *Harvard Business Review*.

Bird, M. (2014, October 8). Retrieved from businessinsider.com: http://www.businessinsider.com/china-overtakes-us-as-worlds-largest-economy-2014-10

Brolly bad show: Chinese sharing startup loses 300,000 umbrellas. (2017, July 11). Retrieved from theguardian.com: https://www.theguardian.com/world/2017/jul/11/brolly-bad-show-chinese-sharing-startup-loses-300000-umbrellas

Buchwald, B. (2015, July 7). *Eight Surprising Facts About the Chinese Luxury Consumer*. Retrieved from forbes.com: https://www.forbes.com/sites/onmarketing/2015/07/07/eight-surprising-facts-about-the-chinese-luxury-consumer/#61a369db74a5

Callen, T. (2017, July 29). *Purchasing Power Parity: Weights Matter*. Retrieved from imf.org: http://www.imf.org/external/pubs/ft/fandd/basics/ppp.htm

China – Ghost Cities. 64 Million Empty Apartments in China. (2015, September 30). Retrieved from globalresearch.ca: https://www.globalresearch.ca/china-ghost-cities/5421229

China cannot accelerate economic growth by increasing leverage, says 'authoritative insider'. (2016, May 10). Retrieved from en.people.cn: http://en.people.cn/n3/2016/0510/c90780-9055625.html

China Focus: China's cultural renaissance inspires lawmakers, a. (2017, March 6). Retrieved from xinhuanet.com: http://www.xinhuanet.com/english/2017-03/06/c_136107384.htm

China Gross Savings Rate. (2018). Retrieved from ceicdata.com: https://www.ceicdata.com/en/indicator/china/gross-savings-rate

China overtakes Japan as world's second-largest economy. (2011, February 14). Retrieved from www.theguardian.com: https://www.theguardian.com/business/2011/feb/14/china-second-largest-economy

China sets 2019 NEV sales quota for automakers at 10 pct of annual sales. (2017, September 28). Retrieved from reuters.com: https://www.reuters.com/article/autos-china-electric/china-sets-2019-nev-sales-quota-for-automakers-at-10-pct-of-annual-sales-idUSB9N1LU02P

China: Inquiry on tainted milk powder. (2014, January 11). Retrieved from nytimes.com: https://www.nytimes.com/2011/01/15/world/asia/15briefs-Milk.html?rref=collection%2Ftimestopic%2FMelamine&action=click&contentCollection=timestopics&region=stream&module=stream_unit&version=latest&contentPlacement=8&pgtype=collection

China's 'four great new inventions' in modern times. (2017, December 17). Retrieved from english.gov.cn: http://english.gov.cn/news/photos/2017/12/19/content_281475982414739.htm

China's dirty little secret: its growing wealth gap. (2017, July 13). Retrieved from scmp.com: http://www.scmp.com/news/china/economy/article/2101775/chinas-rich-grabbing-bigger-slice-pie-ever

China's disaffected Diaosi tribe. (2015, February 3). Retrieved from gbtimes.com: https://gbtimes.com/chinas-disaffected-diaosi-tribe

China's US$1.4 trillion 'One Belt, One Road' set to make bigger impact than US' Marshall Plan to rebuild post-war Europe. (2016, August 6). Retrieved from scmp.com: http://www.scmp.com/news/china/policies-politics/article/2000835/chinas-us14-trillion-one-belt-one-road-extends-beijings

China's Wanda to Buy AMC Cinema Chain for $2.6 Billion. (2012, May 22). Retrieved from bloomberg.com: https://www.bloomberg.com/news/articles/2012-05-21/china-s-wanda-group-to-buy-amc-cinema-chain-for-2-6-billion

China's "sharing economy" up 103 pct in 2016: report. (2017, March 5). Retrieved from xinhuanet.com: http://www.xinhuanet.com/english/2017-03/05/c_136104460.htm

China's bullet trains make five billion trips. (2016, August 1). Retrieved from chinadaily.com.cn: http://www.chinadaily.com.cn/business/2016-08/01/content_26292785.htm

China's car ownership reaches 172 million. (2016, January 26). Retrieved from chinadaily.comcn: http://www.chinadaily.com.cn/business/motoring/2016-01/26/content_23253925.htm

China's Fosun wins bidding for Club Med after two years. (2015, February 11). Retrieved from bbc.co.uk: http://www.bbc.com/news/business-31432322

China's third-party mobile payment market continues rapid expansion. (2017, October 4). Retrieved from xinhuanet.com: http://www.xinhuanet.com/english/2017-10/04/c_136658500.htm

Chinese fashion group has global designs. (2012, May 25). Retrieved from ft.com: https://www.ft.com/content/dba6d4fc-a4c9-11e1-9a94-00144feabdc0

Chinese insurer launches marriage insurance. (2016, August 10). Retrieved from insurancebusinessmag.com: https://www.insurancebusinessmag.com/asia/news/breaking-news/chinese-insurer-launches-marriage-insurance-49661.aspx

Chinese Mobile Phones Dethrone Samsung from Top Position in India. (2018, February 14). Retrieved from sputniknews.com: https://sputniknews.com/science/201802141061649592-chinese-smart-phones-india/

Chinese Outbound Tourism Statistics in 2016: 122 Million Chinese Tourists Make Outbound Trips, Spend $109.8 Billion. (2017, February 3). Retrieved from travel168.net: http://news.travel168.net/20170203/43145.html

Chinese restaurant staff jailed for cooking with 'gutter oil'. (2017, June 12). Retrieved from scmp.com: http://www.scmp.com/news/china/society/article/2091125/chinese-restaurant-staff-jailed-cooking-gutter-oil

Chinese warming up to holiday in Antarctica. (2017, 27). Retrieved from chinadaily.com.cn: http://www.chinadaily.com.cn/china/2017-02/07/content_28120180.htm

Climate Action Tracker. (2017, November 6). Retrieved from climateactiontracker.org: http://climateactiontracker.org/countries/china.html

CNNIC—China Internet Network Information Center. (2016). CNNIC.

Credit Suisse. (2015). *Global Wealth Report 2105*.

Cross-Border Retail Ecommerce Sales in China, 2016–2021. (2017, October 25). Retrieved from emarketer.com: http://www.emarketer.com/Chart/Cross-Border-Retail-Ecommerce-Sales-China-2016-2021-billions-change/212844

Daye, C. (2017, October 10). *Chinese NEV firms feeling bullish*. Retrieved from globaltimes.cn: http://www.globaltimes.cn/content/1069667.shtml

Dehua, C. (2018, January 24). Retrieved from gbtimes.com: https://gbtimes.com/shanghais-average-life-expectancy-reaches-record-high

Dobbs, R., Remes, J., & Woetzel, J. (2016). Emerging Demographics are the New Emerging Markets. *Harvard Business Review*.

Doctrow, C. (2015, October 1). *Fuerdai: Paris Hilton with Chinese characteristics*. Retrieved from boingboing.net: https://boingboing.net/2015/10/01/fuerdai-paris-hilton-with-chi.html

Driest, F. V., Sthanunathan, S., & Weed, K. (2016). Building an Insights Engine: How Unilever got to know its customers. *Harvard Business Review*.

E Jiao (Colla Corii Asini, Donkey-Hide Gelatin). (n.d.). Retrieved from chineseherbshealing.com: http://www.chineseherbshealing.com/e-jiao/

eMarketer. (2016, April 27). *Digital Overtakes Traditional Media in China, but TV Consumption Holds Strong*. Retrieved from emarketer.com: https://www.emarketer.com/Article/Digital-Overtakes-Traditional-Media-China-TV-Consumption-Holds-Strong/1013881

Escabado, J. (2017, May 22). *Nearly $150K Per Post? What You Need to Know About China's Key Opinion Leaders*. Retrieved from forbes.com: https://www.forbes.com/sites/joeescobedo/2017/05/22/key-opinion-leaders-in-china/#388a8e9272ee

Feng, E. (2017, May 10). Retrieved from ft.com: https://www.ft.com/content/04b55fdc-28b7-11e7-9ec8-168383da43b7

Fincantieri and China State Shipbuilding Corporation set up JV for Chinese cruise industry. (2016, July 4). Retrieved from reuters.com: https://www.reuters.com/finance/stocks/FCT.MI/key-developments/article/3400000

Fischer, L. H. (2014). *Leftover Women: The Resurgence of Gender Inequality in China (Asian Arguments)*. Zed Books.

Fish4Dogs takes bite out of growing Chinese market. (n.d.). Retrieved from globalpets.com: https://globalpets.community/news/fish4dogs-takes-bite-out-of-growing-chinese-market

FlorCruz, J. (2010, January 20). *Chinese 'house slaves' grow in booming economy*. Retrieved from cnn.com: http://www.cnn.com/2010/BUSINESS/01/20/china.gdp.narrow.dwelling/index.html

FlorCruz, J. (2011, October 22). *China soul-searching after toddler's death*. Retrieved from cnn.com: https://edition.cnn.com/2011/10/22/world/asia/china-toddler-reaction/index.html

Fong, D., Qian, J., & Xie, Y. (2016, August 29). *In Shanghai, Couples Rush to Divorce to Buy Property Later*. Retrieved from wsj.com: https://blogs.wsj.com/chinarealtime/2016/08/29/in-shanghai-couples-rush-to-divorce-to-buy-property-later/

Frank, R. (2013, November 15). *China has a word for its crass new rich.* Retrieved from cnbc.com: https://www.cnbc.com/2013/11/15/china-has-a-word-for-its-crass-new-rich.html

Fulco, M. (2016, November 21). *Hands off: self-driving cars in China.* Retrieved from knowledge.ckgsb.edu.cn: http://knowledge.ckgsb.edu.cn/2016/11/21/technology/self-driving-cars-china/

Gan, N., & Hu, T. (2017, July 4). *How China's smaller cities are going all out in the race to win young talent.* Retrieved from scmp.com: http://www.scmp.com/news/china/policies-politics/article/2101208/chinas-smaller-cities-offer-cash-incentives-race

GfK. (2015, May 29). *1 in 10 completely satisfied with their looks.* Retrieved from gfk.com: http://www.gfk.com/insights/press-release/1-in-10-completely-satisfied-with-their-looks-1/

Going Social: Durex in China. (2014). *Harvard Business Review.*

GroupM. (2017). *China Media Market Summary.* GroupM.

Guin, U. K. (2009). *The Dispossessed.* Harper Collins Publishers.

Hancock, T., & Xueqiao, W. (n.d.). *South Korean consumer groups bear brunt of China's Thaad ire.* Retrieved from ft.com: https://www.ft.com/content/f3c78afe-821d-11e7-94e2-c5b903247afd

He, L. (2017, April 24). *China's cosmetic surgery boom doesn't look pretty when it comes to profits.* Retrieved from scmp.com: http://www.scmp.com/business/markets/article/2090105/chinas-cosmetic-surgery-boom-doesnt-look-pretty-when-it-comes

Household final consumption expenditure, etc. (% of GDP): World Bank. (n.d.). Retrieved from worldbank.org: https://data.worldbank.org/indicator/NE.CON.PETC.ZS?locations=CN

Huang, Z. (2017, March 20). *Google's Alpha Go now has a serious game-playing rival from Tencent.* Retrieved from qz.com: https://qz.com/936654/googles-alpha-go-now-has-a-serious-game-playing-rival-with-tencents-jueyi-or-fineart/

Hurun Report; Taikang. (2016). *The Healthcare pension Combo Trend.*

Illuminera. (2017). *China's Digital Transformation.* Illuminera Institute.

IMAX. (2016, August 2). *WANDA TO ADD 150 IMAX® THEATRES IN LANDMARK DEAL; LARGEST AGREEMENT IN IMAX HISTORY.* Retrieved from imax.com: https://www.imax.com/content/wanda-add-150-imax-theatres-landmark-deal-largest-agreement-imax-history

imdb.com. (n.d.). Retrieved from http://www.imdb.com/title/tt1397498/

IPSOS. (2017). *2017 MOBILE PAYMENT USAGE IN CHINA REPORT.*

IPSOS; Rudder Finn.(2015). *China Luxury Forecast 2015.*

Jingrong, L. (2017, March 3). *House prices skyrocket in Beijing's school districts.* Retrieved from china.org.cn: http://www.china.org.cn/business/2017-03/03/content_40390802.htm

Jung-a, S. (2016, April 12). *China awash with Korean Wave fever.* Retrieved from ft.com: https://www.ft.com/content/167338ec-fa0b-11e5-8e04-8600cef2ca75

Kai, G. (2016, July 12). Retrieved from chinadaily.com.cn: http://www.chinadaily.com.cn/china/2016-07/12/content_26055052.htm

Kawanao, S., Lu, J., Tsang, R., & Liu, J. (2015). *The Chinese Tourist Boom.* Goldman Sachs.

Kharas, H. (2017). *The Unprecedented Expansion of the World Class an Update.* Brookings Institution.

Knott, K. (2016, January 13). *Chinese celebrities chew their nails for campaign against rhino horn trade.* Retrieved from scmp.com: http://www.scmp.com/lifestyle/arts-entertainment/article/1900650/chinese-celebrities-chew-their-nails-campaign-against

Kroeber, A. R. (n.d.). *China's Economy: What Everyone Needs to Know.* Oxford University Press.

Kuo, Y., Walters, J., Gao, H., Wang, A., Yang, V., Yang, J., …Wan, H. (2015). *The New China Playbook.* Boston Consulting Group; AliResearch.

Lannes, B., Ding, J., Kou, M., & Yu, J. (2017). *China Shopper Report 2017.* Bain & Company & Kantar Worldpanel.

Laydon, J. (2017, August 12). *Film Review: 'Wolf Warrior II'.* Retrieved from yahoo.com: https://www.yahoo.com/entertainment/film-review-wolf-warrior-ii-060837051.html

Leader of China's $9 billion Ezubao online scam gets life; 26 jailed. (2017, September 12). Retrieved from reuters.com: https://www.reuters.com/article/us-china-fraud/leader-of-chinas-9-billion-ezubao-online-scam-gets-life-26-jailed-idUSKCN1BN0J6

Lehrer, J. (2009). *How we Decide?* HOUGHTON MIFFLIN HARCOURT.

Light-Hearted Chinese Olympian Becomes Internet Meme. (2016, August 9). Retrieved from womenofchna.cn: http://www.womenofchina.cn/womenofchina/html1/people/sportswomen/1608/1103-1.htm

Luxury hotels for furry guests boom. (2017, January 26). Retrieved from chinadaily.com.cn: http://www.chinadaily.com.cn/travel/2017-01/26/content_28060825.htm

Mac, R. (2014, September 12). *Alibaba Claims Title for Largest Global IPO Ever With Extra Share Sales.* Retrieved from forbes.com: https://www.forbes.com/sites/ryanmac/2014/09/22/alibaba-claims-title-for-largest-global-ipo-ever-with-extra-share-sales/#1f33fb438dcc

Meena, S. (2017, February 8). *Forrester Data: Online Retail Forecast, 2016 to 2021 (Asia Pacific).* Retrieved from forrester.com: https://www.forrester.com/report/Forrester+Data+Online+Retail+Forecast+2016+To+2021+Asia+Pacific/-/E-RES137063#

Mengwei, C. (2016, July 13). *Divorces up 63% in past decade.* Retrieved from chinadaily.com.cn: http://www.chinadaily.com.cn/china/2016-07/13/content_26067806.htm

Micro-blogging Queen Yao Chen the face of campaign shoot. (2012, November 21). Retrieved from tourismnewzealand.com: https://www.tourismnewzealand.com/news/micro-blogging-queen-yao-chen-the-face-of-campaign-shoot/

Myers, J. (2016, July 25). Retrieved from weforum.com: https://www.weforum.org/agenda/2016/07/china-working-ageing-population/

National Bureau of Statistics of China. (2016). *China Statistical Yearbook 2016.*

Nye, J. S. (2014, November 6). *When will China overtake the US?* Retrieved from weforum.org: https://www.weforum.org/agenda/2014/11/will-china-overtake-us/

PISA 2015 key findings for China. (2016). Retrieved from oecd.org: http://www.oecd.org/pisa/pisa-2015-china.htm

Programmatic Advertising in China: eMarketer's Updated Forecast and Estimates. (2018, January 22). Retrieved from emarketeter.com: https://www.emarketer.com/Report/Programmatic-Advertising-China-eMarketers-Updated-Forecast-Estimates/2002186

PwC. (2016). *China Entertainment and Media Outlook 2016–2020.* PwC.

Rate of diabetes in China "explosive". (2016, April 6). Retrieved from who.int: http://www.wpro.who.int/china/mediacentre/releases/2016/20160406/en/

Reform and Opening Up. (2014, November 18). Retrieved from china.org.cn: http://www.china.org.cn/english/china_key_words/2014-11/18/content_34158784.htm

Roland, G., & Yang, D. Y. (2017, May). *nber.org.* Retrieved from CHINA'S LOST GENERATION: http://www.nber.org/papers/w23441.pdf

Seth, S. (2018, February 16). Retrieved from investopedia.com: https://www.investopedia.com/articles/personal-finance/030415/worlds-top-10-internet-companies.asp

Shang Xia – Chinese Luxury Fashion Brand With a French Soul. (2017, October). Retrieved from martiroll.com: https://martinroll.com/resources/articles/asia/shang-xia-chinese-luxury-fashion-brand-with-a-french-soul/

Shannon, S. (2016, September 27). *On the floor with the daigou, China's overseas shoppers.* Retrieved from ft.com: https://www.ft.com/content/0e0c6a36-330c-11e6-bda0-04585c31b153

Shumei, L. (2017, February 13). *Single men to number over 30m by 2030.* Retrieved from globaltimes.cn: http://www.globaltimes.cn/content/1032677.shtml

Silverstein, M. J. (2012). *Driving Growth – the Female Economy in China and India.* The Boston Consulting Group.

Smith, A. A. (1894). *Chinese Characteristics.* EastBridge.

'Social Commerce' Blossoms on Mobile Taobao. (2016, July 16). Retrieved from alibabagroup.com: http://www.alibabagroup.com/en/ir/article?news=p160726

SODA+Forrester. (2017). *Global Digital Outlook.* SODA+Forrester.

Special Topic Paper: China's Household Registration System: Sustained Reform Needed to Protect China's Rural Migrants. (2005, October 7). Retrieved from cecc.gov: https://www.cecc.gov/publications/issue-papers/cecc-special-topic-paper-chinas-household-registration-system-sustained

(2018). *Statistical Communique of the People's Republic of China on the 2017 National Economic and Social Development*. National Bureau of Statistics of China.

Store, C. G. (2016, July 22). Retrieved from alizila.com: http://www.alizila.com/consumers-get-first-peek-alibabas-buy-vr-store/

Sun, D., Zhou, L., Li, Y., Liu, H., Shen, X., Wang, Z., & Wang, X. (2017). New-type urbanization in China: Predicted trends and investment demand for 2015–2030. *Journal of Geographical Science*.

The Economist. (2018, February 15). China is trying new ways of skimming housing-market froth. *The Economist*.

(2017). *The Future of eCommerce in FMCG*. KantarWorldpanel.

The middle-income trap. (2012, March 27). Retrieved from economist.com: https://www.economist.com/blogs/graphicdetail/2012/03/focus-3

The son of a Chinese billionaire just bought his dog $9,584 worth of iPhones. (2016, September 20). Retrieved from businessinsider.com: http://www.businessinsider.com/wang-sicong-coco-chinese-billionaire-dog-iphone-7-photos-2016-9

The State Council Information Office of the People's Republic of China. (2015). *PRC State Council, WhitePaper – Gender Equality and Development in China*.

TNS. (2008). *The China Source Book*. TNS.

Tough Tasks for China's New Environment Ministry. (2018, March 17). Retrieved from thediplomat.com: https://thediplomat.com/2018/03/tough-tasks-for-chinas-new-environment-ministry/

Uber to sell to rival Didi and create new business in China. (2016, August 1). Retrieved from nytimes.com: https://www.nytimes.com/2016/08/02/business/dealbook/china-uber-didi-chuxing.html

Vinton, K. (2018). Retrieved from forbes.com: https://www.forbes.com/pictures/5997308731358e60d7766b1c/2017-richest-in-tech-top-/#7551c0f63f85

Virtual red packets are most popular way to gift money in China as digital disruption hits tradition. (2018, February 13). Retrieved from scmp.com: http://www.scmp.com/business/banking-finance/article/2133219/virtual-red-packets-are-most-popular-way-gift-money-china

Walters, J., & Kuo, Y. (2016, June 20). *China's Consumers Stay the (slightly slower) Course*. Retrieved from bcg.com: https://www.bcg.com/publications/2016/globalization-center-customer-insight-china-consumers-stay-slightly-slower-course.aspx

Wang, F. (2010, September 30). *https://www.brookings.edu/articles/chinas-population-destiny-the-looming-crisis/*. Retrieved from brookings.edu: https://www.brookings.edu/articles/chinas-population-destiny-the-looming-crisis/

Wang, L. (2015, November 19). *More Chinese couples cohabit before marrying: survey*. Retrieved from chinadaily.com.cn: http://www.chinadaily.com.cn/china/2015-11/19/content_22485696.htm

We Chat About WeChat #5: Red Packets – WeChat's Secret Weapon in Payments. (2016, January 27). Retrieved from wechat.com: http://blog.wechat.com/2016/01/27/we-chat-about-wechat-5-red-packets-wechats-secret-weapon-in-payments/

Xia, C. (2016). Cross-border e-commerce is luring Chinese shoppers. *McKinsey Quarterly*. Retrieved from mckinsey.com: https://www.mckinsey.com/industries/high-tech/our-insights/crossborder-ecommerce-is-luring-chinese-shoppers

Xiaodong, W. (2016, January 25). Retrieved from en.nhfpc.gov.cn: http://en.nhfpc.gov.cn/2016-01/25/c_69360.htm

Xingjian, Z. (2016, July 28). *'So far, the sofa is so far' strikes a chord with overworked professionals*. Retrieved from chinadaily.com.cn: http://www.chinadaily.com.cn/culture/2016-07/28/content_26256174.htm

Yifu Lin, J., & Triechel, V. (n.d.). *Learning from China's rise to escape from the Middle-income trap*. World Bank.

Yutang, L. (1935). *My Country, My People*. Hesperides Press.

Zhaopin: Nearly 80% of China White Collars Trying to Switch Jobs. (2017, February 27). Retrieved from prnewswire.com: https://www.prnewswire.com/news-releases/zhaopin-nearly-80-of-china-white-collars-trying-to-switch-jobs-300413855.html

Zhuoqiong, W. (2016, January 26). *Imports of S. Korean cosmetic products doubled in 2015*. Retrieved from chinadaily.com.cn: http://www.chinadaily.com.cn/business/2016-01/26/content_23244140.htm

Zipser, D., Chen, Y., & Gong, F. (2016). *2016 China Consumer Report*. McKinsey&Company.

Index

A. Sethi, *Chinese Consumers*,
https://doi.org/10.1007/978-981-10-8992-3

The manufacturer's authorised representative in the EU is Springer Nature Customer Service Centre GmbH, Europaplatz 3, 69115 Heidelberg, Germany. If you have any concerns regarding our products, please contact ProductSafety@springernature.com

Printed and bound by CPI Group (UK) Ltd, Croydon, CR0 4YY
27/09/2026
02223596-0001